The Provoker

BIOGRAPHY OF
Bishop Earl Paulk

Tricia Weeks

PROPERTY OF
THE CHURCH ON THE WAY

BX
7990
.169
P388
1986

Copyright 1986
K Dimension Publishers
Atlanta, Georgia

Printed in the United States of America
ISBN 0-917595-09-2

P.O. Box 7300 • Atlanta, GA 30357

ACKNOWLEDGMENTS

Like every ministry at Chapel Hill Harvester Church, the Publications Department is an integral part of that unfolding vision of a Kingdom church which God gave to Earl Paulk in 1960. I sincerely appreciate the work and care of those who have joined their lives to that vision. Many people work daily over Bishop Paulk's manuscripts which communicate the Kingdom message in books, newspapers, magazines, etc.

First, thanks to the excellent Editorial Staff—Gayle Blackwood, Chris Oborne and Gail Smith; Donna Eubanks for typesetting; Don Ross for layout, and Todd Cole, Wayne Henderson and Lee Whanger for photography.

Thanks to proofreaders—Janis McFarland and Jeannie Garthwaite.

A special thanks to Clariece Paulk for raiding family photo albums, knowing just "the picture" telling the story and putting together the pictorial history recorded on these pages.

Thanks to Wes Bonner, Director of K-Dimension Publishers, for his care in technical details related to the finished book.

Thanks to the Paulk family and friends for sharing their lives with me in conversations which I will always treasure. Especially I would like to thank Norma Paulk and Myrtle Mushegan for relating so many personal details and insights.

I also want to thank my husband, Alan, for his love, understanding and encouragement which made writing this book possible.

Most of all, I thank Bishop Earl Paulk for trusting me with the privilege of relating the process by which God called a "Provoker" to the twentieth century Church. God's glory shines through this man's life and ministry. I asked Bishop Paulk to allow me to write his biography in 1983. At that time I knew little about the dynamics of his life story. I only knew the results—the mighty anointing resting on the prophet and the bountiful fruit of his ministry in thousands of people whose lives honor the Lord.

I pray that sharing Bishop Paulk's story with readers will continually perpetrate the message of Jesus' healing, life-giving love in preparing His mature bride for the coming of His Kingdom on earth. God chooses His messengers. God chose Earl Paulk to proclaim Kingdom truth for a time such as this. Amid so many "uncertain sounds" in the Church's camp, thank God for a Provoker with the conviction, courage and fortitude to speak boldly the unfolding revelation of Jesus Christ as eternal King and Lord.

This is a day of Kingdom communication and demonstration to the world. May God bless the message of this one life with everlasting fruit to the glory and honor of our King.

His Kingdom Come!

Tricia Weeks

Pastor John Garlington
September 2, 1937 to January 16, 1986

A Tribute To John Garlington

"There was a man sent from God, whose name was John..." (John 1:6). From the days of John the Baptist into this century God has sent prophets preparing the way of the Lord, alerting those with spiritual "ears to hear" of the visitation of God among them. Pastor John Garlington from Portland, Oregon, was such a man. He saw with single vision the horizon of Christ's Kingdom on earth in a mighty reformation of the Spirit sweeping the Church today. He heard the wind of the Spirit, mysteries of God's Word whispered in unfolding, fresh insights discerned by those who are spiritually minded. He spoke eloquently, powerfully and confidently because he served the Lord as a mouthpiece to His Church.

John attended the first Pastors Conference my church in Atlanta hosted in the fall of 1982. Years later he told me that he tried the entire conference to meet with me. He was eager to share the exciting confirmation of exact things God was speaking to both of us concerning Kingdom truth. Of course, my schedule was totally booked with barely enough time to eat during the three days of the conference.

In October 1984, our paths crossed again. This time we met at a conference at Evangel Temple in Washington, D.C. Bishop John Meares had asked both John Garlington and me to share in that conference. As John Garlington stood at the podium delivering a powerful address, he turned to me and began to prophesy.

I remember listening to his words with tears streaming down my face. His words touched the core of my calling from God. The prophetic direction touched fragile emotions and tender areas inside which are often shielded by bold, hard sayings which God commands me to speak. Something unforgettable happens whenever one realizes that he has become transparent to another person. Either he pulls away by denying that someone else could possibly recognize and share that private pain without abusing such insight, or he merges in an eternal covenant with that person, knowing the joy of fellowship as "those whom God hath joined together . . ." in the ministry. John became my trusted friend, my brother, one who could lift my weariness with a word of understanding.

John labeled me a "Provoker." As one who has worn various labels which I would rather forget, I know in my Spirit that God spoke to me through John Garlington—". . . keep on provoking!"

John Garlington was a "Proclaimer," one speaking to God's people as a voice, a trumpet blasting through seemingly tough exteriors with truth. God gave him an ability to identify ministries and exhort those called of the Lord to special missions in these critical days of Church history. He emphasized that the Kingdom message was a workable message. Through humor and profound insights, he moved people beyond traditions, beyond reading scriptures with surface comprehension, beyond legalistic adherence to status quo Christianity to a fresh, all-encompassing sensitivity and love for Jesus. "Christ in us, the hope of glory!" He gave us vision and hope and strong leadership. He gave us the courage to press on in the quest, ". . . Thy kingdom come on earth as it is in heaven . . ."

January 16, 1986—I was in Charlotte, North Carolina, scheduled to give the evening keynote address at the 1986 Idea Exchange, a gathering of pastors and Church leaders across the nation. I was assigned the topic, "Restoration Theology." Many of these leaders had come to me during the days prior to that Thursday evening. They asked excellent questions about Kingdom teaching. While I sensed resistance from some toward the message of restoration, maturity and unity of the Church, I also sensed more genuine openness and a desire to understand Kingdom concepts from the majority.

I expounded Kingdom theology from the book of Genesis—God's intentions in the Garden—to modern-day mandates from God which the Church must accomplish before Christ returns to rule and reign as King of kings and Lord of lords. I felt like a "Provoker" in every sense of that description! I had promised the Lord that I would neither look at the faces of men nor allow their reactions to alter my course. The speaker following me gave somewhat of the "other side" of "Restoration Theology." Seeds were sown. Decisions were made. Choices were required of many.

Later that evening I received a call which left me feeling shocked and running to God for answers. John Garlington and his beautiful wife, Yvonne, had been killed in an automobile accident in Florida at exactly the time I was speaking. The first reaction to news like that leaves one's mind numb and senseless. The first response is, "Why?" Two so young, so vital, so full of promise and potential, leaving five children! The initial, natural temptation is to challenge God's sovereignty in these matters.

For several days I couldn't find peace in this storm. I opened my spirit to hear from the Lord. I knew that John Garlington lived in covenant with God, understood his own mission and gave his "all" to serve God's people. Why was he taken from his ministry in such seemingly critical days? Then God spoke to my spirit. John Garlington's life was not in vain. John's life continues at another, vital dimension in God's plan.

Jesus told His disciples, "It is expedient for you that I go away . . ." The coming of the Holy Spirit ignited the power of Christ in all those who had depended on Him and followed Him in the flesh. Imagine the shock experienced by those disciples upon hearing about John the Baptist's death. Imagine how senseless Stephen's death must have seemed to the early Church.

I also reflected on the mission of Martin Luther King Jr., to lead his people. His death ignited the fires of equality in generations who made his "dream" their own. "Flesh and blood cannot inherit eternal life." Often one's message is lifted to a greater influence in death than in life—underscoring that message for those who remain as a cause worth living or dying to accomplish.

John Garlington finished his course in victory. He now assumes a new dimension of ministry, cheering us on, giving us even greater cause, hope and diligence. His message lives, making those of us who knew and loved him continue with greater accountability. To whom much is given; much is required. The costs of the Kingdom witness are great. "By faith Abel offered unto God a more excellent sacrifice than Cain, by which he obtained witness that he was righteous, God testifying of his gifts: and by it he being dead yet speaks" (Hebrews 11:4).

John Garlington's message resounds today—greater, stronger, more powerful than ever. Thanks to him, as a mouthpiece of the Lord, I will "go on provoking" until I have no more breath in me or until Christ returns in glory. I am grateful to the Lord for such a privilege. Thousands of others who heard, comprehended and digested the message God gave through John Garlington's life will never back away from its fulfillment. To God be the glory forever!

Our King Cometh!

Earl Paulk, Bishop

PROPHECY

Prophecy to Bishop Earl Paulk
Spoken through Pastor John Garlington
Evangel Temple, Washington, D.C.
October, 1984

It's kind of funny—sometimes God shows me comical pictures. I saw this little scenario in the comic strip "Peanuts." Each year when the football season begins, the little girl holds the football, and the little boy runs to kick it. Each time that he gets there, she moves it and he falls—then he comes back next year.

Something has happened over the years as you've reached out and touched folks, and two things I have sensed, being around you (and I'm kind of glad I won't be around you for awhile).

There is an intense burden in your spirit to see the birth of the Kingdom of God. That intensity bothered me at first. I didn't know what was going on. All of a sudden, I became aware that I was feeling just that intensity in your spirit. And there is such an intensity in your spirit about seeing the Kingdom of God birthed, seeing a visible demonstration of it, that folks who get around you don't really understand. They feel that your orientation is on the Kingdom and not the King. But they don't understand that God has uniquely raised you up as part of a birthing process in the earth. You are literally one of those who is feeling a sense of violence and pressure in your spirit to birth the Kingdom of God.

i

You reach out to touch. Over and over again, you've touched folks who then move the football. But God has called you not only to see the victories and the joys of the Kingdom, but you're one that God is using to fill up the sufferings. That is unusual because we hear so much today about the message of prosperity and the message of victory. But Paul said that we are also called to fill up the sufferings of Jesus Christ.

I see inside your body such wounds and bruises until when the opportunity comes to reach out and heal again, sometimes you are concerned because you are aware of the bruises that come. Sometimes, even while you are reaching out, there is a sense in your spirit that the bruise will come again. I don't understand that. I wish I could give you a word of relief, but it's the glory and the suffering that God has caused you to feel in your spirit.

God wants you to know that you are going to see fantastic things happen in southeastern America. God has raised you up, man of God, as a beacon in that place.

You've been a sign spoken against, but I want you to know that God is raising you up as a spiritual Joseph because as famine begins to fill the spiritual land, men are going to come to you and say, "We don't understand it; we were offended by what you did." But you are going to say like Joseph, "The things you meant for evil, God meant for good." It will not be many days until those who have caused the pain and bruises are going to come back again and say, "We were wrong, God has dealt with us in the night hours. There was an anointing on our ministry that is gone." They are going to come back for healing at your hands.

I just know that until you have fulfilled what God is doing in you, you are always going to feel stretched beyond measure. There is such a sense in my own spirit of what you feel of that urgency of the Kingdom in your heart, that thing in you that just cries out to God to see a birthing go on. It's such an intense thing that you find yourself eating and sleeping the Kingdom of God. You are a man whom God has consumed with that desire. The Kingdom of Heaven does suffer violence, and that violence is going on in your spirit. But you are going to see release after release.

Brother, God is going to unbuckle the Bible Belt. He is going to knock down tradition. He is going to move in such a tremendous way. Even as you've said to folks that thing that God is going to do, He is going to do it! There is going to come a revival in southeastern America that is going to shake the nations. It will be spoken of around the world, and God is going to make your place one of the focuses. God is going to make your place one of the pivotal points. God is going to make your place on the cutting edge of what He is doing in America.

And in the very place where sin, segregation and discrimination have been so difficult, your place will become a sign to the nations of what happens when men move in the dimension of God's Kingdom. And they will come from near and far to hear it. You will be able to say to them, "It's a thing that is birthed in the Spirit. The Kingdom of God does not come by observation; it comes by revelation."

You have said, "Hear me with your spirit," and there is such a cry in you to have folks hear with their spirits, and you wonder sometimes, "Are they hearing?" There are folks sprinkled around the nation who are beginning to hear with the ear of the Spirit and see with the eye of the Spirit, and **God is using you as a Provoker. Keep on Provoking!** The release is going to come.

It would seem, in ways that you cannot imagine, that part of the vision that God gave for the Atlanta area died, but it has not died. It is going to be resurrected, and you are going to see double fruitfulness in the context of what you wanted to see in that city. I see you, Bishop, as a man like Jesus who has literally cried, and God is going to take those tears (He has kept them in a bottle), and you are going to come back, bringing in the sheaves with you. As much as you have known the pressures and burdens, you are going to know the joy of the Holy Spirit and the joy of the harvest. Hallelujah! Hallelujah!

TABLE OF CONTENTS

PROPERTY OF
THE CHURCH ON THE WAY

**PROPERTY OF
THE CHURCH ON THE WAY**

1

CHAPTER ONE

Moses obeyed God and led Israel into the wilderness. Earl Paulk led the people in his church to metal folding chairs sitting on an asphalt parking lot. Beside the redwood and gray stone building where the people met together for ten years, the men of the church put finishing touches on the interior of a huge cathedral tent they had raised the previous week. The "swimming pool blue" structure would easily cover several thousand people. A blazing, late afternoon sun beat down on the tent's durable plastic, creating a permeating glow inside. Hours before a Sunday evening worship service began, people gathered to claim choice seats near the front stage. Arriving early also provided people valu-

The King's Library

able time to socialize with friends.

On that May night in 1983, volunteer parking lot attendants directed the steady stream of cars as they pulled onto acres of parking ground. Hundreds of cars quickly covered the dusty ball field, then parked along the newly-graveled roads winding around the future building site. Shuttle buses circled from distant parking lots. Grateful passengers emerged from the buses pausing near tent entrances. Cars, passing on the road in front of the church, slowed down in heavy traffic. People stared curiously from their cars at all the circus-like activity. This church definitely appeared strange—a startling sight compared to more stately churches along Flat Shoals Road in the Atlanta suburb.

Most people hiked from their cars to the tent. Ladies wearing fashionable, high-heeled shoes struggled in the dirt to keep pace with their husbands' strides. Children ran ahead of their parents. Everyone sensed excitement, smelled the challenge and adventure of a new beginning. People called warm greetings to one another. Their lighthearted comments were filled with good natured exaggeration. Some pointed out the obvious challenges of this new phase in fulfilling a commonly-shared vision from God. Their church always seemed to be constantly in motion, moving under an unseen cloud as God directed His prophet in uncharted paths.

Chairs under the huge tent filled quickly as people gathered from all directions. Expectancy crackled in the air. Numerous voices rose from the noisy crowd in a roar of friendly, blended conversations. Parents directed their children to the adjacent building—the "old" sanctuary—which had been converted into newly built classroom space. While the new classrooms temporarily alleviated overcrowding in the children's ministries, these additions also meant the congregation couldn't reclaim comfortable pews under a roof for Sunday services or Wednesday night teaching sessions. Until a new sanctuary was completed, the big blue cathedral tent was their "church" indefinitely.

Weather conditions alone would test members' spiritual perseverance and physical endurance. No matter how soon construction began on the new building, the people knew they would sit for a time through two-hour services with the summer's sauna heat drenching their clothes with perspiration, autumn's brisk rain splashing down the tent poles, and frosty winter's chilling north winds swaying the billowing blue structure.

In every observable way, people belonging to Chapel Hill Harvester Church could only be categorized as ordinary, middle-class Americans. Like all their neighbors, they worked hard at their jobs all week, sent their children to neighborhood schools, paid their bills, and struggled daily with political, social and community issues. Very few members would be classified as economically rich or poor.

Political views varied among the people. Dedicated liberals would probably label them as "conservatives," and hard-core conservatives would likely call them "liberals." Racial, social diversities adequately qualified this congregation as a middle-American composite. Yet obvious similarities and differences failed to reveal their unity in certain uncompromising, strongly-motivated convictions. After all, these people had joined themselves to an innovative church meeting in a big blue tent sitting on a parking lot. In some respects, at least, they were undeniably radical. They were modern pioneers who were willing to take risks, blaze new trails, press toward new horizons.

Each person in this tent had his own story to tell. Numerous winding paths had brought people to this destination. Their stories were as varied as their names and faces, individually unique and yet corporately interwoven. Some people had loved Jesus since they were children. They prayed and sang "Jesus songs" long before they remembered important leaps of faith in their lives. They couldn't specifically recall that first prayer of salvation, or the first time they knew indisputably the reality of a relationship with the Lord. Some of these people remembered their fathers' daily prayers and being rocked to sleep by mothers singing old hymns to them. They came to this church already convinced that theirs was a special destiny, understanding the mission of their generation in history. Here they recognized a certain sound of the visionary trumpet blasting a message capable of shaking the heavens and jolting the earth. They knew instantly that God had brought them here.

Some people came here in frustration at religion. Lifeless traditions in other churches they attended for many years left them feeling spiritually barren, numbly sedated. At first these people questioned whether any place of worship could fill the voids they felt inside. They had left behind sleeping congregations sitting passively each Sunday on lavish, cushioned pews in adorned sanctuaries. Usually circumstances or un-answered questions in their lives had awakened an inner longing for a deeper reality of God's presence. Some experience—uniquely individual—made them realize they had been spiritually deaf and blind. Sud-denly they wanted answers, hungering and thirsting for life-giving sustenance. The search for reality behind all the repetitious litany and the ceremonial trappings stirred questions within them. That search brought them to this place.

Others came to Chapel Hill Harvester Church from strong Bible-believing fundamentalist or "holiness" denominations. They grew up in strict traditions. Fam-ily Bible reading and experiencing Jesus' presence in their exuberant worship were routine experiences for them. But though Jesus' words proclaimed freedom, joy and abundance in life, they often saw Christian people around them who were bound to constraining rules for no apparent purpose. Girls growing up in these churches were forbidden to wear make-up and forced to adhere to ridiculous dress codes. No one wore jewelry. Young people were taught that movies or sporting events were "worldly" and therefore sinful. Church laws associated spirituality with harsh judg-ment and unbending conformity. True Christianity was defined as "keeping all the rules." After trying unsuccessfully to live by rigid religious traditions, many of these people abandoned their childhood faith in rebellion and guilt.

They were drawn back to Jesus through compassionate, restoring mercy flowing in God's presence. In this church they began to understand true righteousness. The desire to please God awakened in their hearts, renewing relationships with a loving Father reaching out to them. This ministry was unwilling for people to die in legalistic oppression and misunderstanding of God's eternal requirements. As wounded ones learned of Him, they discovered that "His yoke" was easy. Restoration became the delicious fruit of a love relationship with the Lord and His people who were seeking the Kingdom with all their hearts.

Many people reached for the vision of this church as their last hope. They came from circumstances of dark despair and terrifying loneliness. Many of them were forsaken by their families and friends because of terrible choices and deep hurts they had caused. They came to this place as a last resort—with justifiable guilt, emotional bruises and broken lives—hoping for a new start. To them this church represented a City of Refuge.

The crowd under the blue tent blended together several thousand ordinary people, chosen for an extraordinary mission. If Jesus had chosen talented, scholarly, wealthy disciples, His purposes could never have been accomplished in them. In Atlanta, Georgia, like in Galilee long ago, God chose ordinary people who believed He could lead them to a higher realm of life.

Most of Jesus' disciples were childlike in their faith, the kind of people who might jump out of a boat to walk toward Him on the water. The disciples He chose would eagerly organize thousands of people into groups of fifty to feed them a supper of five loaves of bread and two fish simply because Jesus said to do it. They loyally followed a common man who was often misunderstood; a man accused by respectable, religious leaders as being an impostor, heretic and troublemaker. Sometimes His disciples were seemingly reckless, irrational and quick-tempered. They often reacted to challenges with ungodly ambitions and selfish motives. They appeared to have little social grace or polish. Yet, God could have chosen any group of friends on earth for Himself. What made Him trust His heart to certain ones?

God trusted ordinary people with His earthshaking message. First, Jesus trusted His life to a group of Galileans who by all reasonable perceptions were hardly the kind of people usually selected to distribute such valuable treasure. The Jewish Talmud says of the Galileans, "They were more anxious for honor than for gain, quick-tempered, impulsive, emotional, easily aroused by an appeal to adventure, loyal to the end."

Such unimpressive qualities in these people were chosen by God as the raw materials to bend and shape as the Holy Spirit molded them by fire into vessels of honor. These transformed Galileans in the first century "turned the world upside down," accomplishing an impossible mission by proclaiming a radical, double-edged message of choosing life or death.

Jesus lived a Kingdom lifestyle in a daily demonstration with them, walking beside them on dusty roads. He taught them how to bring good news of love, healing and life to the most unlikely, undeserving people. When the Holy Spirit burned the New Covenant into their hearts at Pentecost, these rugged, stubborn Galileans' lives suddenly ignited with power and purpose.

Jesus trusted His message to these Galileans for the same reasons that He trusted twentieth century disciples at Chapel Hill Harvester Church. God's heart has always searched for men and women in every century who would not allow mixture to dilute His prophetic message, the passion of His heart. Jesus chose unlikely "kings and priests" as His closest friends because He knew they had more guts than common sense. Their sensitivity to His voice was uncompromisingly uncommon, but they themselves were ordinary by any assessment. If they could "turn the world upside down" with His radical love, anyone with the desire to join them could share in both the challenges and the rewards. The nucleus of people at Chapel Hill Harvester Church were designer-dressed, business-suited, Buick-driving, computer-listed, outspoken Galileans to the end.

One common confrontation flavored each person's testimony, no matter which path someone walked to get here. The people belonging to this "tent" church had made a bold commitment. They had driven spiritual stakes firmly into their lives. Beyond the spiritual doors of a salvation "born again" experience, or even the baptism of the Holy Spirit opening their lives to God's power and supernatural gifts for ministry, God challenged them further in demonstrating Kingdom life on earth. Other spiritual doors had unlocked inside them requiring even deeper commitments to trust God's voice.

God asked people in this church to decide whether they would pursue the Kingdom which Jesus preached and demonstrated in His own ministry as reality in their lives. God asked whether they would act in spiritual obedience as His witnesses by demonstrating Kingdom lifestyles daily. They were asked to responsibly share Kingdom revelation entrusted to them, boldly proclaimed from the pulpit in this suburb of Atlanta. As God shared Kingdom mysteries with these people, they were called to be responsible stewards by proclaiming the message to the world through the media, Kingdom conferences and a network of churches which would share fellowship with them. Of course, the decision to have a Kingdom heart, open to receive God's direction, immediately confronted a multitude of natural prejudices and fears.

Confrontations required some people to put away racial or social prejudices. All races, cultures and classes of people were genuinely welcomed in this church and were even necessary for its indiscriminate witness. Some people confronted religious prejudices. Sacramental practices which they had piously condemned all their lives were put into proper perspective in this church. The pastors wore clerical collars as a sign of covenant with God. They served the sacrament of the Eucharist in full flowing vestments. After serving Holy Communion, they often flowed in Pentecostal worship with singing in the Spirit, praying for the healing of people by anointing them with oil, laying

23

hands on people in bondage to deliver them, prophesy-
ing, even dancing with uninhibited joy in worship
before the Lord.

God required people to decide whether they would
embrace exuberant young people enjoying worship
songs sounding like loud rock-and-roll music. Other
people decided whether they would reach out in love
and trust to Christians who had committed despicable
sins in their pasts. Many of these people had broken
both God's and society's moral standards in scandalous circumstances.

They decided whether God's restoring love was truly
sufficient for young unwed mothers, men and women
coming out of the homosexual lifestyle, people just
released from prisons, people still fighting addictions
to alcohol and drugs. The song *Amazing Grace* had far
more significance here than simply an old, sentimental
hymn of the church. Everyone was both the recipient
and source of God's cleansing "grace." Restoration
became reality for every sinner and every sin in
genuine application of God's love and forgiveness
through the ministry of His people.

Eventually, some issue forced each person to decide
whether he or she believed God truly spoke through a
twentieth century prophet. Revelation, fresh insights
into the treasures of God's Word, unlocked spiritual
wisdom of the ages. At times the prophet received revelation for God's people through spiritual visions and
dreams which unfolded biblical mysteries. Of course,
strong prophetic truth also stirred questions, criticism
and debate both internally and throughout the Body of

Christ. Misunderstandings were commonplace. Many times the ministry grew weary with ridiculous challenges and accusations. The entire ministry not only paid the price, but also enjoyed the multiplied blessings of moving on the cutting edge of the revelation God spoke to those with "ears to hear" what the Spirit said to the Church.

The eldership of the church provided safety in a multitude of counselors. Men and women called by God discerned and ministered to the needs of the people. Each person had to decide whether to submit to spiritual authority at a level of trust few people were ever taught in their families, other churches or society.

Kingdom demonstration required a personal decision by every person to learn to trust "the Christ" in others. The necessity of trust became the critical issue for every believer experiencing spiritual shaking and testing. Hundreds of people submitted critical decisions in their lives to ministers whom God had called as responsible shepherds. Levels of trust and submission separated fleshly desires from spiritual desires in individual believers' life choices.

Directions for the ministry were never decided by congregational votes. Personal opinions had little influence on spiritual decisions. God spoke direction for the ministry to His designated leaders. Pastors and elders responsibly sought God's direction for the people's lives through fasting, prayer, biblical consistency and the witness of the Holy Spirit within them. People in the church were responsible to demonstrate revelation God gave to them. Through God's written and spoken Word, the counsel of His called leaders and the daily witness of the Holy Spirit, the people grew to maturity—genuine witnesses to powers in the heavenlies and Kingdom standards to world systems.

Prejudices surfaced quickly in people attending this church. Some people reacted to Kingdom theology with hostility. They decided that personal responsibility for Kingdom demonstration was too great. They argued that God's grace sufficiently encompassed generations of Christians who made far less demanding commitments to Him. Sometimes these believers simply attended the services for awhile without making a commitment to "seek the Kingdom" in any way that would alter their lifestyles. They enjoyed the undeniable, divine presence of God in the services; they participated in the extraordinary praise and worship; they admitted that the preaching was powerful and anointed; they never disputed God's calling on the prophet delivering the messages. But these people were "hearers" only. They always burned away during fires of testing.

Arguments against the ministry were very subtle. Internal complaints usually focused on financial decisions, the length of the services, family members in the ministry or doctrinal differences which could not be proven scripturally. Some sincere Christians were unwilling to endure the testing God allowed in a ministry called to be a prophetic voice to the Body of Christ. The teaching here cut deeply into pride, social attitudes and religious traditions which made some people feel secure. Many believers left the church after spiritual confrontation. At the point of making choices for their lives, they discovered that they really wanted to know God on their own terms, meeting their own needs without paying the price of commitment.

No one had to wonder about the message of this church. The Kingdom message was proclaimed not only to the local congregation but also to the world. The construction crew built two stands to support television cameras in the center of the tent auditorium and in an aisle extending from the left side of a three-sectioned stage area. During each service, the television crew worked unobtrusively. Members of the church hardly noticed the production staff's maneuvers. A full-time television department had been in operation for over five years, videotaping almost every service at the church. From those tapes, one service was selected for broadcasting every week on local and national cable channels. Television cameras opened the message and ministry of the church to the world.

Television broadcasting was essential to the vision of the ministry. God had called this church to communicate and demonstrate the gospel of His Kingdom. Television carried prophetic messages across the nation like seeds thrown into a far-reaching, technological whirlwind. Viewers responded enthusiastically to the Kingdom teaching they received each week. Many other ministries regarded the messages as confirmation to similar direction God had spoken to them. The obvious parallels in God's fresh revelation convinced church leaders that the Spirit indeed was speaking prophetically to attentive messengers throughout the Church.

A clear Plexiglas pulpit stood in the middle of the center stage. The pulpit's central position represented the central focus of God's Word to His people. A Communion table also was placed at center stage during the celebration of the Eucharist. From a centralized place of ministry, God's people received revelation, direction and both spiritual and physical healing from the Lord.

The Minister of Worship and Arts, Clariece Paulk, walked with quick steps to a large grand piano sitting on the stage. Clariece had seen many of her most cherished dreams come true. As a child she dreamed of growing up and marrying a pastor. Other little girls played with dolls while Clariece practiced the piano and "played church." Since 1960 when she married Pastor Don Paulk, the younger of the two brothers who founded the church that same year, she had experienced every phase of the struggles and miracles of this ministry. No one was more certain than Clariece that impossible hopes materialized as people prayed and believed God to perform His will.

Clariece was an exceptionally talented concert pianist. She totally commanded the piano, sometimes gently caressing each note and other times plowing into the keys in unrestrained, rhapsodic energy. Clariece sat at the piano projecting symphonic sounds from one instrument as if it were a complete orchestra. However, natural talent and training only partially equipped Clariece to minister in this church. Only God could give her the ability to combine musical skills with supernatural sensitivity as the Holy Spirit directed the music in prophetic worship.

Clariece Paulk's most valuable gift from God was her keen sensitivity and open spirit. She played the piano, planned musical selections and orchestrated the various components of the Fine Arts Department of the church under a mighty spiritual anointing. Clariece seldom predicted all the selections she would use in a service because music and worship "flowed" with the Spirit's direction. God's ministry to His people could never be regulated to a rigid program or plan. But this challenge to spontaneity ignited Clariece's sense of expectancy.

Watching Clariece, one would think that each service was the single most important one in her entire life. She gave her efforts to excellence each time—first to honor the Lord, yet also to challenge the potential of all those affected by her ministry. She skillfully used the piano to cover any imperfections or mistakes of singers, building their confidence. Her servant spirit set an example for everyone working with her. She seemed to have some secret reservoir of energy getting her through endless day and night schedules with consistent resiliency.

The open, lively worship in this church was in many ways an extension of Clariece Paulk's own spirit. She radiated a staccato, upbeat personality. She spoke in rapid phrases with a Southern (Tennessee) accent. She wore frilly, stylish clothes. Ruffles, bows and flowers in her hair expressed a gentle femininity. At the same time she moved boldly and confidently as she ministered in spiritual power.

Clariece was an "idea" person with extraordinary creativity. She was always willing to try new things, allowing time for projects to grow and struggle until they flowed with the Holy Spirit and ministered to people. She nursed the orchestra through its infancy to a place of glory to the Lord. She had oversight of a drama ministry which wrote its own scripts and ministered in productions ranging from clowns and specialized skits to Kingdom comedies, musicals and even children's productions, such as *Kingdom Over the Rainbow*. Under her ministry, a dance company began weekly rehearsals. In time, the dancers began to minister beautiful, physical expressions of worship during the services. Clariece threw all her energy into putting together big, spectacular productions with pomp, glitter and flare. These productions, featuring the combined talents of the Arts Department, presented artistic worship by the "Morning Stars."

Sometimes Clariece's adventurous spirit unnerved the people whom she expected to implement her ideas. For instance, she would spontaneously bring hesitant, unprepared singers or musicians to the platform to minister during a service. She never hesitated to throw a totally new song at the choir to learn by the next service. Because of her confidence and faith, these poor victims were usually amazed at how beautifully they were able to perform whatever she had asked them to do.

Clariece began each service by playing on the piano some familiar song or hymn calling the congregation's attention to a unified purpose: welcoming the presence of their King, Jesus Christ. The lights in the tent dimmed on cue. As she played a hymn, quiet, peaceful reverence fell over the people who until then had enjoyed visiting with friends sitting near them. The music signaled for people to begin to pray. Some interceded for the prophet to speak boldly those things which God had given him to say. Others asked God to meet specific needs in their own lives, to guide them through trials which they had been experiencing. Many people simply asked God to give them open, receptive hearts and anointed ears to hear the message the Spirit would speak to them in that particular service.

The other pastors on the Presbytery walked into the tent from a side entrance. They took their places on the stage in chairs placed in front of the choir facing the pulpit. They came from a time of praying together for God's spiritual direction for the service.

Like the people in the church, the pastors' personalities and backgrounds represented a wide variety. God called one pastor from his retirement after a full career in building and construction. Another pastor was a mother with four children. God called her to a full-time pastorate after she began to minister with anointed gifts of discernment and deliverance to people coming to her for counseling and prayer. Another pastor, a handsome black man with a doctorate, was called to the ministry from a successful dental practice. He allowed dentistry to become a part-time occupation because God had called him to teach the Kingdom message from church to church. Other pastors were called at the peak of financial, business productivity from careers in which they earned two or three times the yearly income of a pastor's salary in this ministry.

Some pastors completed seminary, others did not. All of these men and women were uniquely called with particular spiritual gifts to meet needs in this ministry. All were providentially called by the Lord for such a time as this. Each one of them ministered as an extension of the senior pastor to an ever-growing congregation.

Pastor Don Paulk walked to the pulpit and raised his hands, signaling the congregation to stand. The people sang a favorite song, *Arise, Shine, For Your Light Has Come!* Both individually and corporately, the people purposed in their hearts to enter into God's presence. They came to God according to the psalmist's instructions, "Enter into His gates with thanksgiving, and into His courts with praise. Be thankful unto Him, and bless His name" (Psalm 100:4).

The people in this church easily responded with openness to the moving of the Holy Spirit through praises to the Lord. The singing groups and choirs led the worshippers in various songs, various moods of interaction with the Spirit. On each side of the center platform stood singers who ministered in the services. The Harvester Hour Choir sang hymns and anthems ranging from classical Bach to loud and lively scripture choruses accented with jingling tambourines. Certain selections of the music were physically interpreted by choreographed dancers sweeping across the stage as the choir sang.

Other choir selections flowed with a "gospel" flavor. The "Hallelujah Chorus" began as a predominantly black choir specializing in swaying Negro spirituals or high-energy gospel songs with never-ending refrains like, "Just can't stop praising His name— Jesus!" The racial, cultural variety of these singers added musical versatility rarely captured in an entire choir. The Harvester Hour Choir and the Hallelujah Chorus finally merged into one choir singing all styles of music—no white choir, no black choir—just total, unified rejoicing to the King!

To the left of the center platform stood a nine-member singing group, the K-Dimension Singers. These singers led many of the worship songs during the services. They also ministered special music for television and occasionally traveled with Bishop Paulk on speaking engagements. The K-Dimension Singers combined vocalists from other singing groups: a trio called Promise, members of the Alpha band and soloists on various choir selections. The variety of music, talented voices and instruments lifted in praise to God washed over the congregation in warm waves of celebration.

These singers were not performers. No one sang to entertain the congregation with impressive musical talent. Singers, dancers and musicians simply led all the worshippers, helping people to clear their minds of distractions and open their spirits to express love to God in the intimacy of each person's own individual, yet blended worship expression. Often the prophet had instructed worship leaders that they were called to minister to the Lord rather than "perform" before people. He admonished them, "If your spirit isn't directed toward honoring the Lord, don't walk out on that platform!"

In a sunken area behind the pulpit, orchestra members played instruments accompanying the singers. Sometimes the orchestra played instrumentals or scripture choruses, setting the spiritual atmosphere for people to receive God's Word with open hearts. The orchestra struggled in its beginning. Musicians dusted off instrument cases they had stored away in closets and brought them to church. Many of these musicians had not sounded a note on their instruments since high school days long ago. But God honored their willing hearts, diligence and the desire to worship Him on instruments of praise. Their musical progress was amazing. In just a few short months of struggling in front of an encouraging audience who applauded their fledgling efforts, the orchestra's addition to the singing and worship was immeasurable.

Worship began in the outer courts of God's presence. Praises to God activated the individual wills of believers to put away their concerns and begin to concentrate their attention on the Lord. The outer courts of praise focused the minds of people on Jesus rather than job hassles, problems in relationships or matters needing God's intervention. Expression in outer courts praise was simply willing participation—for instance, clapping hands to music. High energy praise songs motivated people to respond physically by moving their feet or raising their hands. Physical response evoked a willingness within the worshippers to move obediently in God's direction.

As the people became more willing to move toward God, thanksgiving rose up inside them like springs of water that Jesus promised would flow from those who desired His life in them. That flowing spring began as thanks, recognizing God's love and promises with gratitude. Gradually, praise, thanksgiving and love began to pour out of the worshippers in overflowing rivers of adoration toward the Source of love Himself. God's goodness and mercy washed, cleansed, saturated, permeated the people. People felt liberating freedom inside. They sang with grateful hearts about God's creative power, His royal majesty.

Inner courts worship combined praises and adoration to Jesus as the Savior, High Priest and King. In the inner courts of praise and worship, the people recognized the grace of God through the sacrificial Lamb, slain for the remission of their sins. Only His righteousness allowed them to enter fully into God's presence. God's righteousness clothed the people as they drew closer to Him. Inner courts worship cleansed people from their guilt, failures and human frailties, just as the priest washed himself in the brass laver before he went behind the veil into the Holy of Holies. As the people experienced the identity Jesus gave them as His Bride, His glorified Church without spot or wrinkle, they were ready in their hearts and minds to enter into the Holy of Holies to enjoy intimate fellowship with God.

Pastor Duane Swilley came to the pulpit blasting on his trumpet. With the help of other musicians and singers, he led the congregation as they moved individually and corporately through the outer courts of praise. Duane, a gifted motivator, utilized powerful spiritual gifts of exhortation to lead the people. God blessed Duane with many natural assets and talents which he gave back to God by dedicating his life to Kingdom service and ministry. He grew up as the son of a traveling evangelist couple, Wallace and Ernestine Swilley. Duane, his parents and his younger brother, Mark, traveled and ministered in churches all over the world.

This wide exposure to different churches caused many scars of spiritual disillusionment in Duane's perspective toward ministry. When he first attended this church in the mid-1970's, he sat in the congregation as the nephew of the founding pastors without any desire or intention of joining the ministry. But as powerful teaching, genuine unconditional love and healing truth began to confront his restless spirit, the evangelist's call from God on his life since childhood began rumbling within him.

Duane was the leader of Alpha, a dynamic youth ministry in which thousands of teenagers met Jesus for the first time and quickly grew to maturity in the Lord. God used Duane's athletic, handsome appearance and his personal charisma to contradict young people's negative opinions of church as "boring" and Christians as people with dull "losers" lifestyles. Duane Swilley radiated the confidence of a born winner.

As a former Georgia Tech track star, Duane enjoyed competitive, challenging situations. His ministry often took the "cutting edge" path of confrontation and controversy. The Alpha ministry lasered dark areas of bondage in young people's lives with the piercing light of truth. Every Monday night, Duane taught biblical truth with a Jeremiah anointing that broke people loose and shook them up. His early training on the guitar and trumpet prepared him to be an able leader of the Alpha band. Alpha services unleashed bold, electrifying energy with conversion power.

Duane spoke in positive superlatives. His descriptions were peppered with words like "best," "most" and "greatest." Young people often quoted Duane by repeating a word he frequently used, "Awesome!" These tendencies in diction expressed an attitude of urgency, a man perpetually pressing forward to maximize the moment. In worship, Duane's fervor was exemplary. Watching him caused others to consider their own degree of intensity, freeing them by his example to express their own love to God.

Transitions in worship services were never clearly defined. Height or depth of worship depended solely on the willingness in individual worshippers to open their inner rooms, drawing closer to God's light. Many people did not require any degree of prompting to enter into God's presence. Some people drove to church already worshipping, offering songs of praise and prayers of worship to God. Others followed the leading of the pastor standing behind the pulpit, who urged them by his example to disregard emotional barriers to worship.

Pastor Steve Owens was a worshipper able to bridge the outer courts, drawing God's people closer to Him through praise. Inner courts worship prepared people's hearts to enter into the Holy of Holies in total adoration of the King. Whenever Steve sang, he physically personified the psalmist's description, "All that is within me, bless His holy name."

Steve was small in stature but mighty in spirit. His singing voice sounded throaty and professional. His musical style had a "soul" quality with frequent vocal improvisation up and down the scale. Steve could wring every drop of emotion from every word, leaving the congregation hanging onto a song as he chased around the lyrics with his own additional notes and phrases. He was physically active in expressing the emotions of whatever words he sang. He would bend his knees to the beat of the music. Occasionally, he turned his entire body loose in a hopping dance across the stage, expressing a burst of adoration to the Lord.

Steve's singing became a bridge ministry in worship. Significantly, this church served as a bridge back to God in Steve's own life. As a brooding young man, Steve walked away from his Pentecostal upbringing. He married Earl Paulk's second daughter, Joy, and began listening closely to her father's preaching while dutifully accompanying his wife and sons to church. Steve was challenged by the purity of the Word. Steve also received genuine unconditional love from his wife's dad in spite of his intellectual approach to "religion" and guarded emotions in worship.

Steve Owens returned to his childhood faith in a remarkable, turn-around conversion. He recognized immediately that all along God had equipped him with an ability to love people easily, a keen sensitivity to others' perspectives and even a college degree in psychology which prepared him academically as a worthy counselor. Steve began to know a new heartfelt dimension of the heavenly Father's love through his devoted relationship with his father-in-law. Experiencing God's love in one relationship expanded, encompassing thousands. Trusting love for the Lord was the evident motivation as Steve worshipped freely, uninhibited in God's presence.

Steve's goal in leading the congregation in worship was to become totally unnecessary—even unnoticed—by the people. Steve said many times that he believed "leading" worship was totally impossible. How could anyone actually lead others to worship God? Worship could be enjoyed simultaneously and corporately, but the worship experience was always a private matter. Worshippers opening their spirits and entering God's throne room, the Holy of Holies, focused on God Himself. True worship never depended on the efforts of a worship leader or a canned, preplanned, musical format. True worship didn't even require understandable language. In God's presence people sang "new songs" to the Lord in words of love, mingled languages, elusive harmonies and disharmonies, incarnate praises uttered directly in the verbally incomprehensible language of the Spirit.

Some people shouted, "Hallelujah!" while others

clapped their hands. Some people waved their hands above their heads, signifying to God, "My heart is Yours to mold as You will." Hands raised into the air were signs both of surrender to God and of reaching up to One greater, the "Abba" Father, fulfilling every inexpressible inner longing. The intimacy of worship crescendoed in the Bride-Bridegroom oneness in which the finite and Infinite unexplainably merged into one being, one mind, one purpose, one will. The mingled voices rose and fell in waves of worship as the Holy Spirit moved in warm, interactive, intimate personality among His people.

Pastor Don Paulk stood beside his brother as he has done since the early days, over twenty-three years ago, when the vision of this ministry was first born in his brother's spirit. Don was eleven years younger than the man beside him who not only was his brother, but also at times a second father to him. Don and his twin sister, Darlene, were born to the Paulk family in the days when the patriarch of the clan, Earl Paulk Sr., traveled from home much of the time preaching all over the world in a widely influential Pentecostal ministry.

The responsibility for the family's care fell to Earl Jr. who assisted his mother in day-to-day family matters in his father's absence. Don grew up answering to two "fathers" in his own household, both of whom were preachers since brother Earl was called into the ministry at seventeen. That double dose of strict paternal oversight awakened a quick mind and a marvelous sense of humor in Don Paulk. His witty, candid views on life helped ease tensions and sometimes painful struggles in the early days of the Harvesters. Don was noted for his direct honesty in addressing issues facing the church. His perspective had been invaluable to the ministry in recognizing dangers and forcing others to deal with administrative realities which might have gone unattended indefinitely.

Don Paulk was a very talented, popular writer. He served as Senior Editor of *Harvest Time*, a monthly publication sent free to the church's mailing list of over 25,000 people. In his regular column, "Don Paulk's Pen," he described people, events and insights into the ministry with descriptive candor and charm. The combination of the practical view of life dominating Don's perspective, along with his unshakable faith in God's ability to open impossible doors, made his role in the ministry very difficult at times.

Moving cautiously in spiritual decisions, Don Paulk often presented a balanced view to people in leadership who were quick to respond optimistically to any new idea or project. He was determined to lead people only with absolute certainty of God's direction. He was adamantly loyal to the vision of this church as well as to the people God had called him to serve.

The people in the church responded warmly to Don's fatherly concern toward them. He was very sensitive to criticism and persecution that anyone experienced because of their loyalty to the ministry. He was very conscientious about ministry being available to serve the needs of the people. He assumed the role of staff administrator and head of the pastoral shepherding groups. The people at Chapel Hill recognized Don's genuine love for them. His approachable, warm manner made people feel comfortable and at home in the church. No one expressed greater appreciation for those offering their time and talents to the Kingdom than Pastor Don. He let people know that they were personally important to God, the leadership of the church and the vision of the ministry.

Don often walked to the pulpit to open and close the services. He sometimes sang solos with the choir joining him on the choruses. He assisted Clariece by conducting the more formal anthems sung by the choir. Besides preparing the congregation for worship by opening the services, Don often capsuled the entire worship mood in a "final touches" benediction at the end. He spoke with the authority of a founding pastor, yet he had the ability to capture the thoughts of the people, to answer the questions they were asking themselves.

Earl Paulk watched the people in his congregation as they sang and worshipped. He knew that the initial excitement of services in this cathedral tent was short-lived. People always rallied to a new cause in the beginning. They quickly fainted whenever heat, cold or rain caused any discomfort or distraction to them. But long ago, God promised him a people who would survive any test. In his spirit, he knew that many of the people worshipping in this tent were soldiers in a mighty army that God was building across the earth.

Over the past few months, multitudes of people had begun coming to Sunday services. Many people were turned away at the doors because the seating capacity of the sanctuary wouldn't accommodate them in only two morning sessions. Earl Paulk sought the Lord for direction. God spoke to him with clear, specific orders, "Build My Church!" When he met with architects and contractors about building a new sanctuary, he asked God for clear confirmation about all their plans and proposals. God spoke again to him forcefully in his spirit, "Build My Church!"

At last he understood God's orders. God wanted a building of people, living stones, with the spiritual maturity to storm the gates of hell, to overcome worldly kingdoms opposed to God's purposes. Of course, a larger building was necessary and timely. Rapid numerical growth was beyond the seating capacity for three Sunday services in the existing sanctuary. People overflowed the facilities, now totally inadequate to accommodate the worshippers, their children and hundreds of cars. But God's interest focused on His people far more than details of a building program. Undoubtedly, this tent experience would build many people into the church God had ordained.

Earl Paulk read the faces of his congregation. So many of their expressions were fresh, excited, eager to demonstrate the Kingdom of God. So few had any comprehension of the costs. He picked out faces among the masses of people who came to him only a short time ago in desperation, without any solutions—nothing but elusive hope that somehow God would give them a miracle. Now many of those people reached out to others with similar needs, offering living proof of God's sufficient restoration.

He recognized men and women with pioneer spirits. These people tenaciously grasped the Kingdom message and refused to settle for less than God's perfect will for their lives. Many of them had already made significant sacrifices, paid the price in their relationships, finances, careers and other life choices to join the vision of this church. These people had fixed hearts and overcoming faith. They would remain steadfast through trials and persecution. He surveyed the crowd: black faces, white faces, brown faces, all singing in one symphony of praise just as he had seen in the Spirit long ago. Some of the people were "babes in Christ," new Christians needing nurture and tender understanding to survive in the wilderness.

Earl Paulk, a pastor for almost forty years, was a tested, experienced warrior. He acknowledged the risks in this ridiculous tent church. The facts were ironic, contradictory. God had spoken of this ministry having a spiritual impact on the world. No unbiased observer would be impressed with this seemingly ordinary congregation—except perhaps for the number of people. Certainly the facility was unimpressive except for its novelty. Bills for the most recently purchased television equipment lay unpaid on his desk. Earl had obeyed God by giving their old television equipment to Bishop Herro Blair's ministry in Jamaica. Only a firm financial commitment from every person would cause the proposed building to come up from the ground within a short period of time. That commitment was highly unlikely. How easily this wilderness experience on the parking lot could become a well-publicized embarrassment.

He thought about his wife, Norma, who had stood faithfully by him through every test. His three beautiful daughters and their husbands, who worked with him every day in this ministry, stood near him on the platform. He felt the responsibility for his eight precious grandchildren—seven grandsons just as God promised him and one granddaughter, named through a prophetic dream. They fully trusted his wisdom and direction.

So many people entrusted themselves and their families to his spiritual leadership. The man in his mid-fifties felt the weight of these lives that depended on his strength—such grave responsibilities, too great for any man. He knew he couldn't possibly lead anyone who was unwilling to trust God's sovereignty to make provisions for their lives. He felt totally, completely dependent on the Holy Spirit for answers and direction. Human perceptions were so fragile, so fallible. How well he knew all the victories in the past were God's—not his own. The soldier was weary from continuous battle. Without sure guidance from the Lord, the vision of this church was totally impossible for any man to implement. How well he understood Abraham's "hope against hope" regarding the promises of God.

As a loving pastor, Earl Paulk longed to embrace the people before him, to protect them from times of testing. He knew that many of them would fall away. The pastor's heart always responded first to people's needs in their trials. At times he loved people with foolish compassion and understanding, easily forgiving seventy times seven for the same willful offense. He was often criticized for being an "easy touch" for people in trouble. But long ago he asked God to give him unconditional love for His people. God had called him in the foundation of this ministry as a shepherd to "scattered sheep," bringing people safely into the sheepfold. Earl took that charge very seriously—at times becoming an overly-protective shepherd. He was drawn to wounded and brokenhearted people, particularly ministers who were ready to walk away from their callings after being trampled, disappointed and disillusioned.

With the perception of a spiritual father, Earl Paulk clearly saw the warfare in the lives of his people. He wept openly as he watched them, feeling Jesus' deep compassion in His own spirit. So many people lived continuously in chains, bondage and ignorance when Truth could so easily free them. Yet years of ministry forced him to admit that many were dull of hearing. Many followed him, as crowds had followed Jesus, for the bread that he gave them. Some people played spiritual games. They were called to strategic roles in the Kingdom which they either wouldn't comprehend or willingly accept. Disobedience and pride still ruled many people who talked Kingdom jargon but refused "to walk" the same language they talked.

Earl Paulk deeply loved his people. His love for them covered their frailties, excuses and failures. The pastor's heart searched for the "Jesus spirit" in any person. He looked for areas of responsibility where trust could be planted and cultivated. The pastor's heart discerned the totality of one's spiritual condition. He saw someone's spiritual needs without pretense as well as whatever seeds of talent or promise God could develop for ministry. The pastor's heart found places of service where everyone fit into God's master plan.

People easily responded to Earl Paulk's pastoral counsel. Many times during sermons he walked to the side of the podium, leaned on his elbow, and "visited" with the people. During those times, he spoke plainly to them about their personal attitudes and habits. He called these inserted lectures in his sermons "your free part." These fatherly admonitions often struck a humorous tone of Earl's own personal opinions. However, the issues he addressed targeted major areas in people's lives. He frequently called his congregation "Honey," an endearment delighting some people and irritating others. Sometimes he softened hard sayings, pastoral chastenings or prophetic challenges by pleading with the people, "Oh! My dear darlings, will you please **listen** to me?"

Earl Paulk's warm pastoral style and his fatherly concern made his people adore him, but the anointed voice of the prophet ignited unquenchable flames of purpose within them. His words pressed them to the limit of their imaginations. Revelation first intruded into Earl's spirit at a most unlikely time in his own life, during personal crisis in his ministry. Earl Paulk, the prophet, received a heavenly vision out of the smoldering ashes of personal devastation. God unveiled the vision of this church to Earl when he was questioning his identity and calling. His own confrontation with God was as shocking to him as Moses' reaction at the burning bush. Earl backed away thinking that God must be making a mistake. How could God possibly call "a failure" to such an extraordinary mission? Who would he say sent him back to Atlanta to face the humiliation of starting all over again? No one would believe such arrogance or self-abuse could possibly be God's command.

The fruit of the past twenty-three years proved those extraordinary promises over and over. Yet, Earl knew that reality of the heavenly vision was far from complete. Though the vision God gave to Earl in the desert had been confirmed repeatedly and he was grateful for all that God had accomplished, he continued pressing forward without daring to look behind him. Earl Paulk, the prophet, would never back away from fulfillment of the total heavenly vision he had seen in the desert. The loneliness of carrying that vision, even criticism from people closest to him, financial pressures, pressures from "the majority" to settle for less than the total fulfillment of the heavenly vision—nothing would alter his course. His motives had been tested by fire over and over again through accusations, challenges and misunderstandings. He was a man who willingly died daily in his flesh. His life could never be his own again for even one hour.

The prophet's path blazed with the fire of self-denial in deliberate, uncompromising, step-by-step obedience. A prophetic voice to the Church could only walk in total dependency on God's direction. After years of preaching impossible promises to a faithful handful of people sitting on half-empty pews, the vision took root inside them. As their faith soared, so did the reality of the promises. Membership in the church quickly doubled and tripled. Suddenly the ministry, which had struggled for so many years on promises, faced all the problems of needing additional facilities and staff personnel to minister to hundreds of new people who joined each month.

Some signal was given in the heavenlies. God began to send messengers to the ministry. World-known apostles, prophets, evangelists, pastors and teachers came to the church confirming the Word of the Lord spoken for so many years to the faithful few listening to Earl Paulk. T. L. Osborn called the ministry "an oasis in a desert place." Iverna Tompkins called the church "a forerunner," a "lead domino" and a "showcase." Iverna joined the ministry at Chapel Hill for several years as her home church. Iverna's brother, Dr. Judson Cornwall, also moved to Atlanta with his family and became a vital part of the church leadership. Dr. Cornwall continued to minister through writing and teaching to the total Body of Christ.

Carlton Pearson, Bill Hamon and many other men with proven, prophetic ministries encouraged the people at Chapel Hill to realize their mighty visitation of the Lord. The prophetic word repeatedly confirmed that God had established a very specialized ministry in the church. Bill Hamon instructed Earl Paulk to prepare to travel as an apostle to scores of churches raised up under his ministry. Archbishop Benson Idahosa from Nigeria, an apostle whose leadership established over 800 African churches, told the people at

Chapel Hill that their church would become one of five major centers for ministry in the world. Confirmation and exhortation given by God's messengers to the ministry at Chapel Hill Harvester Church thrilled the people. At the same time, God's calling and its repeated confirmations shook them to the sober realities of their responsibilities to God. God had given them much; much would be required.

God began speaking to Earl Paulk to test his total obedience in boldly proclaiming His message. During a summer drought in 1981, weather forecasters made pessimistic predictions about seriously low water tables at the lakes and rivers in the southern states. Weather centers estimated that the perilous situation would take at least three full years of greater than normal rainfall to recover from the drought.

Under a prophetic anointing, Earl Paulk declared to his congregation and to the television audience that God had spoken to him about the drought. He told them that the Lord instructed him to say that what everyone predicted would take three years to remedy, the Lord would perform in only three months.

The congregation spontaneously applauded this bold word from the prophet. Still, many people regretted that he would publicly proclaim such an impossible prediction. Earl Paulk's people dearly loved him, but God had to teach them, like children, to trust the prophetic calling on his life. Only God could teach them that He would speak direction to the church through a modern prophet. Within a few days, the rain fell in torrents across the southern states. The drought conditions quickly changed into a flood from the heavens. Just as God promised, within three months all the lakes and rivers returned to normal levels.

In almost an opposite word from God in calling forth rain from heaven, Earl Paulk promised the people that God would hold back the rain during an outdoor, evangelistic campaign, ALPHA '82, held for three consecutive nights in June of that year. Weather forecasters were baffled the entire week. The rain, which they predicted daily on television, fell on towns and communities surrounding the Atlanta area within a thirty-mile radius. Rain never fell in Atlanta that week. Embarrassed forecasters reported each night on the evening news that the rain would get within miles of Atlanta, and the front seemed to divide and go around the city. Immediately after the last service of ALPHA '82 ended, thousands of people rushed to their cars. As they drove away to their homes, the long predicted rain finally drenched the city.

The Holy Spirit tested Earl Paulk's obedience again in his hotel room in Charlotte, N. C. The night before he was to appear on the PTL program with PTL host, Jim Bakker, God gave him a message to give to the PTL founder. When Earl sat down beside Jim Bakker on the live broadcast, the host asked him about the Alpha youth ministry at Earl's church in Atlanta. Bishop Paulk quickly answered Jim's questions. Then totally in opposition to his own desires in the matter as well as disregarding the opinions of others, Earl said to the host, "Jim, I have a word for you from the Lord."

Earl Paulk prophesied over the founder of PTL that

Jim had been called by God as a world-wide demonstrator of God's Kingdom. He said that the callings of Jim Bakker and Pat Robertson were in the spirit of the two witnesses in the Book of Revelation. They would be used by God to proclaim His Kingdom to the world. Jim Bakker represented the "spirit of demonstration" with his diverse service ministries to lift and encourage believers to receive God's goodness. Pat Robertson represented "the spirit of communication" through ministry gifts in teaching and oration.

Jim Bakker received the prophetic word given to him by Earl Paulk. Immediately he began to minister in power to people in the studio audience. Within a few months, Jim Bakker launched an innovative youth ministry at PTL. He also began making plans to build a home for unwed mothers which he and Earl also discussed that day. Chapel Hill Harvester Church had begun a "House of New Life" for unwed mothers in 1980. A few weeks after the word of the Lord was given by Earl on PTL, Pat Robertson sent his contributors a tape series on Kingdom principles. Within a few months, Pat Robertson released a best-selling book on Kingdom teaching, manuscripts which were being processed without Earl Paulk's having any knowledge of them other than by the Spirit.

God also had given a message to Earl Paulk to give to Demos Shakarian, the founder and president of Full Gospel Business Men's Fellowship International. Demos also appeared as a guest on PTL the same day as Earl. God told Earl to give a prophetic word to Demos Shakarian only after Demos asked him whether God had spoken to him concerning the F.G.B.M.F.I.'s ministry.

As Earl Paulk, Jim Bakker, Demos Shakarian and others rode in a car tour of the Heritage USA property, Demos Shakarian turned to Bishop Paulk and asked him if the Lord had any word for him concerning his ministry. Earl smiled as he realized God's precision timing and preparation. He told Demos that God had indeed prepared him to give a word to the leader of this international ministry. Earl added that he was only permitted to speak it after Demos asked him that question.

Earl told Demos that God wanted F.G.B.M.F.I. to become a greater support to local churches around the world. He said that God had never commissioned the ministry as a separate cause from the work of local churches. Its mission needed to be directed more toward raising up and empowering leaders in small local churches everywhere to lead struggling congregations to confidence in anointed power and ministry gifts from the Lord.

God began giving words for Earl Paulk to deliver in the most unlikely, highly precarious situations. While preaching a Sunday morning sermon in an Atlanta hotel to those who would participate in the 1983 Peachtree Road Race the next day, the Holy Spirit drew Earl's attention to a young African runner sitting in a room among people attending the service. The Lord told the prophet that the young man would be the winner of the race. Earl had never seen this man before and knew nothing about him. He was the smaller of two African runners who sat together in the worship service.

Earl walked over to the young man and told him what the Holy Spirit had spoken. The runner humbly replied that he had prepared himself diligently in hopes of winning the race. The next day, among the thirty thousand runners in the Peachtree Road Race, a young African, Michael Musyoki, was the first place winner. He was so aware of the spiritual significance of his winning the race that he autographed the number pinned to his clothes and sent it by road race officials to the prophet who had spoken to him at the worship service the day before he ran.

God told Earl Paulk that 1983 would be a year of faith and testing in his ministry like never before. The prophet slowly lifted his eyes from the faces of the congregation packed into orderly rows all the way to the back of the tent. He contemplated again for a few moments an unseen place of promise beyond the finite scene before him. He took a deep breath, closing his eyes to visualize an age-old promise, "The kingdoms of this world shall become the Kingdom of our God and of His Christ."

The music stopped. Yes, he was ready. He walked confidently to the podium carrying his Bible and note-book where he had written only a few scriptures that would build a message dropped into his spirit like the title of a song. He would allow God the freedom to fashion that message as a holy offering back to its Source. He would speak boldly to chosen people, royalty, mighty kings and priests—no matter how many or how few they were among the masses of faces—who waited to hear from the Lord with open hearts, anointed ears and ready spirits. His words were sharp, quick and powerful. Through his voice, God spoke to His people with undeniably clear direction.

As a man like any other, Earl Paulk trembled. As a pastor, he entreated, encouraged and covered the fragile frames of people walking by faith, struggling with issues, making decisions at that very hour. But as a prophet of the Lord, his eyes burned with fire and his mouth became a sword of life and death as he obeyed the command that the Lord had branded indelibly with a torch into his heart, soul and mind, "Son of man, prophesy!"

2

CHAPTER TWO

Birth is a mystery. The physiological process can be explained, but a squirming little person's introduction to life is always a miraculous event. Even more miraculous is the little person himself. All people are the seed of generations before them. Fathers and mothers throughout previous centuries have contributed personal potential to one composite human being. Earl Paulk's story began generations before he was born in 1927 to Earl and Addie Mae (Tomberlin) Paulk. Although all seed can be traced ultimately to one common father, Adam, the created son of God, most people discover their most definable traits and characteristics in the generation preceding them. Parents' identities answer many questions about their seed. Earl Paulk's story begins with the life of the man for whom he was named, the single greatest influence in his life.

Baxley, Georgia, in the late spring of 1923 was a place of green acres of flat land, tall, swaying pecan trees and little farms stretched out miles apart along unpaved, sandy roads. Earl Paulk worked diligently to finish the spring plowing under the hot sun. The handsome, stocky nineteen-year-old didn't mind the hard work, but his mind seldom focused on his chores.

Family obligations forced Earl to leave school after the third grade to become a full-time farm hand. Hard times financially in a large family made going to school an unaffordable luxury for the Paulk family's oldest son. Many times Earl Paulk watched younger family members and their friends walking to school. Earl wiped away many tears, promising himself repeatedly that his children would someday enjoy all the advantages in life that he had been denied.

Earl's daddy, Elisha Paulk, was a Freewill Baptist preacher, dividing his time between work on the farm and work for the Lord. Young Earl theoretically admired his daddy's gospel message, but he found religion difficult to accept for himself. He just couldn't promise to keep the kind of sincere commitment and strict rules that his daddy's faith required. In his early teens Earl started going to dances and hanging around other young men in the community who had plenty of ideas on how to spend free time other than sitting in church meetings. Earl enjoyed his friends' antics, visiting attractive young ladies and speculating on all the possibilities the world offered farm boys in the early 1920's. But Earl was a serious young man who probed life's complicated questions and assumed responsibility for other people's welfare. Eventually, the strength of his own conscience, his daddy's prayers and his Bible-centered upbringing overpowered free-wheeling frivolity in his life.

One night Earl went with a friend to a prayer meeting. He was totally convinced that he took his friend to the meeting so he would "get saved." Instead, the major spiritual event of the evening focused on Earl Paulk's own experience of God's power—an unanticipated calling on his life. He sat in a straight-back wooden chair among a few other believers who had gathered that evening to pray. An inner voice began speaking to the young man about a calling from the Lord on his life. The preacher leading the meeting walked over to Earl. In a loud voice the preacher prayed as he gripped Earl's shoulder, "Lord, make a preacher out of him!" Immediately, young Earl jumped up from his chair and walked back and forth across the room, preaching an anointed, spontaneous sermon which was the first of thousands he would deliver.

Now his future hinged on other important decisions and sometimes confusing directions. He plowed the rich soil without giving any thought to his task while sweat saturated his shirt. He occasionally incorporated prayer to God into the running conversation he was having with himself. Finally, Earl Paulk made a decision as to which girl he would marry. He would follow his heart. He would not marry Vertie Mae—the sweetheart whose name was written on the marriage license he had already processed at the county courthouse. Instead he would marry Addie Mae Tomberlin— the beautiful fifteen-year-old girl whom he had met only a few weeks earlier.

Earl Paulk was not usually impulsive. He could hardly believe the way that he had been so quickly, yet totally captivated by Miss Tomberlin. Every reasonable thought in his mind argued for him to stick with his original marriage proposal to Vertie Mae whom he had cared about so deeply. Yet unexplainably, from the first time he heard his brother, Buddy, talk about Mr. Tomberlin's beautiful daughter, he had felt an overwhelming prompting inside which he couldn't quite explain. When he went to the Tomberlins' farm to see Addie Mae for himself, that prompting strengthened into a serious determination to be near her always.

He shocked himself with his unreasonable affections for Addie Mae. Even courting her had become quite a challenge. He had to cross a creek on his horse to get to her daddy's farm. After days of spring rain, the creek would rise so high that he had to undress on the bank, ride his horse across the creek with his clothes held high above his head, then dress again on the other side. He felt so obsessed with such passionate determination to see Addie Mae that his own actions convinced him of how greatly he loved her!

Addie Mae was a beautiful girl. She had high cheek bones, long brown hair and blue eyes that danced when she laughed. Earl Paulk instantly loved her vivacious spirit that made him feel emotionally complete. In all the ways that he was shy and unsure of himself, Addie Mae had strength and inner fire. Her sense of humor challenged his sometimes too serious preoccupation with abstract philosophical issues. She would quickly challenge his profound insights with some spunky verbal twist. When she responded to the things he would say, he sensed a practical perspective to draw from whenever he needed emotional balance and blatant, unrefined honesty.

However, Earl and Addie Mae had one major spiritual conflict. The Tomberlin family believed in the baptism in the Holy Spirit with evidence of speaking in other tongues. Though they worshipped as a traditional Methodist family, they also openly shared with others their belief in the reality of the Pentecostal experience for all believers' lives. They knew that God could work miracles through a believer's faith in the Lord. They had proof of that belief living in their household.

One of the Tomberlins' sons had been healed of a handicapped arm when he went to services at a tent revival conducted in their community by S. J. Heath from Atlanta. J. M. Tomberlin was so grateful to God for his son's miraculous healing that he accompanied his son to the tent meeting the next night. Mr. Tomberlin and the other members of his family were so moved by the power of God in the service, they all received a new spiritual dimension added to their staunch Methodist salvation. J. M. Tomberlin, a respected Methodist steward, never backed away from the validity of that spiritual experience. Evangelist S. J. Heath went back to Atlanta to lead a group of people to begin the 6th Street Church of God. Later, that church was renamed Hemphill Church of God, a church which would play a major role in the life of Addie Mae Tomberlin's oldest son.

Within a few weeks after he met Addie Mae Tomberlin, Earl Paulk returned with his marriage license to the county courthouse to change the name of his bride from "Vertie" Mae to "Addie" Mae. On June 3, the young couple were married in the Tomberlins' farmhouse, standing in front of the fireplace surrounded by their families. The fifteen-year-old bride was hardly prepared for the immediate pregnancy accompanying all the other domestic adjustments she had to make. Emotionally, Addie Mae was unprepared to assume the responsible roles of a wife and mother. Earl sheltered his young bride with loving protection. His mature, dependable strength allowed his bride to remain fresh and childlike in her perceptions. Ten months after the wedding when Addie Mae had just turned sixteen, she gave birth to a baby daughter whom they named Myrtle Olene after a woman preacher both parents admired.

Earl continued to work on the farm to provide for his wife and baby, but his call from God to the ministry was the strongest desire and motivation within him. His intense commitment to preach God's Word stretched his keen mind in developing an extraordinary ability to memorize the Bible. Compensating for his limited formal education, Earl conscientiously absorbed each word of scripture as Addie Mae read aloud to him while they sat by the fire in the evenings after supper. He would quote long passages of scripture back to his wife with verbatim accuracy. Like her husband, Addie Mae had a dedicated vision of ministry. She never once questioned the calling of God in motivating her serious, intense husband's decisions. God's anointing on the amazing memory of this young preacher prompted people in the community to begin labeling him "the walking Bible."

When little Myrtle was three, Addie Mae became pregnant with their second child. Earl hoped their second baby would be a boy. He was preaching more than farming now—traveling about the countryside conducting evangelistic meetings and tent revivals. He had even traveled several times to preach revivals at churches in other states. The baby was due at the end of May, and Earl deliberately stayed close to his wife as the day of the anticipated delivery approached.

Addie Mae felt slight cramps all that day, just enough to alert her that she probably had a long night ahead. When the supper dishes were washed and the sun had gone down, hard labor pains struck. Earl left hurriedly to get Mrs. Campbell, the area mid-wife. The woman had received reports on Addie Mae's condition for several weeks and expected Earl's visit at any moment.

Mrs. Campbell was a well-known Christian mid-wife who had prayed many Appling County babies into the world. As Addie Mae's labor pains became more regular and intense, Mrs. Campbell calmly remarked to the nervous father that this was going to be a very special baby. Finally, the long-awaited

moment arrived. Addie Mae delivered a large baby
boy. Mrs. Campbell bathed the baby and held him up
for his radiant mother to see. The mid-wife prophetically exclaimed, "Mrs. Paulk, this baby is going to be a
preacher!"

Addie Mae smiled at the thought of her tiny baby,
only a few minutes old, already cloaked in his father's
heavy mantle of ministry.

"I'm telling you, Mrs. Paulk. This baby is going to be
a preacher!" Mrs. Campbell exclaimed. "The Lord
spoke to me that you have another preacher in your
family." The baby was born in the same house where
his parents were married. He was chubby with fat
cheeks and broad shoulders. Later his mother would
teasingly blame his wide shoulders for causing the
fragile health with which she suffered most of her life.

Myrtle was less than delighted with this unwelcome
intruder into her exclusive domain. Though her parents had tried to prepare her, she screamed and cried
when she saw her new baby brother. Finally, Addie
Mae asked Mrs. Campbell to bring Myrtle to her bedside so she could spank her. Once Myrtle was thoroughly convinced that she couldn't win, and that she
had no choice in accepting this unwanted addition to
the family, she dedicated her life to serving as his loyal,
responsible guardian. Within a few days Myrtle gave
her total attention to fulfilling all the protective motherly instincts that were possible for a three-year-old to
express.

Choosing a name for the baby boy proved to be a
complicated process. Addie Mae and Earl decided to

name their little boy after O.H. Tollison, a well-known evangelist whom they both loved and respected. They intended to call the baby "O.H." Earl diligently searched the scriptures to find the names of two biblical prophets matching those initials. After an exhaustive search, Little O. H.'s name officially became Othniel Hobab Paulk.

Other family members ignored the initials and the pompous name. They insisted on calling the baby "little Earl." Almost a month after he was born, Addie Mae and Earl finally agreed to drop the initials and join the rest of the family in calling their baby "Earl Jr." after his father. Addie Mae selected "Pearly," a common name in south Georgia, as the baby's middle name simply because she liked it. Years later Earl Jr. regarded his middle name as significant since it reminded him of the "pearl of great price." That meaning became more and more significantly prophetic as Earl Paulk faced crucial choices throughout his life.

Two weeks after little Earl's arrival, his father left for a revival in Hartwell, Georgia. Preaching with Earl Sr. at this revival was the woman evangelist, Myrtle Whitehead, for whom Earl and Addie Mae had named their little daughter. The revival proved to be a mighty move of the Holy Spirit. When Addie Mae received news of all the exciting things that God was doing in the meetings, she immediately wished she had gone with Earl. The revival moved into its second week, so Addie Mae bought train tickets for Myrtle, the baby and herself. They boarded a northbound train from Baxley. Little Myrtle sat beside her mother on the seat, looking out the window, chattering about her wonderful trip. Baby Earl slept for most of the trip on his mother's lap.

The three travelers changed trains in Atlanta. Myrtle toddled along beside her mother, trying to help Addie Mae carry all the baby's paraphernalia. Addie Mae held firmly onto Myrtle's hand while clutching the new baby close to her with her other arm. People making various connections crowded the busy train station. Walking through the mob of people, Addie Mae tripped over a suitcase that someone had thoughtlessly set down. The hysterical mother fell forward on top of her baby. She lunged helplessly, unable to shield the infant from the impact of hitting the ground or from her own weight crushing him.

Addie Mae screamed in terror. She knew without a doubt that she had killed Earl Jr. Alarmed bystanders rushed to rescue the hysterical woman. Several people helped Addie Mae to her feet while others attended the frantic, screaming little girl who had watched both her mother and baby brother fall. Miraculously, the little baby was screaming also. A woman carefully picked up the infant, assuring everyone near her that the baby's insistent wailing was a positive sign. He was thoroughly examined by a crowd of rescuers while they answered all the alarming questions his distraught mother asked them with a trembling voice. The baby appeared to have survived the fall without injury.

Later, safely on the train, Addie Mae, Myrtle and little Earl headed for Hartwell. Addie Mae continued to examine her baby, anxiously praying over him while trying to calm herself and reassure little Myrtle that all was well. She noticed that the baby was bleeding from his navel which had almost healed completely after three weeks. Addie Mae began crying again, trying to keep her emotions and fears from upsetting her little daughter. For months after the fall at the train station, Addie Mae fervently prayed to God that her baby was spared some undetected internal injury. She cared for baby Earl under a threatening cloud of guilt, blaming herself for the accident.

The revival at the church in Hartwell was exceptional, meeting all the raving reports Addie Mae had heard. Earl preached with a mighty anointing that brought great spiritual purging to the little church. However, Addie Mae's memories of that mighty revival were always tinged with personal regret. She continued fighting her own unrelinquishing ordeal.

Earl, his wife and their children stayed in an extra bedroom at a church member's house. During the evening service, rain fell steadily and continued to pour throughout the night. As they were getting ready for bed, Addie Mae discovered a leak in the ceiling directly above the bed where she and Earl were to sleep. She reluctantly got into bed beside her husband. She lay still under the covers, monitoring the water drops rhythmically pelting down upon her.

Suddenly, Addie Mae's feet hit the floor. She grabbed her sleeping baby boy and held him close to her. They plopped down together in a rocking chair sitting in the corner of the room. Earl turned on the light. He looked intently at his wife's fierce expression. With great caution he asked her whether she intended to spend the night sitting in the chair.

"I'll sit in the rain, but I won't sleep in the rain!" Addie Mae snapped back. The evangelist smiled at his wife with an expression of love and understanding. He turned off the light and began to pray for the woman who would always be his "precious sweetheart." How well he understood the overwhelming strain of the life he had asked her to share with him. He promised God that he would always try to be sensitive to Addie Mae's limitations. He would honestly try never to demand greater sacrifices from her than she could bear.

Little Earl Jr. quickly became that special child that Mrs. Campbell had predicted he would be. His chubby cheeks, big blue eyes and unusual sensitivity to people easily won their hearts. Of course, the evangelist's baby always received plenty of attention. He responded easily to love from people—family and strangers alike. Even little Myrtle seemed to understand that Earl Jr. was special. She continued to be very protective and proud of him. As his personal, self-appointed teacher, she treasured all the compliments and praises that others lauded on her little protégé.

In Pentecostal circles throughout the state, Earl was now a well-known, proven evangelist. Among church people and respectable citizens of the community, he was regarded as a fiery, powerful preacher. But among lawless people in the area, he held the reputation of being an unabashed troublemaker. Once after a service, the preacher was held at gunpoint by bootleggers in Appling County while Addie Mae waited in the wagon with the two children. The bootleggers targeted Earl for his adverse influence on their profitable business operations. He was rescued that night by a local man named Hill Perry who had heard about the bootleggers' plans to kill the preacher. Hill Perry showed up at the meeting, pulled a gun on Earl's assailants, and told them to leave the preacher alone. The hero was not a Christian, but he was forever a beloved friend of Earl Paulk. The preacher returned the priceless favor of life years later when Hill Perry was sick and dying. Earl Paulk led the man who saved his life to accept Jesus Christ as his Savior only days before his death. Of course, the family asked Earl Paulk to preach Hill Perry's funeral.

Earl signed ordination papers with the Church of God, bringing his ministry under their denominational authority and covering. In signing these papers, he promised to uphold the church's beliefs with sincere loyalty and perseverance. Earl Paulk was a man of his word. This oath meant his family's personal adherence to church laws which demanded an impeccable code of behavior. Among the more stringent implications of this promise was that the Paulk family would trust the Lord for physical healing rather than depending on medicine or doctors.

Just before his second birthday, little Earl suffered with a terrible case of chicken pox. The severe rash was accompanied by an extremely high fever. He refused food for days. His fever remained constant, holding out even against traditional home remedies which usually brought fever under control. His condition seemed to get progressively worse. High fever caused his little body to jerk with convulsions which terrified Earl and Addie Mae. The parents had maintained a constant, day and night vigil over their son. Both of them wanted to call a doctor. They stood together at their baby's bedside, agonizing over his condition, yet knowing that this was a test of all the faith they talked and preached.

Finally, Earl told Addie Mae firmly that they were going to believe God to heal their baby. Since they had already been praying, Addie Mae knew immediately that Earl was making an affirmation of his faith rather than simply saying what they were going to do. They laid their hands on the baby again and cried out of their spirits for God to heal him. Immediately, the convulsions stopped and his little body became limp. Within a few minutes, the fever broke.

Little Earl began to cry as his mother wiped away perspiration with a cool, wet cloth. With her own tears of gratitude streaming down her face, she asked her baby why he was crying. He was hungry. He wanted some "bo' eggs." Addie Mae laughed through glistening tears as she prepared her baby a huge breakfast of boiled eggs and biscuits to satisfy the ravenous appetite which accompanied his instantaneous, miraculous return to health.

The family traveled with Earl as often as possible whenever he held revivals and camp meetings across Georgia and in surrounding states. They usually stayed in the homes of church members, but occasionally they rented rooms, stretching what little money they had for traveling expenses. One night the family drove into a town to begin a revival with only enough money to pay for the room to spend the night. Addie Mae began getting her two children ready for bed. They were tired from the trip, hungry and complaining since they hadn't eaten any supper. Appeasing their cries for some food, Addie Mae promised her children that if they went right to sleep, they would have a good breakfast the next morning. Neither she nor Earl had any idea how breakfast might materialize. They were totally out of money for food or anything else.

Before daylight, the family was awakened by a knock at the door of their rented room. Earl went to the door to see several smiling ladies holding boxes. One of them asked him, "Are you the evangelist who's just come to town with your family?"

Earl assured the ladies that he fit that description. The lady continued, "The Lord woke me in the night saying that you and your family needed food. We went to the store early this morning to get this to you before your children woke up. I hope you'll accept this as being from the Lord." The boxes were filled with enough food to last for several days as well as a bag of coal to heat their room. Another box contained a hot breakfast for the family. Addie Mae kept her promise to her children because God intervened to honor her faith. Earl Paulk confidently preached God's faithful provision for personal needs at the tent meetings that began that night.

When little Earl was two years old, he went with his daddy to Florida where Earl Sr. was scheduled to preach at the Church of God's annual Florida Campmeeting. Addie Mae wasn't feeling well. She and Myrtle stayed behind in Baxley visiting their relatives. Earl Sr. often put a little chair beside his own on the platform so his son could sit beside him during the church services. The little boy proudly accepted his serious responsibility of "helping daddy preach." Little Earl grew up believing that his seat in church was always placed right beside the preacher he adored.

Earl Sr. delighted in training his baby boy for the ministry. He often preached sermons about "Abraham sacrificing Isaac" and would illustrate the powerful message of Abraham's obedience to God by comparing his own love and devotion for his son sitting in the little chair watching his daddy tell the story to the people. Earl Sr. often called the little boy to him and held him in his arms, dramatically emphasizing Abraham's tremendous sacrifice in obedience to God's command. Through his entire youth, Earl never knew the perspective of sitting among people in the congregation in services where his daddy delivered the messages.

The first few days of the Florida Campmeeting were an exhausting, exciting adventure for little Earl. His daddy took him to get a haircut and bought him a cute little hat to wear. People attending the daily services asked him questions and showered him with attention. They remarked how adorable he was sitting on the platform with his daddy. Suddenly, the little boy had enjoyed himself long enough! Little Earl was ready to end his adventure, expressing his feelings by crying inconsolably. He couldn't think of anything except how much he wanted to see his mother and sister. Earl Sr. tried everything he knew to do to console him, making him promises, offering to buy him candy and ice cream. Finally, the little boy managed to control his crying long enough to look pleadingly into his daddy's crystal blue eyes. With his most desperate appeal, sobbing as he spoke, he told his daddy, "If you was little, you'd want your mama, too!"

When Earl Jr. was three, the family moved to Logan, West Virginia, to assume the pastorate of a little church sitting up on the hill behind their house. The parsonage where they lived was a small, modest little home. Money was scarce in the grip of the depression years. A funeral home was located directly across the street from the Paulk family. Often Earl Sr. would drive the hearse and conduct funerals for people who didn't have a church or pastor, trying to make some extra income for the family.

People in the congregation parked on the street and climbed steps running by the parsonage to get to the doors of the little church. Myrtle and Earl Jr. would stand on the front porch as soon as they saw the first members coming to church. They would talk with the people passing by their house while their mother finished getting dressed and their dad took one final check of his sermon notes. One member of the church, George Lawrence, always brought Cracker Jacks to the Paulk children. Little Myrtle and Earl thought Brother Lawrence was the best Christian in the world! Addie Mae seldom allowed her children to have sweets—mainly because they couldn't afford them.

The family's financial resources were so limited that basic necessities—food and clothing—were usually donated by people in the church. Repeatedly, God would perform some miracle to provide for specific needs they had. Addie Mae sewed the majority of her children's clothes from potato sacks. She would sit for hours and hand-sew little dresses for Myrtle to wear to school. Myrtle was a very perceptive, sensitive child, painfully aware of how poor her family was. She hated school. Not only did Myrtle fight the stigma of being the "holiness preacher's daughter," but also she was convinced that she was the most pitifully dressed child in her class.

A baby from one of the families in the church died, and the baby's mother asked Addie Mae to allow Myrtle to be a flower girl in the funeral. When Myrtle came home from school, Addie Mae told her daughter that the family wanted her to participate in the funeral procession. That afternoon Addie Mae had bought an appropriate dress for Myrtle to wear. They went into the bedroom where Addie Mae had carefully laid out on the bed the most beautiful white dress that Myrtle had ever seen in her life. She absolutely could not imagine her mother buying such a magnificent dress for her.

Addie Mae's eyes narrowed in her most serious expression. She stooped down and stared directly into Myrtle's big blue eyes. In her most threatening tone of voice Addie Mae said gravely, "Now, Myrtle, that dress cost ninety-seven cents and you're going to have to wash lots of dishes to pay for it." Myrtle could not believe that her mother had been so extravagant for her. She gratefully thought of her magnificent white dress every time she stepped up on the box that lifted her high enough to wash dishes at the sink.

The family next door presented a major cultural adjustment for the Paulk family from south Georgia. Their neighbors were a black family. Though Addie Mae fought prejudice in her own heart, she couldn't quite reconcile her Southern upbringing with the ideals she believed were right for Christians to have. She tried to keep her children from playing with the children next door without conveying to them her own unfortunate, ingrained prejudices. Of course, the children ignored her instructions. Mama's rules only made the neighbor children more enticing.

Earl Jr. was fascinated with his dark-skinned playmates. He would ride his tricycle up and down the hill along the fence separating their yards. The pretty little girl next door would come to the fence and watch three-year-old Earl show off as he tried desperately to impress her with his daredevil maneuvers. None of Addie Mae's rules had any effect on his determination to play with the little girl. One day Addie Mae looked out the kitchen window to see Earl Jr. in an embrace, madly kissing the little black neighbor on the mouth. Addie Mae ran outside, grabbed Earl Jr. and scrubbed his mouth out with soap to help him remember her instructions more clearly.

Earl Jr. was a very spiritually sensitive child, responding easily to people at church, Bible stories, praying and singing hymns. Going to church was as much a part of life to him as eating and sleeping. His relationship with Jesus was so real to him that his parents couldn't pinpoint the actual time of his "prayer" of salvation. He often went to the altar when his dad called for people to come forward at the end of his messages. Prayer was as natural for him as talking to his family. "Jesus" was a real friend, included in all his conversations on any topic.

Baptisms were held at a nearby mountain creek as long as the weather stayed warm enough to go into the water. Addie Mae decided not to go to the last baptism of the year. She was pregnant again and felt heavy and uncomfortable. She avoided going anywhere that she couldn't lie down every few hours. Little four-year-old Earl begged his mother to let him go to the baptism with his daddy. She hesitated giving her permission. Earl would be in the creek baptizing the people, therefore he couldn't possibly take total responsibility for watching Earl Jr.

Since Earl Sr. had already promised his son that he could go, he vowed to Addie Mae that the child would be safe. Several of the ladies who were coming with people to be baptized would gladly take care of Earl Jr. Addie Mae bent down over her large stomach to warn her little boy to behave himself and stay away from the water. Again she gave stern instructions to her husband to assign some dependable, responsible adult to look after little Earl during the baptism.

A large group of people gathered at the creek bank. Earl slowly waded into the water until it rose to his waist. He began quoting familiar scriptures he always used as a biblical foundation for baptisms. These passages helped people realize the significance of this sacred, holy sacrament of their faith. The people began moving toward him, one after another. He prayed over them individually, then submerged them in the water with the words, "In the name of the Father, the Son and the Holy Ghost." Many baptism participants emerged from the creek rejoicing with praise and praying to God in their spiritual language. People standing on the bank sang a variety of hymns as the service progressed.

When the last person was baptized, Earl walked slowly to the creek bank. People were beginning to gather their belongings, still enjoying fellowship as they scattered about. People were refreshed through their prayers, singing and watching so many of their relatives and friends participate in the significant occasion. Earl Jr. walked up to his daddy and tugged on his wet pants. The water dripping from his father felt cold. Earl Sr. leaned down to his son who had quietly sat on the bank that afternoon watching the baptismal service with deep, serious concentration. The child said firmly, "I want to be baptized, Daddy."

"Are you sure?" Earl Sr. said with surprise. Little Earl was only four years old. His spiritual sensitivity was remarkably mature, but did he really understand the spiritual meaning of this sacrament?

"Yes, Daddy. I've accepted Jesus. I want to be baptized!" the little boy insisted.

Earl Sr. raised his voice to call back the crowd who were milling about, preparing to leave. The preacher instructed them to gather back at the creek bank for

77

one additional baptism. He lifted his son into his arms. Earl Sr.'s clothes felt cold, uncomfortable and damp against the child's body. The water was much colder than little Earl had imagined. He breathed deeply as his dad walked further into the creek.

When his daddy stopped walking, he turned around to face the people standing on the bank watching them. Earl Jr. looked at his daddy's face, a face which looked much like his mental picture of God. Tears welled up in the preacher's eyes. His dad was seldom sentimental publicly. He usually spent his emotional fire on preaching. Without being told, Earl Jr. knew the depth of his daddy's love for him at that important moment.

"I can hardly express what I am feeling right now," Earl Sr. said, trembling as he looked into his little boy's eyes staring up at him. "I'd rather this boy become a man of God than the President of the United States. Earl Paulk Jr., I baptize you in the name of the Father, the Son and the Holy Ghost."

As Earl walked back to the creek bank holding his soaking baby boy, several people standing in the crowd walked toward the preacher. They asked him if he would baptize them also. More people who had come as spectators and family members moved forward. Until that moment they never expected to participate in the baptism themselves. Earl Sr. wrapped his little boy in a dark, heavy overcoat he had brought with him to wear home. With great joy, the preacher walked back into the water, totally engulfed spiritually in the tender, yet mighty significance of that day in his son's life.

When Earl Sr. walked into the house with little Earl

wrapped in his overcoat, Addie Mae was livid with rage. "I knew this would happen!" she yelled. For the first time little Earl regretted that he had asked his daddy to baptize him. He hated the tension he felt whenever Earl and Addie Mae engaged in any conflicts, especially if he were somehow at the center of their disputes. Now he was going to be scolded, and he hadn't even remembered until that moment the warning that his mother had given him before he left.

Before little Earl could tell his mother he was sorry and take his punishment, Earl Sr. told Addie Mae about the baptism. She looked at the little boy standing in front of her, looking so small in his wet clothes. She had a strange expression on her face, almost as if she had never seen him before. He still thought she might scold him when suddenly she burst into tears. Addie Mae stooped down and grabbed Earl Jr. into her arms. He felt her bulky stomach between them. He realized suddenly that he was getting her wet, but she didn't seem to notice. She only looked at her little boy with warmth, love and childlike wonder. Indeed, he was his mother's very special child.

3

CHAPTER THREE

Life in the Paulk household centered around church activities and close family relationships. The two worlds were absolutely inseparable to Earl Jr. His family moved almost every year. His dad would serve as the pastor of a church for only one or two years at the most. Then the family would receive a new assignment, pack up their belongings and move to another Church of God in some distant state.

Because Earl Paulk Sr. served as such a trustworthy, responsible pastor, solidly true to his spiritual calling, he was appointed the State Overseer of Church of God parishes in five different states. Eventually, he was elected Assistant General Overseer for the entire denomination. However, his iron-clad loyalty to the teachings of the church, as well as the family's constant moving about, called for a tremendous personal sacrifice.

No matter where they were, Earl Sr. always expected his children to be perfect models of behavior. Talking to their friends or any hint of inattention or misbehavior during a church service was never tolerated. Myrtle, Earl Jr. and their younger sister, Ernestine, always knew by conversations in the car on the way home from church whether or not their attention during the services had met their daddy's rigid standards. If Earl Sr. was talkative, they all felt like laughing and singing. But when their dad was quiet and serious, giving quick answers to any questions they asked him, riding in silence would be as painful as the spanking they inevitably received minutes after they arrived home.

Earl Sr. was also very strict about the way his children dressed and the places he allowed them to go. Earl Jr. always felt sorry for his sisters having to wear thick, black stockings and plain dresses compared to the finer attire of other little girls their ages. The Paulk children felt obvious differences between them and their friends. Myrtle was especially aware that "holiness" meant "from the other side of the tracks" to many of her little classmates. Regardless of the class or the teacher, Myrtle continued to dislike school. She passed along that attitude to little Earl Jr. He listened closely to all the torturous details Myrtle told him about her demanding teachers and the mean children who taunted her in her classes. Earl Jr. dreaded the idea of starting to school like an inevitable, long-term prison sentence.

The family had just moved to Michigan. To enforce the idea that he had no choice in the matter, Earl Sr. took little Earl to school that first day of kindergarten. Earl Jr. braced himself to endure a dreadful, agonizing ordeal. He pictured the teachers as looking like wicked fairy-tale witches with long sinister fingernails like those seen in storybooks. School teachers, he imagined, especially enjoyed tormenting little children. He gripped his daddy's hand and held back the tears as they walked into an enormous school building.

When they found his assigned classroom, his daddy knocked on the door. Earl Jr. held his breath. His heart raced. He was shocked to see a beautiful young woman with dark curly hair and warm brown eyes open the door. She smiled at both of them. His daddy pushed Earl Jr. toward her and said, "This is Earl Jr. and he's going to be in your class this year."

The woman slowly stooped down to look directly into his big blue eyes. She gently rubbed his cheek and then patted it with her hand. Almost the instant he began to relax his muscles in grateful, trusting relief, a thought struck him like lightning. "This is a trick! They let pretty ladies open the doors to get you inside away from your daddy! Once they get you inside, the witches are there to torture you!"

Before he could explain his sudden insight into the situation to Earl Sr., he was pushed inside the classroom. Other little boys and girls his own age sat calmly at their tables looking at him. The pretty lady directed him to his seat. Where was the witch hiding? Didn't the other children know the secret? He watched the beautiful lady closely for several hours before he finally convinced himself that she was indeed his very own, wonderful teacher. Once he was completely convinced of her identity, he fell madly in love with her.

His beautiful teacher was an angel sent from heaven, but other aspects of school met his dreaded expectations. The other kids often teased Myrtle and Earl. Without even having to speculate on the reasons, Earl Jr. knew the naughty children picked on them because their daddy was a holiness preacher. Within a few weeks, they were shocked to realize that the antagonizing attention from their Michigan classmates had nothing to do with their daddy's controversial profession. The children mocked the Paulk kids from Georgia just to hear their Southern drawls.

Other aspects of the school routine added to distinctions between the Paulk children and their classmates. Movies were strictly forbidden by the church. Whenever the class was scheduled to see an educational movie or they were rewarded with cartoons, Myrtle and Earl Jr. were instructed to excuse themselves from the class. They went to the library to read a story or sat at an extra desk in another classroom working on a special assignment.

Once Myrtle's class went on a tour through a Coca-Cola plant. At the end of the tour, all the children were given paper cups filled with sample Coke. Since drinking colas was against the church rules, Myrtle found herself in a rather compromising situation. She was too embarrassed to refuse the Coke on "religious" grounds, so she put the cup to her lips and faked drinking it. When no one was looking, she hid the forbidden beverage behind a machine. One of the other students in her class was also a member of their church. He was totally delighted to catch the preacher's daughter joining him in this outrageous transgression of their church's teaching.

On Sunday, Myrtle's classmate told all the other children at church—Earl Jr. among them—the shocking report that "Myrtle drank Coke." For almost two weeks, Earl Jr. enslaved Myrtle into doing all his chores for him. He controlled Myrtle under the threat that he would tell their daddy about her publicly disgracing the church and their family. Finally, the guilt and threats were too much bondage for Myrtle to endure any longer. She hysterically blurted out the whole story to her daddy who was able to chasten and restore her as she begged him for mercy.

Some children at school were cruelly intolerant of the strict moral behavior of the holiness preacher's children. This intolerance was sometimes exaggerated because from an early age Earl Jr. was an outstanding, highly competitive athlete. But unlike other little boys in his class who liked to win, he never bullied other children. At the age when little boys begin proving themselves by testing their physical strength against each other, Earl Jr. ran faster, jumped higher and won any sports contest on the playground. But he repeatedly refused to participate in arguments or take punches. His athletic ability won him many admirers

among his peers—especially among the little girls—
but it also made him a target for jealous show-offs
looking for a challenge.

One cold winter afternoon after school, a group of
boys who were determined to make Earl fight waited
for him in the schoolyard. When they saw him walking
alone, they surrounded him and began pushing him
from one boy to another. The boys verbally taunted
him with insults while they shoved him back and forth.
They hoped this humiliation would somehow hit at
some tender, emotional areas inside him to ignite his
temper. The main issue of contention repeatedly
focused on the fact that his dad was "a holiness
preacher." One boy insisted that Earl Jr. thought he
was "too good to fight!"

Earl Jr. carefully followed his daddy's instructions
by telling the boys to leave him alone. He pushed past
the circle they had made around him and began walking away. Several of the boys grabbed him from behind
and held him while the others took a rope and tied his
hands behind his back. Together they took another
rope and tied the terrified child to a tree at the edge of
the woods. The boys then ran away, laughing with
satisfaction at their long-awaited victory. As he stood
there fixed against the tree, totally humiliated and
crying, he was furious with his daddy's rules. The
preacher's unbending instructions that he not join in
the daily scuffles among his classmates had put him
here. Perhaps this time his daddy had demanded too
much "perfect" behavior.

Within a few minutes, which seemed like hours to

Earl Jr. in his distress, Myrtle came to the rescue by untying the ropes. Earl Jr.'s little girlfriend ran to get the principal. Older, responsible sister Myrtle vowed through clenched teeth that she would unmercifully beat up every one of the boys involved in this prank, no matter what her daddy said.

But Earl Jr.'s humiliation was almost worthwhile when he saw uncharacteristic fury consume his daddy when he heard about the attack. Together they went back to the principal's office to discuss the incident. His daddy was especially furious at the taunting remarks about the "holiness preacher's son." But Earl Jr. was awarded an even more satisfying reaction later at home from Addie Mae. She told her son privately that he had her permission to fight back any time he was threatened. Earl Jr. almost eagerly anticipated being assaulted again, now that any acts of self-defense had premeditated parental blessing.

Because of his unusual sensitivity toward the feelings of other people, even bullies, Earl Jr. learned at an early age that most battles in life could not be settled by fistfights. He was deeply troubled by the inconsistencies and hypocrisy he observed in the adult world—particularly among members in his church. He never understood how some people could seem to be so "spiritual" in their words at church and yet be so cruel to one another where it really counted: in their homes, on their jobs and in their unguarded conversations with one another.

Church politics, vicious gossip and power plays against the preacher—the daddy he loved so much—

greatly influenced Earl Jr.'s plans for his own life. He decided that he would work hard to become financially successful. He would faithfully give great sums of money to the church. However, he vowed he would never live with the insoluble "people" problems his daddy endured. No, Earl Jr. would never be a preacher! This career decision was repeatedly confirmed in his mind through numerous situations in the church which exposed the great hypocrisy among some of the most pious church members.

One Saturday morning, Earl Jr. walked into a busy barbershop in Greenville, South Carolina. All the barber chairs were occupied with customers. Several men sat leisurely in chairs along the wall as they waited their respective turns to get haircuts. Earl Jr. sat down beside a man who was waiting. He casually picked up a magazine. He had just started thumbing through the magazine when he heard the name "Earl Paulk," spoken by a man sitting in a barber chair with a towel wrapped around his head.

Earl Jr. immediately recognized the voice as belonging to one of the featured singers at the church. The man often led the worship just before his daddy preached. As he listened, he was totally stunned by the man's sarcastic tone of voice. Harsh words, glibly spoken about his father in this busy, public place, stabbed Earl Jr. inside as he listened. The barber noticed Earl Jr.'s exasperated expression. He nervously punched the man sitting in the chair. Earl Jr., who for a moment sat immobile, frozen by the impact of such casual, yet insolent remarks aimed at his daddy, quickly threw down the magazine and ran out the door of the barber shop to sort out his anger and hurt.

About the same time he became aware of all the personal attacks on his father's ministry from the very people whom his dad lovingly served, a strong social conscience toward oppressed, abused people in society began to churn inside Earl Jr. Summer visits to his Uncle Reilly's farm in south Georgia opened his eyes to shameful, abusive treatment of poor people. People in rural areas, particularly, passed on a heritage of stubborn racial prejudices from one generation to another. The most confusing aspect of his observations was discovering respectable society's insensitivity toward the downtrodden plight of hurting people. Human misery was ignored, considered to be normal, inevitable and even justified by supposedly Christian people.

Earl Jr. sat on the dusty seat of his Uncle Reilly's old truck as they rounded up the community's black tenant farmers to take them to the tobacco and cotton fields each day to work. He looked at the callow faces of small children standing in the dirt yards. Many of the children were dressed in rags or they had no clothes at all. They silently watched their mothers and fathers climb onto the back of the truck. He was appalled at the rundown, clapboard shanties where large families lived in cramped, filthy conditions. He wondered if the children had any hope of breaking the poverty cycle which was their heritage. When he asked his uncle why these people lived like this, Uncle Reilly flippantly answered his nephew as if to settle the matter, "That's their place."

Uncle Reilly's answer to Earl Jr. was almost benevolent compared to the attitude of other farmers he encountered during those summer visits. Once an elderly black woman working near him struggled under the weight of a large sack of cotton. Earl Jr. immediately put down his own sack and rushed to help her carry the load. Together they emptied her sack onto the scales. He heard someone yell at him, "Put that down!" Later he was scolded for helping the woman. An angry farmer told him, "Listen, boy, you've got to learn that they don't think like we do. They think and live more like animals." Earl Jr. felt sick and disgusted at hearing the reprimand. He could hardly look at the farmer who was saying these things as if he really believed they were true. He couldn't imagine that a grown man could possibly justify mistreating human beings as if they had no feelings.

After returning home to his family, Earl Jr. kept remembering the despicable scenes from those summer visits. In his dreams he would see the shanties, the sad faces of the black children and the hopeless expressions on the workers' faces after laboring all day in the hot sun. He would wake up frightened from seeing the face of the farmer who had scolded him. When he talked to his mother about the cause of these obsessive nightmares, she agreed with him that he had observed tragic injustices. But in her concern for his peace of mind, she added, "Earl Jr., you've got to realize that people have their place in this world. Nothing you can say or do will change that."

Growing up also included times of tremendous joy

and blessings from the Lord to the Paulk family. Shortly after Earl Jr.'s eleventh birthday, Addie Mae gave birth to twins, Darlene and Don. His mother often reminded Earl Jr. that her pregnancy was due to his persistence in his prayers, asking God daily to give him a baby brother. Earl Jr., Myrtle and Ernestine lay on a bed listening to all the disturbing, curious activity in another room of the house as the twins were being delivered at home. Darlene was born first. When they heard the baby cry, the children were relieved that the family's new addition had finally arrived. Then they heard another baby crying. God also gave the Paulk family a little boy. Until that day, no one had even suspected that Addie Mae was carrying twins.

Earl Sr. was the pastor of the largest Church of God in South Carolina when the twins were born. As a State Overseer in the Church of God, he had gained recognition from church and civic leaders throughout the nation as a major Pentecostal spokesman. The Paulk children could hardly believe the respect and place of prominence to which their father's remarkable ministry had grown, even though it had started humbly in near illiteracy and abject poverty. The governor of South Carolina, Strom Thurmond, was one of the first visitors who came to their house to see the newborn twins.

On hot summer afternoons in South Carolina, children easily got restless and bored. They usually finished their assigned chores in the morning. The coveted free time with long days to fill spanned hours of looking for something to do. After the initial excite-

91

ment of vacation from school subsided, the days stretched out long, hot and uneventful.

Bored children always irritated Addie Mae Paulk. She was a mother who insisted her children engage in productive activity, preferably out of her way. When she noticed signs of boredom in Earl Jr., she would suggest some project or chore for him that would channel his boundless energy. Whatever exciting "adventure" she suggested to her children would hopefully occupy them and allow her the leisure time to find a breeze blowing through a bedroom window so that she could enjoy an afternoon snooze.

On one such afternoon, Addie Mae decided that Earl Jr. should accompany his dad on the pastor's regular afternoon visits. After successfully persuading both father and son—neither of whom regarded this plan as particularly appealing for their own reasons—they drove off together in the family's big black 1939 Ford to Sister Arrowwood's house.

By the age of twelve, Earl Jr. had become very skeptical about the spiritual displays he sometimes saw at church. He often wondered why members who gossiped, and even openly criticized his mother and daddy, would be the very ones to shout, pray loudly and "speak messages" in tongues during the worship services. He questioned the loud, uncontrolled, emotional outbursts that some people regarded as spiritual. To a twelve-year-old mind, not only were these displays extremely strange behavior, but also the hypocrisy of some people who flaunted their spiritual gifts planted confusion and doubt in his heart as to their validity.

The one anchor holding him against destructive doubts was knowing indisputably that his daddy's faith was real. The man who preached the sermons on Sunday also lived them every day of the week privately at home with his wife and children. Earl Sr. would not allow his family to criticize people who disputed his ministry. When dinner conversations undermined someone's character for any reason, he would quickly tell his wife and children in a commanding tone of voice to "say something nice, or don't speak at all." They knew that the preacher meant it.

But even though Earl Sr. taught the validity of the baptism of the Holy Spirit, and both he and Addie Mae had often shared their own Holy Spirit baptism experiences with their children, Earl Jr. still wrestled with serious doubts. His father was very reserved about publicly praying aloud in unknown tongues. Earl Jr. decided that the baptism of the Holy Spirit either was not important or was an emotional display which some people needed even though it had very little spiritual significance. He had no desire to become "spiritual" or to pray like the people he observed as examples in church.

The black Ford pulled up in front of a white frame farmhouse. They immediately noticed all the other cars parked in the yard which prepared Earl Sr. for the confrontation inside the house. The entire family gathering at this time of day could only mean one thing. Sister Arrowwood's life had been well-spent. She had been very frail for several months. Obviously the time had now come for her to go on to be with the Lord. The preacher had been expecting this event.

Earl Sr. got out of the car, preparing his spirit for the comfort and strength he would need from the Lord to share with the Arrowwood family. He had lived this scene many times before. Ministry at someone's deathbed had never become simply a matter of quoting appropriate scriptures and verbalizing pat answers to family members. This time Earl Sr. felt such confidence in remembering Sister Arrowwood's gentle spirit. She was one of those shining saints who undoubtedly would "finish her course" with victory. Her death would be very precious to God.

Earl Jr.'s daddy told him to wait in the car as he closed the heavy car door. He watched his daddy walk across a wide porch to the front door, disappear inside, then reappear with other people as shadowy figures through a big screened window at the front of the house. Within a few minutes, Earl Jr. was perspiring and uncomfortable. He felt fidgety. He wished he had insisted on staying home with his mother.

He opened the heavy door, slowly got out and stood beside the car for several minutes. The hot sun beat down on him with roasting intensity. He began to walk very slowly toward the house. He would much rather wait for his daddy in the big swing on the front porch than endure another second sitting inside that stifling car or standing directly in the hot sun's rays. And besides, the swing was suspended in front of the huge window which provided a pleasant perch for him to monitor his daddy's actions inside the house.

He began to swing, trying to create a breeze for himself. In a few minutes he decided to look even more closely at his daddy through the huge open window. He pressed his nose against the screen. At first he was frightened by the scene inside the house. Fascination and curiosity quickly captured his full attention, freezing him to the window. In a bed directly by the window lay an old thin woman with a skeleton face. Her eye lids were closed tightly over hollowed-out eye sockets. She was colorless with white wispy hair and ashy skin blending into her pillow. She lay perfectly still. He was sure she must already be dead.

In the room stood six or eight people talking to each other in soft whispers as if they were afraid of waking the woman. He heard someone say that she was a "godly woman." Someone else said she was "so good to people." One very heavy middle-aged woman walked over to the bed and said, "I believe she's gone," as she put her hand to the old woman's neck, trying to feel some evidence of a pulse.

"No," she answered herself, "her heart is still beating."

A few minutes later, to everyone's surprise, the feeble shell of a woman lifted two frail, bony hands from her chest into the air. Her hands were wrinkled and gnarled, almost transparent with purple veins visible through her paper-like skin. The tips of crooked fingers began to barely touch together to an inner rhythm of some silent song within the old woman's spirit. Earl Jr. heard his daddy say with excitement, "Look, she's praising the Lord!"

And then he saw it! Earl Jr. felt a tingling sensation

rush through his body. Tears began to blur the amazing scene which he suddenly realized he had desperately longed to see. Her lips were moving. He barely heard the words. She was praying in an unfamiliar language. Suddenly, Earl Jr. understood clearly that "unknown tongues" were as real as the prayers that healed his body or the prayers that people prayed when they were saved at the altar of the church. The words were beautiful and holy, sounding like soft music to him.

This languishing, old, country woman moved her lips in the final minutes of her life and spoke to God in words of love that He alone had given her by His Spirit. But in a mysterious, unexplainable way, Earl Jr. knew that she was also speaking to him—or at least God was speaking in these circumstances by bringing him to the bedside of this dying woman. Watching her had settled some questions to which he had been silently, desperately seeking answers. He was somewhat surprised to realize that God had heard his secret thoughts. Perhaps all the doubts and inner questions of his life were really prayers which God would answer in unexplainable, unplanned situations like this.

A quiet, sweet serenity filled Earl Jr. and surrounded him as he stood there with his nose pressed into the window screen. His entire being seemed to be wrapped in a warmth which had nothing to do with the sweltering June temperatures. He suddenly felt as if someone were standing close behind him, silently watching him. He turned around to check for intruders but saw no one on the porch or in the yard. When he pressed his nose to the window screen again, a woman with tears streaking her cheeks tenderly placed Sister Arrow-wood's hands on her chest. Another woman walked over to the bed and tied a cloth around the dead woman's head, as was the custom in preparing a corpse.

Later that same summer, Earl Jr. finally realized the full meaning of the lesson God taught him at Sister Arrowwood's bedside window. Earl Jr. had gone again with his daddy to the yearly Florida Campmeeting, the largest rally in the Church of God. The Campmeeting was held in an open arbored tabernacle with sawdust covering the ground. As his daddy preached, Earl Jr. listened intently to the message.

When his daddy began to talk about the baptism in the Holy Spirit, Earl Jr. pondered each word carefully and asked himself whether he were perhaps too young to pray to receive this baptism. He reminded himself that his mother was younger than he was now when she received the baptism of the Holy Spirit.

The altar call was given at the end of the message for people wanting to receive the baptism in the Holy Spirit. Earl Jr. walked to the far end of the platform, away from a number of other people crowding toward the center of the stage. He hoped he would be unnoticed. The last thing he wanted was attention focused on him concerning a spiritual matter.

As the pastors prayed over the people, Earl Jr. felt a surge of power hit him like a lightning bolt, literally knocking him to the ground. The next thing he clearly remembered was hearing his own voice praying in a spiritual language he had never learned. He got up from the ground brushing the sawdust out of his hair. A crowd of excited, jubilant people surrounded him, shouting, glorifying God, praying in the Spirit and thoroughly enjoying the spiritual overflow of God's power which had fallen mightily on this shy young man of twelve.

Earl Jr.'s early teen years were consumed with weighty responsibility for his family while his daddy traveled. Earl's dad had become one of the nation's leading Pentecostal pastors. Earl Sr.'s ever-growing recognition and influence brought numerous invitations for him to speak at churches all over the nation and abroad. Earl Jr., "the old man" as Earl Sr. proudly called his oldest son, was left in charge of tending the home fires.

Because Addie Mae had stomach problems and suffered often in poor health, she was unable to assume the pressures of sole responsibility for the young children left in her care. Much of the job of parental discipline fell to Earl Jr. in his dad's absence. That responsibility increased after Myrtle enrolled as a freshman at Lee College in Cleveland, Tennessee. Even before he could see over the steering wheel, Earl Jr. sat on a cushion and drove his mother to visit Myrtle at college. He drove his younger sister, Ernestine, to school in his own dilapidated car. She became so embarrassed to be seen in the car that she insisted her brother let her out to walk the last block to the school building.

Little Don and Darlene slept with Earl Jr. every night, one lying on each arm. He also had the unpleasant task of spanking them whenever Addie Mae decided they needed it. Finally, he shared the responsibility of caring for a fourth little sister, Joan, whom he adored and protected with deep affection more like a young father than an older brother. Joan completed the Paulk household.

When Earl Jr. went out for football during spring practice at Bradley County High School in Cleveland, Tennessee, he knew he was going to have trouble. The coaches, players and all the students began to excitedly make state championship predictions about the team they would have in the fall. Their optimistic predictions were primarily pinned on three players: Jimmy McCoy, a running back who eventually became a football star at Tennessee State; Herbert Walker, who eventually played football at Vanderbilt; and Earl Paulk, a six-foot-tall tailback who could run like the wind.

All three football stars were the sons of Pentecostal preachers. That fact alone insured problems for the talented trio as well as for their fathers. The church was very rigid about school activities which young people were allowed to join. Sports participation was not considered a wholesome activity. Competitive athletics were considered "worldly" and therefore never sanctioned by the church.

Earl Jr. spent many hours talking to his daddy about the reasons the church embraced these seemingly ridiculous rules. Conversations on playing football would gradually drift to other legalistic issues like make-up, jewelry and movies. Earl Jr. would ask his dad the reasons that women in singing groups could come to their church wearing make-up. His daddy would even compliment their "spirituality," yet he would never condone wearing make-up for women who were Church of God members.

His dad listened patiently as Earl Jr. expressed his frustrations at the inconsistencies and rules he had questioned all his life. When Earl Jr. finally finished venting his side of these debatable issues, his father would softly answer him, "Earl Jr., I don't know whether some of these things are right or wrong. I simply know that I've made a promise to uphold certain teachings of the church. As long as I'm committed to my denomination, I'll keep those standards the best that I possibly can."

Earl Jr. was not really satisfied with his father's answer but felt no bitterness toward him because of the preacher's steady, consistent demonstration of all the things he taught from the pulpit each Sunday. He also knew that his father really listened with genuine respect to his views. Earl Jr. watched him as he thoughtfully considered all his son's challenges, weighing the arguments scripturally to discern the truth. Even though his father's final answer would always be the same, that answer carried far more than a benediction ending the discussion. His predictable answer was never said simply to patronize or appease his son. Earl Sr.'s loyalty to the church was a stronger truth to his son than all the "do" and "don't" rules which irritated him.

All the Paulk children knew that their private and public lives were constantly under close scrutiny. Their dad had taught them that they were always expected to answer to the church for their behavior in any situation. Once Earl Jr. was at a party at a high school gymnasium where some kids were dancing. He and several of his friends played Ping-Pong at the other end of the gym the entire evening. When Earl Jr.'s dad heard about the dancing at the party, he insisted that Earl Jr. come to the podium at the Church of God headquarters' church to apologize. Earl Jr. publicly confessed to having been at the party and asked forgiveness for any embarrassment he might have caused the denomination.

One Sunday morning, Earl Sr. told the congregation that he would ask for a public apology from the next person who disrupted church services by talking. As soon as the words were spoken, Myrtle figured that she would be the one to apologize. As she sat in the choir, someone asked her a question. She answered quickly just as her father turned around to see her talking.

All the next week Myrtle pleaded with her father to give her another chance. He remained firm in his resolve to make her apologize publicly. Finally realizing that her tears wouldn't change his mind, Myrtle began asking God for rain on Sunday so the morning crowd would be smaller than usual.

The church was filled with people that Sunday morning. Myrtle could hardly look at the congregation as she sat in the choir in agony, dreading the moment her daddy would call her to the rostrum. Finally, he turned to look at her in the choir and said, "Myrtle, I think you have something to say to the people this morning."

Myrtle walked slowly to the podium with her head down as if she were going to her own execution. Her countenance visibly bespoke her deep distress and pain. She looked at the unsuspecting congregation who stared questioningly back at her. Before she could say a word, she burst out crying hysterically into the microphone. The whole church was perfectly quiet except for Myrtle's loud uncontrolled lamentation. People in the church began crying with her. Myrtle never did regain enough composure to apologize for talking during the service, but the entire church experienced repentant intercession that day because of Myrtle's unexplained broken heart.

Earl Jr. was unable to test his ability as tailback on the Bradley County football gridiron that fall. Officials closed the school because they didn't have enough funds to operate. Rather than allow Earl Jr. to waste a year of education until the public schools reopened, Earl Sr. enrolled him in a private Christian school. Bob Jones Academy was located in Cleveland, Tennessee, where the family lived that year. As a student there, Earl Jr. could earn both high school and college credits simultaneously.

Some of Earl Jr.'s most important lessons as a student at Bob Jones Academy were not written in books or learned in the classroom. Earl Jr. always knew that he could run very fast. His extraordinary athletic ability constantly threw him into a dilemma with the church's teachings on sports participation. Rather than viewing sports as "worldly," Earl Jr. saw his participation as a way of gaining credibility and respect through the natural talent God had given him. He never needed to question his motives for having such a highly competitive spirit. He wasn't interested in accumulating trophies, medals or personal accolades, but he was very intent on recognition and respect for the Pentecostal cause he had always represented to the world outside the doors of the church.

Perhaps those humiliating childhood memories of being taunted as the "holiness preacher's son" emblazed within him a burning determination to be a winner. Almost obsessively throughout his life, the cause he represented pushed Earl Jr. to press beyond whatever achievements he could gain through natural abilities alone. He insisted on proving excellence within himself, doing better than his best at every challenge. Credibility for his cause became the primary desire of Earl Jr.'s athletic achievements. That consuming motivation carried over into academic pursuits and personal relationships as well.

One of the state's most outstanding track stars, Henry Nettles, ran every afternoon on the track at the Bob Jones campus. Earl Jr. would go down to the track after his classes to watch Henry practice. Later at home, Earl Jr. would time himself running against Henry's running times that day. Henry held numerous track records in the state, so matching his running times set very high standards for Earl Jr. After several weeks, Earl Jr. gathered the courage to talk with Henry. With some hesitation he asked Henry if he would race him to the fifty-yard-line on the football field.

103

Henry was accustomed to frequent challenges from fresh, hopeful track stars, and he readily agreed. Earl Jr. ran barefooted against Henry just as he had practiced at home. When Earl Jr. crossed the fifty-yard-line ahead of Henry, the record holder was impressed but also a bit bewildered. He thought that this challenger must be an agile sprinter who had caught him off guard. Henry immediately suggested that they run against each other again in some laps around the track. Those laps would test this young upstart's vigor in maintaining his remarkable pace.

Several laps later, Henry was shocked to realize his challenger had stayed right beside him. Earl Jr. ran with a smooth, easy stride and a winner's determination. He quickly became Henry Nettles' fast-running, fast-learning protégé, and they grew to be close personal friends. Henry eagerly gave Earl Jr. his first real track coaching and encouraged him to pursue competitive track at the collegiate level.

Another important lesson Earl Jr. learned at Bob Jones Academy was from the founder of the school, Bob Jones Sr. The founder often spoke at the chapel service the students attended every morning. Earl Jr. was impressed with the man's open candor in sharing his wealth of ministry experiences and innermost thoughts with the students. Bob Jones never apologized for his bold opinions and his high spiritual values. Earl Jr. especially admired Bob Jones for humbly admitting how unlikely he was to be the founder of a school since his own education had been so limited. He instilled in the students the recognition of an education as a great privilege, a God-given opportunity.

Bob Jones had a saying that especially intrigued Earl Jr. The man would look intently at the students as if he were speaking some secret wisdom that they would need to know as a key to get them through life. He would say, "When you come to the end of your rope, tie a knot and hang on!" Earl Jr. would smile when he heard the man say it. But something sounding like an untold story resounded in Bob Jones' voice, something hidden far deeper in the man when he said it than Earl Jr. could possibly understand at the time. That little phrase contained a mighty lesson, a golden key, more theology than many of the volumes on church doctrines Earl Jr. would read years later.

Earl Jr. remembered Bob Jones' chapel lectures at many appropriate times in his life. Whether the respected leader knew it or not, he gave Earl Jr. and the other students valuable insights they needed when the "end of the rope" was no longer a trite little expression. Earl Jr. remembered Bob Jones' saying on many turbulent days in the ministry when the only alternative to falling over the edge was to "tie a knot and hang on."

Bishops have to start young

The Paulk Family
(Left to Right) Back Row: Ernestine, Myrtle, Earl Jr.; Front Row: Addie Mae Paulk holding Darlene, Earl Sr. holding Don (Baby Joan had not been born)

Mama and Daddy Paulk
at 1501 Parkwood Ave.
Charlotte, N.C.
(1942)

Tender young lad (1938)

Marriage of Bishop John Meares and Mary Lee Bell (1944)
(Left end) Earl Paulk Jr., age 17
(Front row, left to right) Martha Miller, Clariece Miller
(now Paulk), age 6

"Yes, Lord, I'll preach."

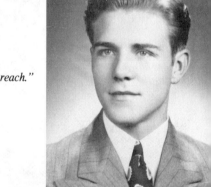

Earl Paulk Sr.
In those days called "The Walking Bible"

Addie Mae (Tomberlin) Paulk

Norma and Earl
First Year of Married Life

"I have my songs and I'm ready to sing."

Pastoring in Moultrie, Georgia (1948)

Rebecca Mae

Susan J

Roma Beth

Pastoring at Hemphill Avenue Church of God
(Now Mount Paran Church of God)

4

CHAPTER FOUR

The Paulk family moved back to Greenville, South Carolina, the next fall. Earl enrolled in Furman University as a college freshman at fifteen. He finished high school a year early and began college with credits already earned from his classes at Bob Jones Academy. He went out for football again and easily made the college team. But this time during the early season practices, Earl's daddy took a firm stand against his son's sports participation. The Church of God in Greenville was large and prestigious. Southern Conference football always dominated conversations every fall among people in the Greenville area. Earl's playing football at Furman would never go unnoticed by people in the church.

Understandably, Earl was crushed. His coaches had encouraged him about his running ability and potential contribution to the team. He had already developed a close friendship with Skeeter Coyle, a Southern Conference football and track star. Other players extended warm acceptance and mutual respect for Earl's athletic ability. He longed to share with them his best effort in helping their team win the conference.

After he worked through the painful disappointment of quitting the team, Earl went to his dad with a request. Would the preacher consider permitting his son to run track at Furman? Earl had carefully prepared his argument to be convincing. He pointed out to his dad that track was virtually an unnoticed sport. College track meets usually generated very little public support or publicity. After initially rejecting the idea, Earl Sr. reluctantly consented. He gave his permission more because of Earl's submissive attitude in quitting football than because he agreed with his son's participation on the track team.

Earl Sr. soon regretted giving in to his son. Earl became a celebrated athlete on campus, regularly winning medals and trophies. He set several Southern Conference records and also participated in class politics, serving on student advisory boards at the university. One Sunday morning, Earl was startled by the heavy thud of a newspaper hitting his chest, jolting him awake. He opened his eyes to see his father standing over him in a distinctive, rigid posture. His jaw jutted out firmly; his eyes blazed. By the telltale signs in his dad's countenance and carriage, Earl knew immediately that he was in big trouble.

"So no one will know that you're running track, huh? No publicity! You promised!" Earl Sr. turned around briskly while still speaking and walked out of his son's room, slamming the door behind him.

Earl opened the newspaper with a sinking feeling. Without having to search, he saw a large picture of himself emblazoned across the front page of the sports section. In the picture he was finishing a race, setting a new Southern Conference record. His head and arms were thrown back in that dramatic moment when a runner breaks the tape and crosses the finish line. Under his picture, large letters printed the name, "Earl Paulk."

Athletics represented only one area of Earl's life which caused him continuing inner conflicts. He had fallen deeply in love with Esther Green, a Furman beauty queen who almost perfectly matched every item of his mental criteria for the ideal woman. Many of her qualities suited him perfectly—physical attraction, personality, cultural interests and intellectual achievements. But even though her family attended a Pentecostal Holiness church with genuine commitment, Esther often made Earl feel very uncomfortable about his own spiritual values.

Esther's image completed all the sophisticated plans Earl had chosen for his life. She opened artistic worlds to him. They went to the opera to see Rise Stevens. Both of them tried out for a major school drama—though Esther was upset when Earl landed the male lead, while the casting director overlooked her for the female lead. Esther admired Earl's athletic abilities, intelligence and popularity on campus. He had introduced himself to her one afternoon after she had watched him play in an intervarsity football game. She was proud to be dating a member of the elite Student-Faculty Co-operative Committee and the president of the sophomore class. She particularly admired Earl's determination to become financially successful. He had confidence and ambition. She would squeeze his hand and tell him sweetly, "These are the hands of a surgeon."

Because he adored her, Earl tried desperately throughout their courtship to minimize any spiritual incompatibilities between them. Esther's church permitted a much more liberal lifestyle than the Church of God where Earl's dad was the senior pastor. Esther's stylish clothes, make-up, pearl ring and necklaces drew critical attention whenever she accompanied Earl to services at his church. Whenever anyone asked Earl—as they often did—whether he was studying to become a preacher like his daddy, he could feel Esther's muscles tighten as she pulled away from him. He would quickly answer that he had decided to become a civil engineer and give generous financial support to churches.

Their most heated discussions focused on Esther's beauty titles and modeling opportunities. As president of the sophomore class, Earl had sponsored Esther in the Miss Furman contest which she easily won. Along with the Miss Furman title came public appearances, modeling offers, celebrity recognition and pressure to enter other beauty contests. Earl strongly objected to her modeling bathing suits. They discussed his reservations at her aggressive pursuit of all the vain trappings associated with the glamour-girl, beauty queen image. But Esther disagreed with her boyfriend's perspective.

At what appeared to be the most serious time in their relationship, just as they were beginning to admit their deep love for each other and everyone was assuming that they would eventually marry, Earl responded to God's calling him into the ministry. The drastic transformation of all his goals, along with the sincere reaffirmation of the lifelong, ingrained values of his church, began closing doors of passion in his emotions.

Almost overnight, Earl became a totally dedicated, insensible Pharisee. He became willingly obedient to every law of the church, regardless of his long-held personal questions or opinions about them. As a painful first test of his calling into the ministry, Earl deliberately cooled his feelings for Esther. He realized that his love for her would demand a lifetime of divided loyalty and spiritual compromise. His calling dominated every personal decision. He willingly would pay any price to wholly follow the Lord.

Earl had felt unsettled all Sunday afternoon. That evening he was still restless, sitting as usual in the choir between his mother and Myrtle at the Greenville Church of God. His daddy preached vigorously to a capacity crowd in the large church. As Earl listened to the strong content of his father's message, a voice in his spirit spoke to him, "If you do not accept the call on your life to be a minister of the gospel, your father's ministry will end during this service."

Earl was shaken by the strange words diverting his attention from the sermon. He looked quickly at his mother sitting beside him, then scanned the familiar faces of people sitting quietly in the congregation. He tried to reassure himself. What a ridiculous thought! Then the voice spoke again and said to him, "If you need a sign to know that I am speaking to you, I will give you one."

Immediately, his father stopped preaching. Earl Sr.'s hands grasped his head as if he were going to faint. The preacher leaned against the podium with his eyes closed, holding his head. He said almost in a whisper, "I feel like I'm standing in a cold bucket of water. Pray, Christians! God is doing something here."

From the back of the church, Earl saw a brilliant light that began to move horizontally over the people who were in prayer, oblivious to the strange sight. It looked like a fiery ball moving very slowly across rows of the congregation. The light continued to move across the crowd in the back of the church. It traveled up a center aisle to about three rows from the front platform. All at once, the light traveled speedily through a window to the outside.

Earl sat frozen, terrified and thrilled. Even in a breathless state of shock, his heart racing, he knew that he must somehow respond to the astonishing sign that God had given to him. He leaned over to his mother who was praying and asked her if she had seen anything strange over the congregation. She looked at him for a moment, wondering if she had heard him correctly, and then she answered, "No, but I'm very concerned about your daddy."

Earl replied, "Mother, I've got to say something." He got up and walked steadily toward his father who had seemingly regained his composure and stood at the pulpit in concentrated prayer. The preacher looked totally surprised when his son touched his arm and asked him for permission to speak to the people. Earl, an unwilling leader, usually resisted speaking in church. His mother had enlisted him to help her teach the older women's Sunday School class, and he also led the youth group. From his early teens, he preached as the Junior Pastor in the children's church, but still he avoided the center spotlight, especially his father's pulpit.

Without a trace of hesitation or fear, Earl faced the people directly. Their eyes were fixed on him, expecting him to give some explanation for the strange interruption of this service. His voice sounded strong and sure. "I must tell you that God has called me to be a pastor, to preach the gospel. I intend to do as God has called me. I ask all of you for your prayers."

The people spontaneously praised and thanked God for Earl's announcement. As they responded in unison, a woman loved by the people in the church as a faithful intercessor got up from her seat and walked toward the pulpit. Earl and his beaming father backed away from the podium as the woman moved in front of them.

"Brother Paulk, you know I rarely speak out like this.

I know what I'm going to say will sound very strange. Regardless of how this sounds, I must confirm the words that Earl Jr. has spoken. As we were praying, the Lord told me to open my eyes and look over the people. I saw a light—almost like a ball—come into the back of this church. It traveled down this aisle and went out that window. I knew in my spirit that God was calling a preacher in this church tonight, but I didn't know who that person was. That call was undoubtedly to Earl Jr."

As the people responded in amazement to the woman's words by clapping their hands and praising God, another woman sitting on the other side of the church got up from her seat. She also walked to the microphone and looked at the people as they became quiet, giving her their attention. "I believe that God wants you to have a confirmation about what has happened here tonight. I also saw the light come into the back of the church—just like this sister said. I assure you I will never doubt the things that have happened in this place tonight!"

Already burning inside Earl were permanently branded the words of confirmation, "Never doubt!" As he reflected many times on that momentous night in his life, he knew that his call from God to the ministry required a dramatic, supernatural sign to shake him from his own stubborn will. Affluent ambitions had grown as solid, definable goals within him. However, Earl could never easily walk away from a calling which so specifically marked his life as belonging to God. Years later, at a time of personal defeat in his ministry when his whole world crumbled around him, the Spirit of the Lord brought him back to that night in Greenville, South Carolina. That same inner voice spoke again concerning his calling, and he heard those words echoing inside him, "Never doubt!"

Immediately after his call into the ministry, Earl began traveling and preaching every weekend. With classes at Furman during the week and preparing to preach on Sundays, Earl had little time left for Esther. The intensity of their relationship quickly wavered. Esther believed that Earl's feelings had changed toward her because he was jealous of a correspondence she had maintained with a boy in the war.

In a bold unspoken message to Earl, Esther declared alternate choices for the direction of her life. She entered the Miss Greenville pageant which she won. She went on to win the Miss South Carolina pageant. Later she was chosen the first runner-up in the Miss America contest. She confided to Earl's parents after he married that she would have given up anything to please him if she thought for a moment he still cared for her.

Meanwhile, Earl directed all his efforts to becoming the dedicated minister that God had called him to be. As the son of a well-known Church of God leader, many opportunities to speak opened easily to Earl. News about his calling spread rapidly among the pastors in his denomination. Also, the Ministerial Club at Furman University elected him to be their president, the first Pentecostal student ever to hold that office in the Baptist college.

One Saturday morning, Earl took a bus to Union, South Carolina, where he was invited to speak at a youth rally at a local Pentecostal church. He sat down on the bus beside an attractive young lady. After introducing themselves they soon began a lively conversation. The girl started trying to impress him with her vast knowledge on religion when she learned that he was a ministerial student at Furman.

She told Earl all about this strange church in her neighborhood. She said that people in this church used brooms to "beat the devil out of each other." She continued to tell him that often she stood outside the church looking through the windows to see people rolling around on the floor. Many times these people performed weird rituals in their services which she described in detailed, shocking eye-witness accounts.

Earl decided to spare his new friend the embarrassment of finding out that he was the guest speaker at that particular church that night. This conversation confirmed to him the wild misconceptions of Pentecostal beliefs among people in more sedate denominations. As they got off the bus in Union, a large poster announcing the youth rally with Earl's picture on it hung prominently in view of the departing passengers. No one could avoid seeing it. The girl took one look at the poster and suddenly realized she had reported outlandish exaggerations to "one of them." She took off running as fast as she could down the street without looking back.

Weekend evangelism surfaced the natural preacher in Earl, a role he had lived vicariously through his father all his life. He preached one of his first sermons at his brother-in-law's church. Myrtle had married a handsome, soft-spoken Armenian, Harry Mushegan, whose family escaped persecution and the eventual slaughter of Christians in the Russian villages where they had lived. Harry's family settled primarily in California as prosperous cattle farmers. After living on the West coast for a year, Harry and Myrtle moved back East to minister at a church in Tennessee.

Another weekend, the State Overseer sent Earl to a little church in Crow Creek, South Carolina, located about sixty miles from Greenville. The church had recently dismissed its preacher because of financial problems. For that reason, Earl didn't know exactly what sort of reception to expect from the congregation. He drove up to the church in a borrowed car about thirty minutes before the service began. He went inside the small building and started a fire in a pot-bellied stove sitting in the center of the room.

Earl had decided that no one was coming when a woman walked into the church and sat down. Earl introduced himself to the woman. She smiled, assuring the young preacher that others would be along in a little while. Within minutes, a few women sat on benches scattered throughout the room, while their husbands stood outside at the wagons and cars, smoking and visiting and waiting for their wives to "get religion."

Earl asked Zeno C. Tharp, the State Overseer, to allow him to continue going to Crow Creek on a regular basis. He felt challenged to try to rectify the somewhat humorous behavior of the Crow Creek congregation. He asked the women to start coming to church a few minutes earlier to allow him some time to socialize with the men standing in the church yard.

Within a few weeks, Earl's strategy began to work. He stood outside at the cars with the men talking about the weather or farming until time for the service to begin. Then he excused himself from "socializing" in a very friendly, non-threatening manner to go inside the church to preach. His warm, "no pressure" approach began to work on the reluctant bystanders. A few men finally began to follow the young preacher inside the church for the services. Eventually, all the men were coming inside the little church. The congregation at Crow Creek quickly doubled in size and their finances began to recover.

One aspect of Earl's early ministry bothered him greatly. He wasn't fully prepared to handle the sensitive social situations which repeatedly happened during his weekend traveling ministry. Whenever Earl preached revivals or youth meetings, he attracted a large following of young ladies. Teenaged girls suddenly grew very spiritual at the sight of this young, handsome guest preacher, a college boy at Furman.

His family teased Earl whenever he returned home from these weekends by asking him, "How many girls were saved this week?" Though he laughed at their good-natured comments and admittedly enjoyed certain aspects of the flattering attention his sex appeal generated, he also searched for some permanent solution to the problem. This repeated situation had became a nuisance in the ministry of this serious young evangelist.

Since his call into the ministry, Earl determined more than ever that he would represent genuine spirituality. He was extremely sensitive to the motives of those who responded to his ministry. More than anything else, he desired that people experience a true, life-changing encounter with the Lord. He could never accept what looked on the surface like a spiritual breakthrough in someone's life when he knew in his spirit that the person's underlying motives aimed at some far less significant goal.

One Sunday night Earl arrived home late from a weekend of ministry. The house was dark and quiet, his family obviously already in bed. Earl tapped lightly on his parents' bedroom door until he heard his mother answer him. He quietly opened the door. As usual, Earl Sr. immediately asked him for a report on the weekend. He told his parents how well the services had gone and gave them the regards of the pastor at the church where he had preached. Then he added quietly, "I'm going to get married within the next few weeks, within a month at the very most."

His parents wanted to laugh, but something in the serious tone of his voice kept them from regarding his words as merely a joke. "Who are you going to marry, Earl?" Addie Mae asked. Perhaps his relationship with Esther had rekindled and he hadn't told them.

"I don't know yet," he replied softly as he closed the door.

The next few days Earl's parents observed their son,

somewhat amused, yet also perplexed at the serious resolve in the young preacher's decisions for his life. Sitting beside his mother in church the next Sunday night, Earl leaned over to her and whispered, "I might just marry Norma Davis." Addie Mae laughed and shook her head as Earl smiled at her. She was amazed at how casually her son could make such a momentous comment.

The Paulks had known Norma Davis since she was a little five-year-old girl. Her father had died suddenly on a trip out West when she was only two, leaving her widowed mother with six small children to raise alone. Whenever Earl Sr. served as the pastor of the Greenville church, he had always given little Norma special affection and attention. In reciprocating his irresistible love, Norma claimed Brother Paulk as her surrogate father throughout her childhood. But the pastor was not the only member of the Paulk family that the little girl had grown up adoring. As long as she could remember, Norma Davis had been in love with Earl Paulk Jr.

Norma's house was located on the route between the church and the Paulks' house. Norma rushed home from church and posed prettily on the front steps as she waited for the preacher's car to drive by her house. She was much too shy to ever actually approach Earl with her feelings for him. Many other girls in the church felt the same way that she did. But she quietly moved close by him at church activities, hoping that he would notice her.

The first time Earl actually beheld Norma Davis'

beauty—the way she had always dreamed he would—
was far from the glamorous, romantic setting she had
always envisioned. Norma's mother did the very best
that she could on the meager salary she earned working in a textile mill. The family struggled financially,
close to destitution. Not only were their resources
insufficient to meet basic needs, but also two of the
Davis sons had severe physical handicaps. One of the
boys was deaf and another was frequently stricken
with epileptic seizures. They required special daily
attention from Norma, their responsible little sister
who cared for them while their mother worked.

Earl now regularly assisted his dad in pastoral
responsibilities by serving the parish. He often took
food to Norma's house since the church befittingly
helped the family to stretch what little money they had.
On one of those pastoral calls, Earl noticed, as if for the
first time, the stunning girl with big blue eyes and
smooth fair skin. She stood dutifully over the scrub
board at the kitchen sink, washing the family's
clothes. Her manner was quiet, soft and gentle, a true
servant. But she also possessed an unexplainable
attraction beyond striking physical beauty or the
sweetness of her spirit. Norma Davis personified an
ironclad strength and steadfastness that drew Earl to
her.

At a church social Earl asked Norma if he could drive
her home. She had come to the party with another boy
in the church. Without any hesitation, she uncharac-
teristically broke her date with the other boy so that
she could leave the party with Earl. That first evening

together confirmed the strong attraction between them.

Within a few days of their first date, Earl asked Norma to marry him. On that evening he asked Norma to go with him for a drive in the country. When he first approached the subject of marriage, Norma was thunderstruck. Was he playing with her emotions? She was unsure whether he were really serious. He was so unemotional, far too rational for a young man proposing marriage. He had never even kissed her!

Earl told Norma that he didn't love her the way he knew he would with time. He felt the potential for a deep, abiding love for her that would continually grow. He also told the bewildered girl that if she consented to marry him, she must understand that she would never be first in his life. As a minister's wife, she must willingly honor his calling from God as his primary, unrelenting priority.

Norma's one lifelong dream had always been to be the wife of a minister. She had loved the church from her earliest memories. The church had been her "father" substitute, and Norma had trusted God's direction through her pastor for every decision. God had given her a beautiful singing voice which she often used in the music ministry at church. She sang alto as a member of a quartet called "The Happy Four." God had sovereignly prepared her to understand this complicated young man and this strange marriage proposal. Norma had sat in the congregation on the night when God called Earl into the ministry. She was as certain of his calling from God as Earl was.

Norma consented to every inclusive clause of this exceptional marriage proposal. Even with the conflicting emotions she felt inside for reasons she couldn't yet comprehend, Norma wistfully agreed to everything Earl asked her. She knew with all the faith possible for a seventeen-year-old girl that somehow God would take care of every aspect of her ambiguous future as this man's wife.

That faith was tested. Earl asked Norma to allow him to visit every girl he had ever seriously dated just once more. At the conclusion of those visits, he intended for them to be married immediately. Again, Norma trusted Earl's motives in this unorthodox request. He spoke every word so deliberately, undoubtedly premeditated and significant. Norma knew that he had considered carefully every aspect of their future plans. These details were somehow necessary to the kind of life he would build with her. Norma felt their lives strangely merging in accordance with some higher, spiritually-directed design, unlike traditional plans of other young couples headed for the altar.

They needed to tell Norma's mother about their engagement. Norma and Earl drove back to Norma's house and walked together into the bedroom where Mrs. Davis slept. Norma's mother had been confined to bed for several days with influenza. She was delighted to have this unplanned visit from the young pastor. Before Earl approached the purpose of his visit, he sat down on the edge of the bed and prayed for Mrs. Davis' speedy recovery.

After praying with her, Earl sat down on another bed

in the room and began sharing with Mrs. Davis his desire to marry her youngest child. Mrs. Davis, a deeply spiritual woman, gave Norma and Earl her wholehearted blessing. Through her tears, she expressed gratitude to the Lord for His continuous provision and faithfulness to her family. Her Norma truly deserved the best.

When Earl told his mother the news, Addie Mae Paulk was elated with the expected announcement of her son's engagement. Earl predictably kept his word that he would marry in only a few weeks. Norma frantically confided to Addie Mae that the whirlwind courtship and engagement left little time to realize what was actually happening to her. Every detail related to the wedding was arranged so quickly. Addie Mae laughed sympathetically with the young bride-to-be. She told Norma that Earl Sr. had done the very same thing to her!

Norma and Earl easily could have planned the largest, most elaborate wedding that Greenville had ever seen. Their guest list could have included hundreds of people and state and national dignitaries. Instead, Earl wanted a private, simple wedding. The couple chose the sentimental significance of having their ceremony in the little farmhouse in Baxley, Georgia. They planned to stand in front of the fireplace where Earl Sr. and Addie Mae had been married years before, the same house where Earl was born.

Earl Sr., Myrtle and her husband, Harry Mushegan, were already in Baxley holding a revival. Addie Mae announced the news of Earl's impending wedding over the telephone. Myrtle cried when she heard about her brother's sudden plans. All three family members expressed astonishment at the immediacy of the event. They had known and loved Norma Davis almost all of her life.

Both Earl's and Norma's families drove down to Baxley for the wedding. Since the revival was still in progress, even on their wedding day, both Earl and Norma attended the evening service held in a high school gymnasium. Norma sang *Just A Closer Walk With Thee* as confirmation of the meaning of that day to her. She looked radiant in her white linen suit, glowing with the aura of a young bride marrying the love of her life.

The old farmhouse was stuffy and crowded in the suffocating heat on a Fourth of July night in 1946. Family members filled the house, packed into the small rustic rooms. People stood at open windows and crowded doorways. Earl and Norma stood in exactly the same spot where years before Earl Sr. and Addie Mae had taken vows pledging their lives to God and to each other. In adherence to the Church of God teaching, the marriage vows were pledged without exchanging wedding rings.

The newlyweds smiled adoringly at each other as they pressed through well-wishing family members out the door of the little farmhouse. They stood on the front porch while relatives took turns hugging them and wishing them lifelong happiness. Suddenly two men dressed in workshirts, overcoats and jeans rolled up to the knees ran barefooted toward the house yelling,

"Earl Jr., we want to meet your bride!"

Norma anxiously searched Earl's face to see if she should run back into the house. Norma usually avoided personal attention, and she had endured more than her share of a glaring spotlight focused on her for one day. Earl laughed, pulled his bride to him and whispered, "These are two of my cousins who love to play jokes on me. Just greet them like they were royalty and they'll love you forever. If you act like you're shocked, they'll never let you forget it."

By that time the cousins stood at the edge of the porch. Norma aggressively opened her arms and reached out to both of the men saying, "Hello, I'm Norma, Earl's wife." Both of the men suddenly seemed very quiet and embarrassed. As Earl had predicted, they thought their new cordial cousin was really some woman!

After the wedding, Earl Paulk kissed his beautiful bride for the first time ever. The romantic honeymoon consisted of the wedding night at a motel in Baxley, Georgia, a bus ride the next day back to Greenville, and a blissful week of privacy at the Paulks' house. The rest of Earl's family graciously remained in Baxley continuing the revival and visiting all their relatives to give the newlyweds the entire house to themselves.

As Earl had promised, his love for his young bride grew daily. They spent hours in deep conversations, planning together for the ministry God would give them in the days ahead. Norma learned intimately the nature and spirit of her tenacious husband. With increasing understanding and reverence, she also began to comprehend the depth of the commitment which she had made to Earl and to God.

As Earl had warned her, Norma realized repeatedly through daily situations that her husband's first allegiance would never belong to her. That realization, which might have caused resentment in a woman with less faith than Norma's, only made her stronger. God certainly had trusted her to share the life of a man with a unique mission. Like the spirit of a young woman from Nazareth named Mary, who daily watched the mysterious blending of the natural and the spiritual in the son God had given to her, Norma Paulk often silently contemplated her husband's determination. This very human man with many weaknesses was absolutely consumed with a desire to know and serve God. Like Mary long ago, Norma Paulk pondered many things in her heart.

5

CHAPTER FIVE

A fellowship hall, converted from the old, original church, sat across the street from the Church of God in Greenville. In addition to a large social room which once served the congregation as a sanctuary, the back part of the building included a small apartment. The old church kitchen completed the compact residence where Earl and Norma lived while he finished his senior year at Furman.

Earl and Norma were typical newlyweds—poor, happy dreamers. They worked part-time at Southern Franklin Process Company, a textile mill which dyed yarn. For additional income, Earl accepted an appointment to serve as the State Sunday School and

Youth Director. The weekend job paid him a total of $100 per month. Half of that income automatically belonged to the State Overseer who had generously financed Earl and Norma's car. Any additional money came through "love offerings" from revivals and weekend preaching as an interim pastor or guest evangelist.

For all the advantages Earl enjoyed as the son of Earl Paulk Sr., his ministry struggled financially because of his father's success. Many Church of God pastors considered Earl Paulk Sr. to be at the very top of the denomination in influence, responsibility and income. They knew that Earl Paulk Sr. sent his children to college. The ministry grew and flourished at the Greenville church, one of the largest and most prosperous in the denomination. With those factors coloring their perspective, local pastors in smaller, virtually unrecognized churches seldom regarded Earl Paulk's son as a young struggling college student, totally living on his own with a wife to support.

Many times Earl preached weekend revivals for nothing more than meals and a place to sleep. After one such revival at a little church in Charleston, S.C., Earl and Norma stood together on the church steps after the pastor and his congregation had extended their warmest thanks and driven away. The couple counted a few dollars between them, realizing their gas tank was sitting on empty. Embarrassment had kept them from admitting their need for cash. They hoped to receive "a gift" during or after the final service. Earl tried to fight feelings of disappointment—even anger. Surely they deserved some small remuneration after a full weekend of ministry everyone had assured him was "such a blessing" to them!

Norma asked her husband what they were going to do. Earl tried to reassure her while he held off his own panic with internally ingrained, male responsibility. He quickly assessed the situation, praying for direction. Earl checked their options, weighing their needs against their pride in asking for help. He decided finally that they would sleep in the car. The next day they would swallow any remaining pride and borrow money from the pastor or a church member for enough gas to get home.

As they walked across the parking lot, a car pulled up in front of the church. A man got out of his car hurriedly, yelling as he rushed toward them. He said that he was so relieved that they were still there. He wanted to send Earl's dad the ten dollars he owed him for a book he had purchased from him several months earlier. With money faithfully provided in their dire circumstances, Earl and Norma spent the God-sent provision at the nearest gas station and drove back to Greenville that night.

Earl maintained an exhausting schedule. He attended classes each day at Furman, worked afternoons and evenings at the textile mill, studied every spare moment he could find and spent weekends on the road in ministry. But ministry was never relegated simply to a weekend job. Evangelism flowed continuously, instilled in the intricate fiber of Earl's character. Whenever he talked to people, they heard about the

Lord. He had particularly challenging opportunities to plow rocky ground at the Southern Franklin Process Company.

When he first began working at the mill, he felt conspicuously out of place. His language was clean and he couldn't comfortably relate to the jokes his fellow workers enjoyed and told repeatedly. Earl promised himself that he would not come across as a sanctimonious preacher, but at the same time he refused to compromise his values to fit in with the gang. He prayed for opportunities to minister to his fellow workers and gain their trust. Within a few months, six of the men working closely with him had made commitments to Jesus Christ. One of those men later became a Baptist pastor with a growing church in the Greenville area.

One unforgettable October night, Earl and Norma woke suddenly to the sound of an explosion that shook their apartment and rattled the windows. Earl bolted out of bed, prepared to fight some unknown enemy. He ran to the window, thinking wildly that perhaps a gas truck had exploded or an airplane had crashed. Instead, his mind was jolted with the sudden realization that flames engulfed the church across the street.

After calling the fire department and his father, Earl threw on some clothes. In his shocked, nightmarish state of mind, each second he spent dressing seemed to pass in slow-motion. He ran irrationally toward the burning building. The fire was intense. Consuming flames spread rapidly. He looked through the sanctuary windows just as the platform area collapsed in a blazing inferno beneath the weight of a grand piano.

One pulsating thought beat repeatedly through his mind, "Get the important church documents from an office file cabinet!" Some of those records were minutes of significant quarterly conferences which were of historical importance. The files also held some Financial Committee reports—important, documented records which were valuable to the entire denomination. Earl knew that he had to risk getting those documents out of the church if he could find a way.

The fire consumed the building with an uncontrollable appetite. Earl ran into the office wing located behind the sanctuary. An outside door leading to the office was mysteriously unlocked. Suffocating smoke rolled out the door as he entered the room. His eyes immediately began stinging. He held his breath. He blindly felt his way across the room to the files. Indiscriminately grabbing all the folders he could carry, he crawled across the floor. He gasped painfully for air. Suddenly, all sense of direction vanished. He strained with all his might just to remain conscious.

While sirens screamed in the night, a fireman threw a heavy axe through the office window, striking Earl on the head and arm. Excruciating pain surged through his body just before he lost consciousness, adding hopelessness to his already deranged state of shock. However, the broken window provided him with precious oxygen as smoke billowed through the jagged opening to the outside. A fireman finally opened the same door that Earl had used and found him lying on the floor near the window, still clutching the precious documents. The fireman dragged him out of the building. Within minutes, the roof on the office wing of the church completely collapsed in flames.

Later that night, Earl watched his dad's broad shoulders shaking as he wept over the ashes of the church he had so lovingly fathered. His dad leaned against a telephone pole, crying from the depth of his soul. The preacher's face wore the strain of grief and loss as well as the heavy responsibility ahead. Now he must lead a heartbroken congregation beyond the devastation smoldering before him. Earl quietly whispered consoling words of hope to his father, promising that they would build a bigger and better church than this one had been.

Within a few days, spokesmen from local mills and city officials campaigned on the radio and in newspapers to rebuild the church as a community project. Working people, most of them members of other churches in Greenville, donated money to begin the new building. Daniel Construction Company responded to the community appeal by graciously offering a special building contract to the church. A traveling Baptist evangelist, J. Harold Smith, offered the use of his auditorium located in the downtown area for the church's weekly services. He rarely used the theater during the winter months.

But the people at the Greenville Church of God decided to challenge unpredictable weather by meeting in a large tent. They erected the tent a block away from the future church's construction site. For two years— including icy cold winters and summers of sweltering heat—the congregation met together for services in that tent. They watched eagerly the slow, steady progress on their beautiful church building. Just as Earl had said to comfort his father, the new church was a far bigger, more beautiful edifice than the building destroyed in the fire.

When Earl graduated from Furman with a bachelor's degree in history, E. L. Simmons, president of Lee College in Cleveland, Tennessee, immediately contacted him. President Simmons offered Earl an attractive teaching position at the denomination's school. The college was opening its first year of operation on the former Bob Jones Academy campus which the Church of God had purchased to expand their facilities.

Earl felt absolutely no desire to teach. His goals and intentions focused totally on his calling to be a pastor. However, he willingly trusted the direction of his ministry to the leaders of the denomination. They unanimously encouraged him to accept the teaching position. Earl's college degree made him a choice young leader in the church. They viewed him as a young man with versatile talents and academic preparation which could meet a variety of needs within the denominational structure.

Earl and Norma obediently moved to Tennessee. Lee College's curriculum also included instruction for students in their last two years of high school. As a first year teacher, Earl taught 356 students—more than any other faculty member. The school's greatest staff needs were in the physical education department. In addition to teaching P.E. classes, Earl became a health and history teacher in the high school. He also taught Old and New Testament Survey, American History and Church History in the college division of the school.

Meanwhile, Norma stayed busy at home as well as taking classes in shorthand, typing and piano. She was preparing herself to help Earl in the church they hoped to serve eventually. Few pastors employed church secretaries in the late forties and a pastor's wife who played the piano always assured him of a worship leader he could trust. A pastor felt a tremendous boost of confidence whenever he could flow comfortably with his pianist. Norma's natural, musical ability enabled her to learn piano very quickly. She took every possible opportunity to prepare herself for the versatile role of a pastor's wife. They prayed confidently each day that Earl's teaching career would last only temporarily.

Earl enjoyed the year of teaching much more than he ever believed he would. However, the most important decision he made that year regarded continuing school as a student—not as a teacher. Even before graduation at Furman, Earl considered enrolling in seminary to pursue a more comprehensive theological understanding. Few preachers in his denomination earned college degrees, much less advanced seminary training. Many conservative leaders in the denomination argued that education—like participation in sports—was a worldly endeavor which hindered true spirituality. Some preachers regularly ridiculed the idea that seminary training enhanced the ministry of a godly man. A few ardent fundamentalists argued an extreme position— that God was unlikely to call a well-educated man into the ministry. They equated academic ignorance with an advantage in doing God's work and hearing God's voice.

Earl agreed that a seminary degree did not determine a man's calling into the ministry. He vehemently disagreed, however, with the hostile anti-education prejudices perpetually imposed by many evangelical pastors and church members. He questioned their underlying fears for such an aversion to formal education. Their pride—bragging because they lacked a college degree—seemed as unjustified as other denominations who boasted of high educational standards for their ministers.

Earl believed that truth could stand any test and still remain true. He wanted an opportunity to test Pentecostal doctrines against historical traditions and various theological beliefs. He also wanted to understand the biblical basis for doctrines and sacraments practiced by other denominations. He believed that many denominations held great truth in their doctrines which his own church ignored. But he often questioned the reasons that many Christian leaders denied the power of Pentecost as a viable experience for every believer. Earl knew that if he ever hoped to influence the thinking of Christians both within and beyond his own denominational doors, a seminary degree would give his voice notable credibility. Personally, he felt compelled to allow his own faith to undergo an objective, academic test.

Three seminaries accepted Earl's applications for enrollment: Princeton University, Southeastern Baptist Seminary and Candler School of Theology at Emory University. Emory University offered Earl a scholarship which he readily accepted. Earl and Norma moved from Tennessee into a little cabin owned by Earl Sr. at the Church of God campground in Doraville, a suburb of Atlanta, Georgia.

Earl held the distinction of being the first Pentecostal-born student ever to attend Candler School of Theology, a renowned Methodist seminary. He quickly learned that seminary classes were as challenging as he had anticipated. His predominantly Methodist professors and classmates afforded him many opportunities to express Pentecostal theological views. As many times earlier in his life, Earl found himself clarifying misconceptions of "holiness" churches in class discussions. More than ever he accepted the responsibility of worthily representing his heritage to people on the fringe of the Pentecostals' tremendous, yet sometimes unrecognized and unappreciated influence on the total church.

God repeatedly used Earl Paulk in creating a spiritual bridge between Pentecostals and other Church leaders. He eagerly learned—broadening his knowledge from a variety of sources. Earl was an insatiable student of the Bible, hungry for any spiritual enlightenment that anyone was willing to share with him. Two decades later during the widespread Charismatic outpouring of the Holy Spirit in which many Catholic and Protestant doctrinal boundaries proved to be insignificant as the Spirit moved, Earl received letters from several of his Emory classmates. These Methodist pastors credited open Charismatic receptivity in their churches to their lasting impressions of the outspoken Pentecostal student who sat with them in seminary classes. Many of these Methodist pastors had received the baptism of the Holy Spirit themselves. They wanted Earl to know about the exciting dimension of power that this experience brought to their ministries, their people and their personal lives.

Seminary classes met Tuesdays through Fridays at Emory to allow seminary students to minister at area churches on weekends. Earl traveled to various Georgia churches on weekend assignments from the State Overseer. Most of the churches he visited needed an interim pastor or guest speaker for a rally or revival.

One of those churches needing an interim pastor was Shannon Church of God, located near Rome, Georgia. This little church was recovering from a scandalous incident which had shaken its congregation. The pastor of the church resigned after a bitter fistfight with a church member. Supposedly the pastor had spouted off some insulting remarks about this member's wife.

The State Overseer warned Earl of this regrettable situation at the little church when he made the assignment. With much prayer to find ways to bring peace and healing to the disillusioned people, Earl delivered strong messages on spiritual warfare hurting "little ones." He believed God directed him to speak boldly. After one of these fearless sermons, a church member asked Earl and Norma to join his family for lunch.

The young preacher and his wife sat at the table with

139

the family in amicable, lively conversation, enjoying a delicious Sunday feast. Earl casually mentioned how difficult the disruptive situation at the church must have been for all the victimized members of the church. He noted how divisive such a childish incident as a fistfight between the preacher and a member became to innocent people. He added that Satan often used such incidents to destroy people's faith and the work of the Lord in a church.

Suddenly all the simultaneous chatter around the table halted abruptly. A thick silence fell over the room. With a serious expression the host peered directly into Earl's eyes. The man told Earl, "I'm the member who was fighting with the preacher." Earl choked on the food sticking in his throat while everyone at the table watched him mentally pick himself up from the floor.

Earl also spent several months at a little church in Moultrie, Georgia, which experienced remarkable growth during the short span of time he ministered there. In only four months the little congregation of twenty-five people grew to several hundred members. An evangelical outpouring in the little church ignited the open hearts of the people. They excitedly invited their neighbors to come to the services. Soon the church was unable to seat all the Sunday morning congregation. They stood along the walls and sat in chairs crowded together in the aisles.

During the Moultrie revival, God asked Earl a question which determined the destiny of his ministry. Earl was in prayer, worshipping the Lord, when the Spirit asked him, "What do you want from Me?" The question was unexpected and startling in its implications. At that moment, Earl knew God would grant anything he asked. He knew that the Spirit offered him the same opportunity He had given to Solomon—the choice of wisdom, wealth, fame, power . . . Earl answered carefully, "Lord, that I may love Your people. Give me that unconditional love that You have for them." Within moments the confirming evidence of love beyond natural compassion or affections engulfed Earl Paulk as he ministered to specific needs of people in the congregation. Only years later did Earl also realize the bitter cup accompanying the knowledge of such agape love—an irrevocable gift from God.

The Moultrie church requested that Earl be assigned to them as a full-time pastor. He was also offered a full-time pastorate at a church in Buford, Georgia, much closer to the seminary.

The Buford church offered Earl his first real opportunity to use well-ingrained ministerial skills. Finally he was able to give himself to people under his total care for an extended period of time. He and Norma moved into the small parsonage near the church. They quickly began to love the hardworking people whom they were called to serve, a dream which had finally come true. Norma relaxed much more among the people in her own ministry to them. She played the piano for the services and felt comfortable in her role as the pastor's wife. She developed close relationships with the parishioners. They confided their problems to her, depending on her ministry almost as much as Earl's.

Since the Buford church provided Earl and Norma

their first extended pastorate with some financial security, Earl finally agreed with his strongly-maternal wife that their lives were stable enough to start a family. Norma wanted children from the beginning of their marriage, but Earl insisted on waiting. He wanted them to be in a position to enjoy all the pleasures that came with parenthood while comfortably meeting the responsibilities.

Norma's first pregnancy was a time of fulfilling anticipation. Her thoughts and concerns turned inward to love and nurture the new life within her. Pregnancy held special meaning to Norma for many reasons. More than ever, their ministry at the Buford church caused Norma to realize the demands on a dedicated pastor's time. Family and personal concerns often pulled against Earl's desire to meet his congregation's needs satisfactorily. Undoubtedly, the responsibility for parenting this baby would primarily belong to its mother. She knew God had prepared her from childhood to cope with the lonely hours and the demanding schedule of their lives in the ministry.

Seminary classes met Tuesdays through Fridays from early morning until noon. Earl attended his classes in the morning, then studied, counseled, prepared his sermons and visited people in his congregation during the afternoons and evenings. He gave almost obsessively conscientious attention to caring for members in the Buford church. He knew that any neglect or failure in meeting their needs would be attributed (at least in his own mind) to the time he devoted to school.

Few people in the congregation actually knew that Earl attended seminary classes. He felt such total allegiance to his ministry as his first priority that he permitted very little time for himself. He avoided any possibility of criticism from the people for being unavailable in emergencies or when someone needed him for spiritual counseling.

Some women in the church told Norma about one of their members, Mrs. Daniels, whose husband physically beat her because she attended church services. When Norma reported the situation to Earl, he immediately contacted the woman and asked her about the unsettling rumors he had heard. She admitted to her pastor that her husband beat her repeatedly for coming to church. However, Mrs. Daniels said that God promised her the strength to endure the abuse she received. She believed that her husband's salvation depended totally on her own spiritual perseverance. Earl recoiled at the physical and emotional price this woman seemed willing to pay, yet somehow he trusted her resolute spirit in the matter. He admired her unwavering courage. Unable to convince her to take an alternative solution, Earl daily covered Mrs. Daniels in prayer and reminded her repeatedly to call whenever she needed him.

A member of the church called Earl one afternoon to tell him that Mrs. Daniels' son, a child about twelve years old, had been severely gored by a bull. Because of the unusual situation in the Daniels' household, Earl had never visited the family's home. As he walked toward their house, he saw Mr. Daniels standing by a tree in the front yard. He walked over to the man and introduced himself. Earl immediately felt hostility rise against him. The man glared at him with intense hatred. Mr Daniels growled, barely moving his lips, "What are you doing here?"

Earl replied softly that he had heard about the little boy's condition and had come out of concern for their family. The man stared angrily at the preacher. Earl walked with firm determination into the house to console and pray with Mrs. Daniels for her son's life. The child miraculously survived the attack. He and his mother continued coming to church under continuous threats and physical abuse.

Years later when Earl ministered at a church in Atlanta's inner city, Mr. and Mrs. Daniels made a special trip to the church to share the good news with Earl about Mr. Daniels' salvation. God had honored this woman's years of dedicated prayer—in spite of constant warfare with no evidence of victory. Her perseverance overpowered spiritual forces of darkness which had controlled her husband. Mr. Daniels warmly embraced the pastor he had so completely despised. He apologized humbly to Brother Paulk for the years of hatred and regrettable abuse he had inflicted.

Norma's mother and brother visited in early September, knowing that the baby was due soon and Norma needed someone to be close to her in the days near her delivery. Norma had felt very uncomfortable that evening. She hesitated to tell anyone how she felt because she didn't want to cause any premature excitement over the big event. When she was totally sure her discomfort was real labor, she woke Earl. In the early morning hours he drove Norma to the hospital with the typical nervous anxiety of a father-to-be.

The baby was born very quickly for a mother undergoing her first delivery. Because the baby was so large, the doctor tried to slow down the contractions. He allowed Earl to stay with Norma throughout the entire labor experience. Earl left the room only at the actual moment of birth. He returned a few moments later to greet the new mother and their beautiful screaming daughter.

The baby weighed over nine pounds. They named her Rebecca Mae, "Rebecca" after Earl's grandmother on his father's side and "Mae" after Earl's mother, Addie Mae Paulk. Many years later Earl believed that his daughter's name was significant to his ministry for greater reasons. The Genesis story of Abraham's servant finding a wife for Isaac gives a detailed account of the qualities in the young girl, Rebecca, who completely met the servant's demands for the girl who would marry his master's son. God revealed to Earl that those same qualities were necessary for the Bride of Christ who is betrothed to God's Son. Earl often referred to the last day's Church as the "Rebecca" Church, the Church that would birth the Kingdom of God on earth as it is in heaven. He taught the revelation that Sarah's conception was to birth the nation of Israel, but Rebecca's conception will birth the mature Church of Jesus Christ which will usher in the ultimate Kingdom of God in the last days (Genesis 24, Romans 9:10).

Little Becky slept in a portable bassinet under the piano during church services as Norma played the songs and hymns for worship. Whenever Becky got fussy or hungry during the services, a precious couple in the church who were close to Earl and Norma, Mr. and Mrs. L.A. Wilson, took little Becky out of the church to allow the service to continue undisturbed.

For his last two years of seminary, Earl, Norma and Becky moved back to the campground in Doraville to live in the Youth Parsonage. Earl served as State Sunday School and Youth Director of Georgia just as he had in South Carolina during his senior year at Furman. He traveled around the state to different churches on weekends to supervise and motivate activities in various youth groups. Of course, continuous traveling taxed his demanding schedule in seminary as well as his physical stamina and their family life. However, Earl did have more time to devote to his classes and his wife and daughter during the week.

Widespread exposure to youth groups at various churches in the state established Earl as somewhat of a "youth" spokesman to the leadership of his denomination. Young people he met across the state increasingly voiced frustration at the legalistic doctrines of their church. Legalism in dress and strict codes of behavior made them feel more like misfits in society than confident young people with "good news" to share. Church laws caused them to question whether Jesus Christ was "the answer" for the problems in their lives. Church rules only created more problems for them. While trying to hold them to the authority of the church for their own sakes, Earl objectively tried to explain reasons for certain traditions and standards. He gave positive explanations to the same questions he had asked himself for so many years.

Earl's open, straightforward approach to these issues without any signs of condemning kids for asking questions won their trust and devotion. He became their champion and authority on church issues. They looked to him to influence changes in needless, oppressive church laws. But Earl knew that they would eventually learn that the power structure of their denomination did not easily tolerate debate, radical changes or controversial ideas.

When he campaigned for the denomination to build a swimming pool for the young people at the Church of God campground in Doraville, the leaders labeled him everything from a young liberal intellectual to a trouble-making communist. The Church of God strictly ruled against boys and girls swimming together in the same pool. They referred to public swimming pools as "mixed bathing." Repeatedly, Earl heard them say that changing times and social trends did not "lower the standards" which the church adamantly upheld. As he swallowed adverse reactions to his proposal from the older, unbending, denominational establishment, he promised himself that he would never allow rigid laws to make him uncaring, insensitive and unthinking.

But in honoring the integrity of his life's choices and ministry, Earl clung as closely as possible to the well-worn philosophy his father had always espoused. He made solemn promises as a pastor to uphold church teachings and laws. Regardless of the lack of biblical support or his personal opinions, he would somehow work with diligent dedication within the denominational structure where God had unquestionably called him to serve.

Many doors opened to Earl upon graduation from seminary. Several churches where he had ministered notified him that they would gladly have him return as their senior pastor. All the revivals, youth rallies and guest preaching inevitably made him a popular, influential voice throughout the southern churches in the denomination. The approval of the membership at various churches carried substantial weight with those making pastoral assignments at denominational headquarters.

Among many calls to pastorates, Earl received an invitation from Hemphill Church of God in Atlanta, a church where he had conducted a revival. Hemphill unquestionably stood as one of the largest, most respected churches in the denomination. However, some controversy had recently split the church. The volatile nature of Hemphill's problems created an unstable membership, somewhat less than the "grand prize" for a young pastor that the church would have been in its glorious past.

With a proven record of handling controversy and challenges, Earl accepted the assignment to Hemphill Church of God. He, Norma and Becky moved into the parsonage next door to the church. He began a ministry at twenty-five years of age in a pulpit normally filled by seasoned pastors who had paid their dues to rise to the top of the denominational structure. Amid all the congratulations from his family and friends on such a choice, impressive assignment, Earl felt the lonely, sober reality of facing struggles far beyond his abilities or preparation. Every foundation in his life would soon be tested and shaken. He needed faith like never before. When he was alone in his thoughts, he tried to understand—even rationalize—the intense trepidation he felt deep in his spirit. Disregarding natural fears, for the second time in his life Earl Paulk ran into the fire.

6

CHAPTER SIX

His body ached with exhaustion. A protective inner calm finally lulled him into a place of numb emotions and thoughts. Earl closed his eyes hoping to escape even the darkness of his bedroom. As his body began to relax, suddenly his mind raced with a thousand particles of light colliding like all the unfinished details of the day. He shifted his weight searching for a comfortable, relaxed position. He tried to pray. Without instant inspiration, he concentrated instead on some scriptures he would quote to someone dangerously close to a dark subconscious tunnel of despair. He felt himself almost swallowed inside the tunnel where feelings grow cold and life's goals evaporate into effortless indifference.

After only one year as pastor of Hemphill Church of God, his energy was spent. The constant tugging from one group of people to another with seemingly impossible demands and insatiable needs had frayed his confidence and wounded his spirit. He wanted desperately to please them all. He devoted himself to being the shining example of the "perfect pastor" everyone demanded. Inside he struggled to separate the pastoral image that one person required of him from the roles demanded by other parishioners. He vainly sought solutions to their differences that wouldn't betray his conscience and yet would allow people on every side of an issue to love him.

His role as resident peacemaker placed him in the center of a continuous war zone. He stood as a defenseless mediator against biting accusations, suspicions and resentments hurled from every direction. He listened patiently for hours to people voicing their fixed opinions. When they finally allowed him to reply, he could almost visibly watch his words bounce off the stubborn places inside them. Dissatisfactions on any issue were eventually blamed on the preacher. He constantly asked God the reasons his prayers failed in these situations. But instead of hearing answers from God, Earl only blamed himself.

The pastor carried the divisions among his people inside him like his own personal failures. He fasted for extended periods of time, searching for solutions. His clothes swallowed his bony frame. After prolonged fasts, Norma would beg her husband to eat again. Earl sought penitence for everyone through his own stringent disciplines with the unbending will of a Pharisee. He imposed extreme self-denial on himself while obsessively trying to meet childish demands from everyone else. The divorce of a couple from a highly respected family in the church provided a central focus for the restless congregation to vent their various frustrations. This divorce split the congregation into uncompromising factions. The divorcing couple were well-known gospel singers. Their singing ministry, records and personal appearances had established public association of commercial-quality gospel concerts with weekly services at Hemphill Church of God.

In addition to insoluble issues surrounding the divorce and the congregation's opinions about them, Earl routinely faced a congregation expecting professional musical entertainment at every service. He tried to gear the focus of the music ministry to become a harmonious continuation of the teaching and preaching of God's Word. Instead, he finally admitted that many people had joined the church primarily for the music. Some members preferred attending a church with featured singers and a little preaching added to fill the minutes until noon.

Attempts to balance the spiritual diet of the services tested the spiritual maturity of the congregation. Many members resented the young pastor's efforts. They clearly preferred entertainment to challenging teaching. Somehow Earl managed to maintain a good relationship with the family at the center of the divorce controversy. Family members continued to minister during the services. When the family finished singing and Earl walked to the pulpit, hostile people scattered throughout the congregation got up from their seats and walked down the center aisle out the doors of the church. With that introduction, Earl preached his heart out to people who remained for the message.

Other changes Earl initiated received more favorable responses from the people. In keeping with his inbred abhorrence to showy, public displays, Earl stopped the practice of raising money by asking members to stand up or raise their hands to pledge some specific amount. He promised church leaders that the budget of the church would increase if he simply appealed to the people to give their tithes and offerings to the Lord as an act of worship. Within three months, the new policy proved itself to the church leaders. The young pastor also earned new respect from the congregation when the budget of the church tripled.

Earl held firmly to his comprehension of spiritual authority, developed within him at an early age. He spoke candidly to the elders of the church shortly after he assumed the pastorate. He willingly submitted his ministry to receive their wisdom and spiritual counsel. Hopefully they would help him avoid some of the apparent problems threatening the church's stability. He realized his youth could easily be perceived as a weakness in his role as the senior pastor. Personal support and input from the established, older church leaders were critical to the people respecting the decisions he would make.

Most of Earl's and Norma's personal and social

friendships emerged from people in this older echelon of church leaders. These parental relationships offered the young couple stability, security and ample personal and professional advice. But Earl began to think and respond to life emotionally like a much older man. The combination of administrative demands, continuous controversy among his people and his determination to be the "perfect pastor" at all costs gradually suppressed natural, normal appetites of a vibrant young man in his late twenties. The dedicated Pharisee quickly became an animated mannequin going through the motions of ministry.

Not only was he war-weary with the daily battles at his own church, but denominational leadership continued to oppose changing church laws he fought to eradicate. He made a speech at the denomination's Ordained Council concerning wearing wedding bands. This speech addressed specific problems encountered by wives in his congregation whose husbands were away in the Korean War. These women shared with their pastor some uncomfortable situations they had experienced, emphasizing their need for a visible sign of marriage covenant in their husbands' absences. Not only did the speech fail to penetrate the hard core establishment's thinking, Earl was practically laughed off the podium for suggesting such a break with the church's unbendable traditions.

Ironically, one of the other speakers at this Council who most strongly opposed Earl's "wedding band" proposal spoke about his own recent travels to Church of God congregations in South Africa. He emphasized the South African Christians' "great spiritual maturity and zeal for the Lord." Earl sat in the assembly thinking that everyone knew South African members of their denomination wore wedding rings. He wondered how this official could have traveled among these people—admiring their spiritual maturity—and never have even corrected them for what he supposedly regarded as a sinful practice. That sort of obvious hypocrisy insulted his respect for church leaders.

Whenever Earl's furious reaction to the denomination's inconsistencies churned bitterness inside him, Earl Sr. gently confronted his son's challenges with soft answers. Earl Sr. reminded the young pastor to give himself totally to his calling by concentrating on the positive aspects of his daily service to God. Earl Sr. assured his son that God would honor his submission to spiritual authority—even to rules contradicting his personal opinions—if he would trust God to deal with the leaderships' consciences and believe that God controlled all of the steps of his ministry.

The young pastor took his father's calming words to heart. Earl repeatedly returned to Atlanta, obediently submitted—as much as he possibly could be—to all the Church of God mandates and laws. A few weeks after his "wedding rings" speech, a precious older couple joined his church. Earl responsibly reminded the wife that their denomination disapproved of her wearing a wedding ring. The woman sweetly smiled at her young pastor as she stretched out her hand. She looked confidently into his eyes and replied, "Brother Paulk, my husband put this ring on my finger before you were born. I've never taken it off."

Because he had openly spoken his own beliefs at the Ordained Council and therefore felt no betrayal in his conscience, Earl bought a gold band for Norma to wear to her obstetrician's office. Now visibly showing in her second pregnancy, Norma had felt the questioning looks of other women sitting with her in the waiting room for appointments with their doctor. Norma repeatedly heard all Earl's frustrations in discussions advocating wearing wedding bands. She felt no condemnation that the ring she wore to the obstetrician's office might jeopardize her good conscience or her relationship with the Lord.

Susan Joy Paulk, called "Joy" by her family, was born in the early morning on July 15, 1953. Earl never felt that he should ask the Lord to give him a son. On the other hand, Earl Paulk Sr.—proud of his own "Junior" following in his footsteps—felt that Earl needed a son to carry the mantle of ministry to a third generation. Ironically, Joy became a tomboy at an early age. Though petite and very feminine, she became the competitive son substitute by inheriting her dad's athletic ability. She excelled in sports and easily cultivated strong peer relationships as a very popular, independent young lady. Like her name, Joy became a gifted comedian whose ministry included dramatic insights acted out as good medicine edifying the Body of Christ.

Norma's reaction to Joy's birth typified a mother having her second child. Norma wondered how she could possibly love two children with the same consuming intensity she had loved her first baby. Postpartum blues set in almost immediately. Norma burst into tears when Earl told her about finding little Becky hiding behind the door, crying and asking for her mama.

The new baby was a welcomed, much-needed reprieve from the never-ending wilderness where Earl dwelled daily. At those desert places in his life when he couldn't find rest from everyday pressures, he felt parched and barren inside. Reading the scriptures and prayer were absolutely void of emotion. If he had followed his feelings, he would have resigned. Many times he wondered what spiritual help he could possibly offer his people. Then unexpectedly God would lead him to some well of water to sustain and refresh his calling. After months in the desert, he would walk for several days in green pastures beside still waters.

Through a friendship with Pastor Ralph Byrd, senior pastor at Faith Memorial Assembly of God, Earl received an invitation to serve on the Atlanta Christian Council's Executive Committee. Besides opening doors in exchanging ministry ideas, working toward common community goals and interdenominational problem-solving with other church leaders, the Council also opened participation in a highly respected television ministry to Earl.

Television exposure in the Atlanta area thrust Earl into the forefront in the early days of the Charismatic Movement throughout mainline denominational churches. Television viewers enjoyed the sermons of this handsome, well-educated Pentecostal preacher. His messages often advocated the baptism of the Holy

Spirit as a desirable, valid experience for every Christian. Earl's direct preaching style and confidence opened many opportunities for ecumenical ministry. Services broadcast from his church shattered long-held stereotypes in the minds of many viewers about wild Pentecostal "holy roller" preachers and congregations.

Inevitably, people from other churches seeing the broadcast visited Hemphill, primarily on Sunday nights. They enjoyed the free-flowing, upbeat worship and listened intently to the fiery Pentecostal preacher's challenging messages, delivered stronger in person than by television. A woman in a staff position at the First Baptist Church in Atlanta asked Earl whether she should leave her church after receiving the baptism in the Holy Spirit at the end of a service. Without hesitation, he advised her to stay in her home church and share the blessing God had given to her life. He assured her that as the Holy Spirit opened the hearts of those around her, they would ask her about the new vitality they noticed in her life and ministry.

Many pastors on the Atlanta Christian Council's Executive Committee were inhibited in front of television cameras. Their personal distractions during the taping of the programs caused their congregations to regard television production as an intrusion on their usual services. These pastors frequently cancelled their turns to appear on the hour-long, weekly television program, broadcast live from the various churches.

The secretary of the Council, Jo Ann Adams, knew

that Pastor Paulk had no misgivings about appearing on television, and he consistently preached interesting, quality sermons, well representing the standards and goals of the Council. Because she could always call him on a moment's notice whenever another pastor cancelled a scheduled appearance, Earl became one of the most frequent speakers on the program.

Television exposure brought Earl public recognition as a well-known pastor throughout the Atlanta area. Coinciding with television broadcasts, radio became the medium bringing him prominence as the national radio spokesman for the Church of God. Walter Bennett, a CBS producer who also produced Billy Graham's *Hour of Decision,* asked six Church of God preachers to submit tapes of their sermons. From those tapes, the producer selected one preacher as the national radio spokesman for the denomination. The denomination informed Earl that he was chosen because his voice lacked strong regional identification, probably because his family frequently moved from state to state throughout his childhood.

The denomination recorded the National Radio Broadcast each week at the Church of God headquarters in Cleveland, Tennessee. Earl traveled from Atlanta to Cleveland and back every week for almost two years. He recognized that God was opening new, important channels in his ministry's outreach and influence, but he still struggled at Hemphill with dissensions and denominational politics. His congregation continuously divided into warring factions over numerous issues. One member of the Hemphill Church

Council, also a member of the Finance Committee of the church, particularly opposed Earl's spiritual ideologies. The man consistently reacted to his pastor's convictions as being "too liberal." He bitterly opposed Earl's views on racial and social issues as well as openly criticizing his administrative decisions.

Atlanta was like a volcano ready to erupt during the fifties. The seemingly calm social order began hearing the first rumblings of pressure from underground racial unrest. The first stirrings of the Civil Rights Movement, which later focused the eyes of the world on the city, quietly organized for turbulent confrontations. The governor of Georgia was a close personal friend of a Hemphill Council member frequently opposing Earl's "liberal ideas." This govenor was publicly regarded as a man with strong segregationist views and political insensitivity to oppressed people, particularly those from racial minorities.

When the federal government first issued edicts forcing schools throughout the nation to open their doors to racial integration, the public reacted with fury and defiance. Without united political voices, and too few politicians willing to lose elections over defending groups with little to offer them in campaign contributions, the school integration controversy simmered for almost a decade. The issue boiled over finally in rioting, demonstrations and life-threatening reactions to school busing in the violent sixties.

From early childhood, Earl felt drawn to people who were abused by society. He easily empathized with anyone denied basic human rights for any reason. He always fought prejudice, believing strongly that every person was a valuable creation of God, born with spiritual potential, specific purpose and eternal destiny. Without totally understanding his ability to comprehend their feelings, Earl deeply identified with social entrapment as a result of the circumstances into which people were born. He spoke boldly to his all-white congregation, insisting that racial equality and equal opportunity were God-given rights to everyone. The sharp edge of his words cut into the core of his congregation's prejudices and racist politics.

Racial issues in Atlanta exploded with a mandate from the federal government to integrate Atlanta schools. City and school officials retaliated with threats to close the schools rather than force black and white students into classes together. Atlanta newspapers reported the daily debates between school officials and Washington legislators.

In what seemed like negotiations, but were actually a deliberate delay tactic, political leaders formed committees to investigate the conditions and note the differences in "white" and "black" schools in the state. These people argued that they already had "equal, but separate" school facilities. They said that racial integration would simply create an undesirable social problem with no educational advantages for anyone. Earl agreed to serve on one of these investigating committees along with a state congressman, a city official and several influential business leaders.

The committee received a list of "white" and "black" schools to visit. From the beginning of their tours, they were notably impressed with the consistent standards found in these schools. However, the selectivity of schools on the list irritated Earl. He knew the motive of this selection of campuses was intended to prove the dedicated racists' "equal but separate" arguments. Earl suggested to his group that they also visit several unlisted schools in more remote, rural areas of Georgia. With resistance from a few members of the committee, they finally relented, accompanying the pastor to these schools. From the beginning of their visits to these randomly selected schools, the group was absolutely appalled at the contrasts they observed.

Many rural black schools were heated with pot-bellied stoves. Little children huddled around these stoves trying to stay warm. Many children wore their coats in class all day. The group observed antiquated facilities and frayed, torn textbook materials in one school while another school in the same area would have the latest lab equipment and new books. Sanitary conditions varied. Some schools lacked indoor rest-room facilities. Recreational equipment, libraries and cafeteria facilities in white schools far surpassed those in the randomly selected black schools. But similar equipment and facilities were only minor issues in Earl's mind. He couldn't bear to observe the fear in black children's faces as the committee walked down the halls of their schools. Somehow, in spite of being told repeatedly for years that he could do nothing to change appalling social injustices, God had given him a responsibility to speak for these children, the opportunity to expose publicly the improprieties of their environments.

The Atlanta Christian Council devoted extensive discussion and prayer on action they should take on the school integration issue. In an act of moral conscience and responsibility to God, Earl Paulk joined some other members of the Atlanta Christian Council by signing a document called the Atlanta Manifesto. This edict condemned the attitude of local school officials in threatening to close schools to avoid racial integration. Pastors signing the Manifesto knew they faced tremendous opposition and personal, public slander. "Nigger lover" labels were frequently hurled at the pastors signing this controversial document. Misunderstandings of their motives drew criticism from both black and white communities, segregationist leaders and of course, their own congregations.

When local newspapers published the Atlanta Manifesto, Earl received furious reactions from some members of his church. Friends of the governor of Georgia as well as strong segregationists among his people mumbled that either they or the preacher would have to leave the church! Without any regrets for the stands he had taken, Earl merely added these complaints to his already overwhelming list of daily pressures and threats. Some people did leave the church over this issue. They believed the preacher had finally overstepped his boundaries of influence by taking this bold political stand.

At a time when Earl never knew greater success and influence in his ministry's outreach, he experienced feelings of internal defeat at his church. Love, dedication, discussions, sermons, fasts, prayers and petitions for peace in the church failed to appease or unify his people. Though most of the members adored the preacher personally, the preacher himself felt like a failure. He asked God continually how he could lead Hemphill to become the church he knew God wanted it to be. His people knew how much he wanted unity. Yet, he had done everything he knew to do to bring them into one mind and spirit in vain. Closer to home, he often carried guilt toward Norma and his girls with so little quality time to give them. Whatever his schedule required at any given moment, Earl felt as if he should be doing something else. Whenever he was working, exhaustion distracted his thoughts, making him believe that he would have a better perspective if he only had a few hours to rest. When he tried to sleep, the pressures caused him to lie awake staring blankly into the darkness asking God for answers.

Besides regular television and weekly radio broadcasting as well as the counseling and preaching responsibilities of his pastorate, Earl was writing an extensive layman's theological treatise on Pentecostal beliefs. Charles W. Conn, editor of the *Church of God Evangel*, and Reverend Lewis J. Willis, editor of *The Lighted Pathway*, both encouraged Earl to write a book in simple, layman's terms explaining basic Pentecostal doctrines. He had written several articles for both of their magazines. With the help of his secretary, Ruth Holt, Earl wrote a book called *Your Pentecostal Neighbor*, published by Pathway Press in 1958. Years later this book would be regarded as an important treatise of the Pentecostal movement just prior to the Charismatic outpouring throughout denominational churches. The book remains a widely quoted reference source by other writers on historical Pentecostal beliefs.

Earl wrote two other books published in 1960. *Sunday School Evangelism* emphasized practical preparation for church members to lead others to know Jesus Christ. Earl believed that Sunday School must equip all Christians to be "soul winners" in their spheres of influence. *Forward In Faith Sermons* contained fifty-two messages he had delivered on the *Forward In Faith* broadcasts. Response to the radio program poured into denomination headquarters. The broadcast had grown to over fifty outlets including Alaska, Hawaii, Costa Rica, Central America, Jamaica, Barbados and the British West Indies. Earl had become, as his book cover read, ". . . one of America's most accomplished gospel preachers."

In another bold ecumenical move which many pastors considered highly controversial at the time, Earl offered his church to host Atlanta's first Full Gospel Business Men's Fellowship International meeting. Earl recognized the value of this organization in motivating spiritual leadership in local churches to build Christian fellowship across denominational lines. The Atlanta chapter of F.G.B.M.F.I. began meeting monthly at Hemphill Church of God. Years later, the Atlanta F.G.B.M.F.I. met in local hotel ballrooms and remains one of the strongest, largest chapters within the international organization. Several of the men from Hemphill, who led the Atlanta chapter of

F.G.B.M.F.I. in those first meetings, still lead the organization over twenty-five years later.

Earl's ministry appeared impressive in its extent and diversity, but the pressures continued to be overwhelming. Many times he walked to the pulpit on Sunday mornings without inspiration or feeling the slightest ability to lift anyone's spirit. He arranged sermon notes in front of him, prepared routinely after crying out to God for some "word" to speak. Often he felt almost abandoned, as if the heavens were closed to him. He stared blankly at the people sitting in neat rows dressed in their Sunday best apparel, waiting for a message from God to give them the strength, encouragement and inspiration he didn't have for himself, much less for them.

Then the flow sovereignly began, rising from some deep, hidden reservoir in his spirit. He looked into the eyes of his people, drawing strength from those transmitting their love and trust in his calling. His confidence in the Lord ignited the gift as a combustible substance. Gradually, a familiar warmth rose inside him to become a powerful, urgent proclamation spoken with confidence. Within moments a spontaneous sermon, God's word to His people in that hour, resounded on the people's ears with a bold anointing. A spiritual stride fell upon him, or perhaps the gift had been nurtured from childhood—imparted day by day through the words of his father's prayers over him, or perhaps even sovereignly woven into his inner parts from the womb.

This preaching experience happened repeatedly. He

left the pulpit, amazed and grateful. He could never trust his emotions to anticipate God's ministry to His people—even ministry from God to himself through his own mouth. He received encouragement and direction with the congregation. The people often extolled the excellence and power of his preaching, but no one knew better than the preacher that God deserved all the glory.

Multi-faceted inner conflicts added to his gratitude for God's faithfulness to him. He resisted admitting even to himself the emotionally tangled webs subtly trapping him in a system that betrayed so many of his lifelong ideals of what he believed God intended a church to be. The easiest thing to do would be to go along with the party line and deny his conscience. He grew up knowing the strategy to face problems which determined whether a pastor had a rough or smooth ministry. He searched for painless solutions to his own dilemmas. How could he possibly resign from a denomination which had provided him such visible prominence and token respect? What about the heritage of his father's remarkable ministry which had been passed on to him? What was he to do with his dad's dreams for his bright future as a leader in the denomination?

Earl realized that questioning his loyalty to the denomination made him vulnerable in his ministry to the people. He ministered with guarded discretion as a man totally out of balance emotionally, wondering how long he could endure the strain. He often felt guilty endorsing so many rulings of the church which left him battling and debating the issues in his own mind. He wondered if his ministry were becoming a sham to God—shining with success on the surface, but hiding the dark truth of failure deep within himself.

Voicing any beliefs conflicting with the denomination only frustrated him more. Was he growing afraid to challenge the denomination and even, if necessary, to stand alone for truth? His answers to himself made him feel compromising and hypocritical—two characteristics he had always abhorred in others and vehemently denied in himself. Could it be that he was becoming a replica of those people he had grown up vowing never to parallel? Was he saying one thing and believing another? Was he selling out his convictions for acclaim and approval from people who were impressed with his talent and promising him higher stakes? Honestly answering those questions caused him to despise the man he felt himself becoming. He groped desperately for solutions. More than ever, his desire to be true to his calling from God made him want out of the mire of religious bureaucracy. But would there be any hope of ministry awaiting a free man? The examples he had witnessed through the years left him little hope.

Horror stories circulated continuously at denominational headquarters about pastors whose ministries were in trouble for a variety of reasons, usually reported with the pastor at fault. The denomination regarded negative reports from a minister's congregation as cause for investigation and many times disciplinary rulings to pastors who had violated the party line in any way. A pastor unable to prove his innocence after the denomination received reports regarding the pastor's morals or his failure to keep denominational standards was virtually finished in his ministry. The Church of God regularly forbade pastors to preach, even if they admitted to making mistakes and vowed repentance. The pastor forever wore his guilt in denominational circles like an invisible, immovable brand. Future pastoral assignments—if they were made at all—were doled out for the least desirable churches and locations.

Of course, the denominations' stringent actions in such matters devastated the families of those ministers. Most pastors' wives grew accustomed to criticism. They knew well that ministry to people on such a vulnerable level of confidence almost always involved emotional risks during the healing process—especially for people who felt love-hate ambivalence toward the pastor who made them face their problems and admit their own guilt in order to repent, receive forgiveness and start again. Reports criticizing pastors often began with emotionally scarred people transferring their own unresolved guilt by pointing out to others some weakness in their pastor. Earl was certain that many times the real issues—denominational politics and loyalty—were hidden beneath complaints resulting in pastoral reprimands.

When a pastor was guilty of violating denominational standards, his wife and children survived their private, personal pain far more easily than the public disgrace from their denomination. The denomination offered them sympathy, but no one dared respond to their crisis with spiritual covering, loving restoration and reconciliation back to service in the ministry. Christian people talked "grace" and "forgiveness," but mistakes in ministry always meant public shame. God might forgive and restore a wounded soldier in His army, but the denomination indignantly refused.

Earl often regretted the history of insensitive rulings from the hierarchy of his denomination. He could recall numerous cases in which he believed denominational leaders exhibited a lack of compassion. The consequences were devastating for mistakes in ministry— ominously threatening to Earl who doubted his future loyalty to a system he no longer supported in his heart. Such disillusionment made him feel as if he were leading a double life.

While still trying to maintain the "perfect pastor" image, Earl warned his father that he wanted out of the denomination. Earl Sr. tried to assure both Earl and himself that his son's unrealistic idealism was surfacing again, that his frustrations would pass if he waited them out. Surely Earl Jr. could realize the opportunities he had within his grasp. He could easily influence internal change in church rulings in time, if only he didn't react irrationally to inconsistencies in their denomination, which admittedly needed to be addressed.

But one thought pressed Earl in refusing to disregard his gnawing disillusionment. What if God were calling him out of the denomination? What if his resignation were somehow God's plan, the leading of the Holy Spirit? Immediately, he answered himself with ingrained defenses. Of course, leaving the denomination would be wrong! Of course, his father was right! He would have his chance to change the system within the system—if only he could wait. As in the past, could he simply concentrate on his successes until then? No, the positive blessings from God to his ministry made standing for truth even more important to him.

His greatest inner conflict centered on the people he served at Hemphill Church of God. He loved the people dearly but wondered every day if he could ever bring them into unity and move them beyond their old-line traditions and doctrines. He knew that many of his ideas for ministry would push some of them too far—press them with radical changes and social confrontations. The miracle of his ministry was the devotion of his people to so many "new ideas" he had introduced and implemented. Yes, he had fought battles to birth every one of them. Still, he knew many members would react in dismay at the extent of his "radical" ideas for ministry if he were to share them.

Was it love that made him protect them from the jolting convictions burning inside him, or was it fear of the consequences of sharing those convictions? Was he a responsible leader or a coward holding onto status quo acceptability for the sake of security? If only he could find solutions to reconcile the conflicts without any of his people being hurt or disappointed in him. The one constant check inside him when he felt he couldn't endure another moment was his love for his people.

Pastoral dedication finally caused all the conflicts

and issues to converge. Earl had been counseling a young couple in his church who were experiencing marital problems. Many of the undercurrents of their problems began to make Earl feel very uncomfortable with his growing involvement in their conflicts. Instead of reconciling their disputes, he felt himself becoming more and more of a participant in them. Instead of settling issues, he was becoming one more issue added to a seemingly irreconcilable list of problems.

When Earl realized he could no longer offer this couple help or solutions, he called for help. He told his State Overseer that he was becoming emotionally entangled in a counseling situation which needed objective, outside mediation. He wanted some spiritually mature leader to intervene and offer him an acceptable escape from exclusive responsiblity in solving this couple's disputes. A person in spiritual authority could easily open some alternative in counseling before his role as referee became more of a complication to the marriage. Especially because of the growing emotional attachment of the wife, Earl no longer felt that he should be the one to defend her views in marital disputes with her husband.

The State Overseer's reaction struck Earl like a sharp, unexpected slap across the face, leaving him feeling stunned. The man emphatically informed the pastor that even admitting to a precarious situation like the one he described would be the same as an admission of guilt in their denomination. He charged that the best thing Earl could do would be just "to handle" the situation. He promised in a well-meaning gesture to pretend Earl had never said anything to him about needing help.

This refusal for help triggered an overwhelming sense of defensive anger in Earl, followed by a flood of all the suppressed frustration toward his denomination that he had "handled" for almost thirty years. Mentally recalling Earl Sr.'s philosophy simply to trust God and obey the rules no longer soothed his fury. The State Overseer's reply confirmed all those buried feelings of being trapped. Was a call for help really the same as an admission of underserved guilt that could ruin his and his family's lives? Was this the example of compassion and covering espoused by his spiritual leaders? If so, he definitely wanted out.

Without answers on what he should do first, anger smoldered inside him. Buried, destructive fury surfaced in thoughts and actions that would have shocked him before now. Driving from Tennessee after the radio broadcasts, he recklessly accelerated his car going around curves. He told himself that death would be an honorable solution to his dilemma. He felt simultaneously abandoned and trapped by the church. Where was a door of escape that would spare his family undeserved distress?

Norma gave birth to their third daughter on February 7, 1960. Little Roma Beth Paulk blessed her daddy's life at a time when he felt least deserving or capable of fulfilling his responsibility to the tiny baby. Beth was the delicate daughter, soft-spoken and tender. She grew with a poet's sensitivity and a writer's perception.

Beth's birth occurred during a time of great spiritual warfare over her family. Like hope from heaven, Beth became a gift from God to her family through a life reflecting peace in the storm and a song soothing troubled hearts.

Earl Sr. and Addie Mae visited their children in Atlanta on the Saturday that Beth was born. Earl Sr. proudly announced Beth's arrival the next morning during the service at Hemphill. He told the congregation that the parents had named their beautiful baby girl "Debra Diane." No one ever quite figured out where he picked up that name for her.

Uncontrolled, destructive feelings of despair continually surfaced in Earl. Instead of judgment and condemnation for the needs of people challenging all the laws in life that he had always defended, he understood for the first time the loneliness and compulsion of willful sinners. No one felt more desperate than someone who had lost hope, locked away in unchangeable circumstances. No wonder rules meant so little to trapped people.

Of course that was the reason "harlots and publicans" immediately recognized Jesus as their friend, their only hope. Any consolation or escape from their desperation flickered elusively in their lives, no matter how drastic that escape from circumstances might be in its consequences. Tidal waves of compassion for hurting people in a man so completely out of balance physically and emotionally became detrimental to Earl's decisions in ministry. At times he reacted to situations with extreme measures of compassion—

almost trying to overcompensate with grace toward others for the lack of understanding toward his own hurts. For the first time in his life, the proud Pharisee with all the pat scriptures answering any situation was shaken without answers, groping within himself for deeper understanding of those scriptures to make some sense of his own life.

He made every effort to escape the smothering circumstances that jeopardized the ministry at the church. Searching for a way to maintain dignity through an acceptable solution, he requested that the church release him to do the radio broadcasts in Tennessee on a full-time basis. He grabbed at any possible way to alter his path and gain his freedom gradually without hurting hundreds of people he loved. Instead, the church voted unanimously to keep Earl as their pastor. They urged him to continue doing the broadcasts as a part-time responsibility.

Earl Paulk had served at Hemphill Church of God for eight years. Those years brought him all the accolades of a remarkably successful young pastor by anyone's criteria. Inside, Earl was convinced that he was a thirty-three years old failure chasing an impossible dream which refused to go away. He poured out his feelings of love in a letter to the people in the church along with his regrets for failing to prepare them for his leaving which he blamed on himself. He gave the resignation letter to his State Overseer to read to the congregation. They would hear the letter on a warm August Sunday morning, hours after the family had packed their belongings into a rented trailer and left town. Many people in the church would have physically prevented their pastor from leaving if they had known his plans.

The house and the furniture belonged to the church. Clothes and a few other personal items comprised all the belongings the family had to take with them from the past eight years. Everyone cried as the life they had known snapped shut abruptly, like their suitcases and the doors of the car. Becky, Joy and little Beth shared in the tears and finality of those moments without needing an explanation.

They drove through the night to Myrtle and Harry Mushegan's home in Daisy, Tennessee, to make some decisions about the next steps to take. With the monotonous engine of the car as the only sound, Earl confronted his own thoughts. He remembered another time in his life when he felt the same abrupt abandonment as this. On that night, God severed him from all the ambitious plans he had made for his life by calling him into the ministry. How strange that he would think now about that night in Greenville long ago, while every minute drove him further away from the church God had given him to serve. Still, remembering the night he was called to be a pastor flickered in his mind like a glowing light amid all the dark uncertainty of his other thoughts.

The congregation never heard the letter left for them with the State Overseer which expressed Earl's deep love and loyalty to the people at Hemphill Church of God. He explained the complicated, regretful reasons for leaving and he hoped they would forgive him for his failures. He prayed they would remember the many blessings from the Lord during their eight years together.

Members of the church council met before the service and agreed not to mention the letter to the congregation. They reasoned that reading the letter could generate too much justification—even devotion—for Earl himself. They decided that people should feel the hurt and rejection that their pastor's leaving would cause them without any explanation from him. They merely announced to the people that their pastor and his family left abruptly in the middle of the night to avoid a scandal. The possible connotations of "scandal" were left to speculation in the minds of the people.

Because the congregation never heard Earl's own words to them in his letter, naturally the people immediately felt betrayed and confused. The announcement of their pastor's leaving fell like a large rock thrown into a pond, rippling the surface in every direction. Rumors quickly devoured the image anyone might have had of the tender, hard-working young pastor whom they had loved. Many forgot the love he expressed to them numerous times in eight years, pouring out his best efforts to serve them and help them grow in the Lord. Suddenly their pastor became a stranger, a calculating impostor who had selfishly taken their trust and affection and left them without a word.

In the car headed for Tennessee, the pastor himself felt cruel strippings of his ministry even miles away from a disillusioned congregation. The shattered man driving the car accepted responsiblity for his own decisions, yet he wondered how to rebuild on those foundations of truth left within him which could not be shaken or destroyed. Except for a precious wife sitting silently beside him holding a peaceful baby, two confused little girls now sleeping in the back seat, and a trailer packed with everything they owned hitched to the car, all else that Earl treasured on earth had been stripped away, irreparably broken and left far, far behind.

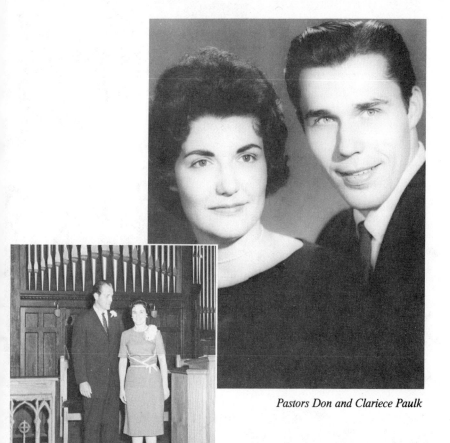

Pastors Don and Clariece Paulk

Earl and Norma before the beautiful pipe
organ in first church home—
836 Euclid Avenue, Atlanta, Georgia

The Harvester Trio
Norma, Don and Clariece

Enjoying a few days in Florida with the
girls.

Second church home (1965)
850 Euclid Avenue
Atlanta, Georgia

The Sanctuary Choir (1965)

Oldest daughter Becky is married
(1969)

Daughter Joy preparing to walk down
the aisle (1971)

Church Staff (1973)
Earl, Clariece, Don
(seated) Dottie Bridges

Aerial view of first building phase
(first six acres)

Beth, you're my baby."

Daughter Beth on her wedding day with
Paulk grandparents (1977)

"Oh, Atlanta, Atlanta . . ."

Yolanda King and Earl Paulk at the Martin Luther King, Jr. Arts Festival

Earl Paulk being interviewed concerning the murdered children in Atlanta

Fellowship with Atlanta pastors:
(l to r) Dr. Sam Coker, Dr. Bill Self, Bishop Earl Paulk, Dr. Frank Harrington

7

CHAPTER SEVEN

Myrtle and Harry Mushegan's house in Daisy, Tennessee, sat at the bottom of a large mountain. In Daisy, the Mushegans enjoyed serving one of the most prosperous churches in their ministry. In fact, the denomination headquarters had notified Pastor Mushegan that he would be honored at the next Ordained Council for the impressive numerical growth and spiritual blessings so evident in the church. At that same council, Myrtle had been asked to serve as chairperson for the Ladies' Day meetings.

Myrtle Mushegan had never felt greater fulfillment or security than she did in their ministry at the Daisy Church of God. In the beautiful Tennessee mountains, living in a spacious home which the church provided, Myrtle devoted her time to working beside her husband in the ministry as well as meeting all the demands of a busy housewife and mother to their three children, Harolene, Alan and Janet. But for the past several weeks, Myrtle Mushegan had gone about her work preoccupied and deeply troubled. All her thoughts projected far away from her own daily routine in Daisy. She had fasted and prayed continuously for her brother, Earl, unable to concentrate on anything besides the perilous uncertainty which overshadowed his ministry and the church he served in Atlanta.

Earl had called her from Atlanta a few weeks earlier to say that he, Norma and the girls, along with their parents, Earl Sr. and Addie Mae Paulk, were coming for dinner. Myrtle was elated. Visiting with so many family members at their table was a rare delight. Immediately she began planning their dinner together, making meticulous preparations for these special guests.

The moment they arrived, Myrtle sensed the restless anxiety among them. The serious mood in the group contradicted all her expectations for the family gathering. No one talked beyond formalities or offered any explanation for the impromptu visit. Rather than press them with her questions, Myrtle busied herself in the kitchen with final preparations for their meal together. Earl asked Harry to walk with him up Daisy Mountain, located directly behind their house. After the two men left, Myrtle called her mother into the kitchen.

Myrtle asked Addie Mae for an explanation for their

strange mood, hoping for answers to calm the gamut of fearful speculations running through her mind. Addie Mae avoided answering her daughter, simply telling her that Earl was "trying to make some decisions." Realizing that such an answer only increased Myrtle's apprehensions, Addie Mae promised her daughter that either Earl or Harry would explain the situation to her when they returned. Meanwhile, Norma and Earl Sr. sat together on the living room sofa in silence. Norma cradled six-month-old Beth close to her while the other children enjoyed their evening together, oblivious to pensive adult contemplations overshadowing interaction among the rest of the family.

After a quiet dinner with tension impeding the usual lively banter that Myrtle had eagerly anticipated, the dinner guests left for Atlanta. Then Harry told Myrtle the details of his conversation with Earl on the mountain. As he began explaining to her, repeating the things Earl had shared with him, Myrtle grasped the full consequences to her brother's ministry. How well she could personally relate to her brother's frustrations and feelings of entrapment from a lifetime of overbearing laws and expectations. Those same feelings were buried within her, tempered only by unshakable family loyalty and positive blessings from God derived from the many aspects of sound gospel which their church consistently taught. She had found peace for herself many times in concentrating on God's blessings in the lives of so many beautiful Christian people in their denomination who genuinely loved the Lord.

But Myrtle also knew the denomination's intolerance toward anyone leaving the ranks for any reason. Undoubtedly, the denomination would focus on some "problem" in Earl's ministry and blame his leaving on moral behavior or character flaws. Idealistic convictions or criticisms of policies were hardly an acceptable explanation—especially for a pastor whom many old-line leaders had regarded as a "liberal radical" since his days of study at seminary! She knew well that some people had waited anxiously for her brother to topple off his pedestal. Myrtle also realized that Earl, like any pastor, had made mistakes through the years and certainly had disagreed with enough people to build a formidable case against him. Could he emotionally endure the consequences of a decision like this? Could his family endure walking away from lifelong, reliable security? Could they survive under the shadow of unfavorable opinions from the people they had known and loved all their lives?

Myrtle asked herself how Earl could have even allowed these conflicts to push him so far. Was he wrong for trying to "go along" for so many years, waiting and wanting desperately for childhood wounds to heal? She had watched him try to teach and defend the rulings he had always questioned. Would he now risk jeopardizing his ministry and the security of his family? If he left the denomination, he had no assurance of preaching again. With a tarnished reputation and an uncertain future, how far could elusive dreams—even dreams from God—take a man without tangible help?

Myrtle reflected on the strict, protective upbringing

she and her siblings shared in the Paulk household. Earl's formative years had been an undeniable paradox. A strict code of behavior carefully sheltered Earl from "the world," yet he had shouldered the weight of adult responsibility almost from childhood. He never really enjoyed his youth as other young men who were given the freedom of choices, whimsical pursuits, exploring and stretching their creativity. He had walked a straight line of rigid responsibility; and yet, in his inner world lived a dreamer, a crusader for worthy causes, challenging all the wrongs of the world, believing for miracles against impossible odds.

Unbending standards, ingrained from birth, programmed submission into all the Paulk children. They understood "doing whatever was expected" until the pressures of their inner conflicts thrust them into an intolerable crisis, a breaking point. Undoubtedly that was the crossroads where Earl found himself now. She knew most of all that she must seek the Lord. God would speak answers to her spirit that she desperately needed. Like many times before, God would provide peace for her to face the shattering fears and questions in her heart.

The more that Harry and Myrtle Mushegan searched together for direction through prayer, fasting and meditating on God's Word, the more determined they grew in defending Earl against any reactions from their denomination. They spoke with him frequently by telephone. They offered him spiritual encouragement and their faith in God's will in leading him through this difficult period of transition. Understanding that he needed to find specific direction immediately, they also offered their house as a refuge when he and Norma decided to leave Atlanta.

After days of seeking the Lord with open hearts, God assured the Mushegans that He was in control of these circumstances. Their discussions also brought them to personal decisions concerning their own role in this matter. They would answer denominational reactions according to one uncompromising resolve which they would defend to any extent necessary: Earl's ministry would continue with or without the blessing of their denomination. Spiritual calling, much less an anointing of the Holy Spirit, did not depend on denominational structure or affiliation. Anointing rested in adherence to truth and obedience to God in fulfilling one's calling. Harry Mushegan even felt personal inner tuggings of the Holy Spirit as Earl talked with his brother-in-law over the telephone about the possibility of starting an independent evangelistic ministry. Of course, Earl spoke only of possible options for himself outside the denomination. He was totally unaware that voicing speculations quickened the Holy Spirit's confirmation within his brother-in-law's heart.

Harry Mushegan began carefully reexamining the rigid denominational mandates which had dominated most of the decisions in his own ministry. He shared so many of Earl's dreams. He, too, had always believed that the Church must demonstrate loving restoration and compassion toward those who were in trouble— including ministers who were burdened, weary or wounded in battle. He would boldly defend his brother-

186

in-law's view of denominational conflicts on that basis. Hopefully, he could serve as a mediator in resolving the matter peacefully with the denomination's leaders. Perhaps Earl would receive understanding and covering from their leadership, breaking the pattern of public accusations which usually resulted. Considering that pattern of reprimand grieved Harry. No one in the denomination could deny the mighty calling and faithful service of Earl Paulk's pastorate at Hemphill. Perhaps he could influence enough people to recall his brother-in-law's years of dedication.

Earl, Norma and their three girls arrived at the Mushegans' house in the early morning hours before daylight. The trailer packed with their belongings symbolized the finality of the life they left behind them. In spite of Earl's and Norma's feelings of being suspended between a painful ending and a new beginning, the Mushegans maintained their own plans to attend the Ordained Council in Memphis, Tennessee. Myrtle and Harry intended to participate in the leadership roles honoring their ministry. Perhaps their availability would help to answer the complex Hemphill issues, certain to be discussed. The denomination would undoubtedly make immediate decisions concerning new leadership at the church. Meanwhile, Earl and Norma sorted out their own thoughts secluded at the Mushegans' house, babysitting all of the children and praying for God to show them the next step.

At first, the Ordained Council sessions met Harry and Myrtle's worst speculations. Everywhere people questioned one another concerning the reasons Earl

Paulk left Hemphill Church of God. Myrtle and Harry felt the spotlight on them, curious stares and strained greetings overshadowing previously warm relationships as they attended the scheduled assemblies and various meetings. In keeping with their resolve to God and each other through days of spiritual preparation, they projected positive confidence in answering all the questions and stares. More than ever, walking directly into a raging storm of conjecture, they knew they had heard from the Lord. Their confidence rested in knowing He would provide sure solutions and direction.

Church leaders from Hemphill attending the Council rushed to Harry and Myrtle to discuss the situation at their church in Atlanta. One after another they confided to Earl's sister and brother-in-law that their pastor had been "set up" in many situations causing him to feel futility in his attempts to implement innovative ministry at their church. They admitted to knowing the source of planned confrontations to wrestle control of the church's direction from the young pastor. Assuring the Mushegans that most of the members in the parish solidly supported Earl, they remarked that his political involvement alone would never have turned the majority of the congregation against him. However, his stands on civil rights had drawn harsh criticism from a few key leaders in the church—leaders who wanted their pastor's influence destroyed.

Few people understood the complexity of Earl's denominational conflicts, much less his perspective in ministry. Of course, Earl regularly fought opposition to new ideas, but he would never have imagined the extent of hostility brewing against his leadership. These enemies believed that only "a moral issue" would totally destroy the devotion of the congregation toward their pastor. One Hemphill leader vowed to Harry and Myrtle that he would personally confront the gossip unleashed in Atlanta. He assured them that he knew for a fact that Earl was the target of a conspiracy.

Encouraged by supportive comments and promises discussed with Hemphill leaders attending the Council, Harry and Myrtle returned home to Daisy to share their hopes of peace with Earl and Norma. All those hopes shattered quickly. Within a few days Harry Mushegan responded to the blaring horn of a car parked on the road at the end of the long, winding driveway in front of his house. He walked down the hill toward the car where three of the denomination's leaders waited for him. The men rolled down the car windows, still sitting in the car as they delivered a message. They got right to the purpose of their visit. The spokesman sternly reprimanded Harry for allowing his brother-in-law and his family to stay with the pastor in a parsonage owned by their church.

Harry reminded the men of the "Good Samaritan" parable. He said firmly that he couldn't just put the family out in the street until they made definite plans and had provisions. One of the men quickly retorted that Earl Paulk was not the church's problem or responsibility. The care of his family was "Earl's problem." They insisted that Harry tell his brother-in-law to leave his house at once.

The defiant spirit in these men stunned Harry Mushegan. He was silent for a moment, carefully considering each word spoken to him. Then he answered firmly, "I'm sorry, but I just won't do that and you can take that message back to the denomination for me." He walked back to the door of the "denomination's" house, feeling the reverberating impact of their orders to him concerning Earl and the repercussions of his reply to them. Those insensitive judgments were spoken by spiritual leaders in his denomination, men whom he had respected highly until that moment. Perhaps it took such words to finalize the momentous decision he had contemplated for several weeks.

That evening Earl and Harry talked together several hours as they searched for definite direction from the Lord. Earl felt terrible about the pressure and conflicts he had caused in Harry and Myrtle's lives, but Harry refused to allow Earl to carry guilt for the Mushegans' decisions. The men began to pray, opening their spirits in tears of brokenness to God. They relinquished their own wills, contrite, pliable to however God would move in their spirits with a word or some direction. Both men sensed that these prayers held the significance of an Old Testament altar of sacrifice where God would meet with them, driving immovable stakes where they could return again and again to understand events unfolding in the days ahead. As they cried out to the Lord in intercession, both men took their wallets and placed them on the floor between them. Together, they made a covenant of spiritual unity, binding their lives, their families, their possessions and their futures in an eternal bond. The oneness of their covenant superseded the close family ties that they had always shared.

With open hearts the men began to express their longings for a ministry of restoration for people who felt abandoned and bruised. They shared scriptures as the Holy Spirit stirred their minds. God began driving that stake in their lives through His Word. They remembered passages that expressed the calling of God in their hearts to a ministry of compassion. They felt called to minister to "scattered sheep" referred to in Matthew 9:36-38. One of the men read that passage aloud, knowing somehow that the words were spoken as God's audible direction to them: *"But when He saw the multitudes, He was moved with compassion on them, because they fainted and were scattered abroad, as sheep having no shepherd. Then saith He to His disciples, 'The harvest truly is plenteous, but the laborers are few; pray ye therefore the Lord of the harvest, that He will send forth laborers into His harvest.'"*

The name "Harvesters" from the passage represented the compassion of Jesus at seeing people who were scattered "like sheep without a shepherd." Immediately Harry called some of his relatives at the Armenian Church in Los Angeles, California. He told them to expect the two families to arrive in a few days for a series of services. They would seek God's will each day of this trip. God would further confirm the ministry of the Harvesters and open doors to specific direction.

Then Harry called the State Overseer of Tennessee and made a recommendation for the pastor to replace him at the Daisy Church of God. Within hours he began receiving calls from other pastors in the denomination warning him of the dangers of his resignation. They suggested that perhaps sympathy or family loyalty had caused him to overreact. Disregarding their well-meaning advice, Harry Mushegan assured them that his heart was fixed to follow the sure leading of the Holy Spirit. He blessed his brothers in the Lord for their concern and wished them well.

Myrtle and Earl's younger brother, Don, also decided to join the group in their initial evangelistic endeavor to the west coast. Twenty-two year old Don had just graduated from Lee College, called and licensed in the Church of God for the ministry. He began working with his dad after graduation from college, but as the events surrounding Earl's career became a major family crisis, Don informed his father that he wanted to support Earl in whatever direction he took. The first step in that decision meant joining his brother's and sister's families on their trip out west. Further ramifications of that decision meant Don's own break with the family's denomination.

At least one aspect of Don's plans to travel called for a tremendous sacrifice from him. Her name was Clariece Miller, a beautiful concert pianist from Cleveland, Tennessee. They had set their wedding date for December l6th. Clariece stayed behind in Cleveland, working as a sixth grade music teacher in a local elementary school until the wedding. Don and Clariece met during their freshman year at Lee College, but didn't date seriously until their senior year. After a summer romance, Don insisted that Clariece transfer to the University of Chattanooga to be near him. She had left Tennessee to study her sophomore and junior years at Wheaton College in Illinois.

Clariece totally supported Don's decision to join his brother and brother-in-law. She knew Earl Paulk from the times she occasionally played the piano for the National Radio Broadcast. Clariece grew up as a dedicated member of the Church of God, but her love and call to the ministry ignited during summer vacations at her Uncle John Meares' church in Washington, D. C. When she spent the summers as Uncle John's guest pianist among the predominantly black congregation of his independent church, Clariece knew that this church exemplified a freedom of the Spirit that really glorified God. She couldn't pinpoint theological reasons for the spiritual freedom in the church, but the worship at Evangel Temple lifted her to a dimension she'd never experienced anywhere else. Her uncle, John Meares, had left the denomination long ago to begin the church in Washington's inner city. Those treasured summer memories caused Clariece to fully support her fiance's decision.

Earl and Harry packed their families' belongings into rented trailers hitched to the bumpers of their cars. Harry left behind many personal belongings—an extensive collection of books, for instance—because he didn't have room in the trunk of the car or trailer. He couldn't afford the added weight of transporting these items across the country. Driving westward into the vast unknown, the families left Daisy knowing that they would never return as the same people.

193

Three pastors, two wives and six children crowded
into two white Chevrolets to begin a new work for God
called the "Harvesters" on a blistering August day in
1960. If they had not been certain that God had spoken
to their spirits about the work they were beginning, the
trip alone would have shaken any trace of self-reliance
they might have harbored. The children soon grew
restless in the seemingly endless confinement of the
car. The heat was unbearable, draining the group
physically and emotionally. Little Beth cried constantly with an upset stomach. They couldn't run the
cars' air conditioners extensively for fear of over-
heating the engines.

Earl rented a U-Haul trailer which came equipped
with a spare tire. Harry rented a National trailer with a
contract for a spare tire if he should need one, redeem-
able from the nearest National Rental dealership. Earl
noticed when they left Tennessee that Harry didn't
have a spare tire. He and Don teased Harry about the
contract in his pocket. Of course, the National trailer
actually did blow a tire crossing the desert. Harry's
"contract" inevitably became an infamous family joke.

They used the U-Haul spare tire to get them to the
National Rental dealership. All the way to the dealership Don held up the contract to every passing car and
yelled, "Hey, don't worry, folks! We've got a contract!"
Don Paulk salvaged everyone's sanity on the trip with
his priceless witty comments and comical verbal
twists. Don had inherited the Tomberlin good looks
and an invaluable sense of humor from Addie Mae.
When everyone else was ready to turn around in frus-

tration and exhaustion, Don Paulk observed some hysterical irony of their uncertain plight. Like good medicine, they all drew strength in therapeutic laughter
from Don's personal renditions of this cross-country
trek. The three men rotated driving the two cars. Long
miles allowed each person to battle subjective thoughts
about the uncertainty of life ahead of them. Reminders
of the loss each one left behind took its emotional toll at
various times for individual reasons.

While driving late one night, Earl thought again
about the rapid changes in their lives within only a few
days. Everyone else in the car slept, allowing him
moments of inner seclusion. In the dark quietness Earl
began crying, allowing tears to flow freely after fighting to contain them within himself all day. Suddenly,
he felt someone breathing in his ear. Ten-year-old
Becky whispered, "Daddy, why are you crying?"

He swallowed, trying to gain composure in his voice.
Becky whispered again emphatically, "Why are you
crying, Daddy?"

"I was just thinking about something that made me
feel sad, sweetheart. Everything is all right. You go
back to sleep."

Earl wiped tears off his cheeks and took a deep
breath. He thought about how much his children loved
and trusted him. Where was God taking all of them? He
knew that God had given them the name "Harvesters"
a few nights before when he and Harry prayed for
direction. But in spite of a few facts he believed about
the present, and many truths of overcoming faith he
had preached almost all of his life with fervor and

certainty, he still felt despair when he tried to answer certain questions determining his future.

He couldn't avoid facing obvious truths. He was thirty-three years old. Tangible security of the past was gone now. Doubts about this decision filled his mind at times, screaming accusations against him. What if he had made a terrible, unalterable mistake? Perhaps his ministry was finished after all. If necessary, perhaps he could teach at some college again. He was still young. Perhaps he could learn new skills. Perhaps he could apply for some job totally unrelated to the ministry. What could he do? He thought about how his resume would read: "Bachelor's degree from a Baptist college; Master's degree from a Methodist seminary; television and national radio preacher; author of three books and numerous published articles; pastor for eight years at a large Pentecostal church in Atlanta; strong advocate of civil rights and church reform . . ."

In those weak moments he felt the tears begin again as he thought about the work he had poured his life into and the people he had loved as much as any young pastor ever could. What were they thinking now? Did they know how much he loved them? Did they understand the reasons he had no choice in leaving them? Perhaps this trip was really a dream after all, only an undeniable warning to make him consider his options more carefully. He would wake up soon to the same daily challenges which he had faced for eight years as senior pastor at Hemphill. After all, leaving his people was hardly in character for him. Everyone knew him as the preacher with guts and fortitude who tried new things and spoke out when everyone else feared reactions from the opposition. Then he remembered the anguish of those months, weeks and days before he left. Leaving Atlanta, leaving the denomination, took more courage than anything he had ever done in his life.

That denomination had cradled him, raised him and provided him a place to minister when he was only seventeen years old. But now the umbilical cord was irrevocably cut. The shock of that severing began a new life, but the uncertainty of his identity now—an identity crisis with consequences affecting many lives—left him running like Moses into the desert. Like Moses, he questioned all the unexplainable dealings and callings of God in his life, including God's judgment for his own mistakes and many hurts and misunderstandings resulting from this choice. As he watched the road roll out before him in the night, he willfully disciplined his mind, deciding to concentrate only on the distance ahead—the future as far as he could see by the car's headlights.

Eventually they stopped at a motel for the night, too tired to go another mile. Earl carried the kids and some luggage to their rooms. Finally, he stretched out on the bed to sleep for what seemed like only minutes. Sleep drowned out the blaring voices asking unanswerable questions, allowing him to be free from the pain of thinking too much. He closed his eyes at last, grateful for physical exhaustion and the miles already behind them.

Days on the road with lively family interaction were

easier than facing the quiet nights. Family conversations remained positive and encouraging. One attribute the Paulk family learned long ago was the art of ministering to each other in a crisis. Except for confinement in the car and irritating heat, the older kids regarded their trip as an adventurous vacation, a cross-country excursion of sight-seeing with their cousins.

Each of the adults added their own special flavor to the pioneer experience. Don's personality—youthful optimism with humorous commentary—lightened all the dark realities. He was clearly a gift from God to his family at a time when his support and perspective helped all of them endure the most taxing conditions. Harry and Myrtle Mushegan served as parental caretakers of the group, solid and dependable decision-makers. Their attitude toward the situation conveyed confidence in God's higher purposes and plans for their lives. Norma was quietly supportive, spending most of the long hours on the road nursing and caring for Beth. Norma's unshakable faith always came through in any trial, but she was also very sensitive to Earl's emotional turmoil. Her trust in his having made the right decision for them was like a soothing ointment applied to any doubts or confusion Earl felt.

Underneath the laughter and family interaction, undeniably deep sadness gripped Earl's mind. He couldn't fully understand the source or meaning of such pain, but it wouldn't go away. His certainty of future promises and hopes couldn't dispel the darkness of an ominous shadow falling over his spirit. When he fought the feelings, relief came only by concentrating closely on words about "scattered sheep" which God had given to Harry and him. That passage of scripture opened hope to him like a door to an elusive, undefinable possibility of feeling fully alive again, perhaps even more alive than ever before.

As the group approached the Arizona state line, they decided to stop overnight in Phoenix en route to Los Angeles. Harry's brother, Nap, and his wife, Dorothy, would surely welcome the travelers with warm hospitality. A home atmosphere would provide a haven from their exhausting pace for a few hours. The mothers welcomed the prospect of using a washing machine for the children's clothes. Though Harry hadn't been able to contact Nap and Dorothy to tell them they were coming, he assured everyone that his brother's family would be delighted to accommodate the group of travelers who now felt and looked like a band of gypsies.

Nap Mushegan opened the front door of his house as the two cars pulled into his driveway. He walked steadily toward the passengers spilling out of the cars, stretching themselves. Without a trace of surprise in his voice, Nap smiled and calmly said, "I've been expecting you. I knew that you were coming here, and the Lord has made provisions for you."

For all the faith and surge of assurance those words inspired in the exhausted travelers, their positive spontaneity took a sharp nosedive. Nap began repeating some dismal reports he had received over the telephone from Atlanta. Several callers had telephoned to inform him of recent events surrounding Earl's leaving Hemphill Church of God. One caller, the same man who had promised Harry and Myrtle that he would expose the conspiracy against his pastor, now warned other pastors about Earl's tarnished ministry—adding unbelievable lies to his warnings.

Hearing the content of those lies sent Earl's spirit and mind reeling. Suddenly he felt deathly sick inside and understood for the first time the strange battles he had fought every mile of this trip. He was waging intense warfare intended to destroy him with words from these callers which hit him like shrapnel from an explosion. Gradually the pain grew dull, leaving him feeling numb, shocked, emotionally paralyzed in his mind for his own protection. He shielded himself from all consciousness of the conversation around him, standing like a man in a vacuum among other people, close enough to touch yet millions of miles away. He could barely hear their voices as they went on talking.

How could friends do this? Scenes from the past eight years flashed in rapid succession in his mind: the struggles they had worked through together; the projects and decisions of the church; the comfort and love he had given to their families in various situations; warm feelings of friendship; times of comfort when the pressures seemed almost insurmountable. Had they forgotten? Were these words really from his brothers in the Lord, leaders he had trusted? All self-accusations for any of his own failures now drowned in a flood of betrayal and lies so distorted from the truth of his own mistakes that the words threatened to poison him with bitterness! If only he could understand their motives, satisfactions or reasons for attempting to destroy him and his family.

His mind was frozen, too numb with shock to speak or cry or respond other than staring blankly at all the others. Gradually he began to hear the words Nap Mushegan was speaking. God had shown Nap an alternative plan to their evangelistic endeavor in Los Angeles. The Lord had spoken to him while he and his family were on vacation just a few days earlier. Nap said the Lord assured him that the families were coming to Phoenix, and God had made specific provisions for them to settle there. Their trip to Los Angeles was not intended to launch the evangelistic ministry they envisioned. Nap was totally convinced that God had led them to Phoenix to begin a new church.

Nap had just been offered a little church building on one of the main streets in downtown Phoenix by a wealthy member of a small prayer group he led. The prayer group recently moved their meetings into the quaint church building, a charming facility surrounded by swaying palm trees. Now the church needed to conduct a series of nightly services to ignite the growth and ministry which Nap believed the Lord had promised to give them.

And that only began God's provisions for them with nearly perfect timing! Nap's family had almost completed building a new house, filled with new furniture they were purchasing. Within two weeks they would move into the house, leaving behind a furnished three-bedroom ranch house with a small furnished guest house behind it for the two families to occupy. The tiny guest house had been built to encourage long visits from Harry and Nap's father, Pop Mushegan. Now that guest house, a western stucco with a bedroom, bath, sitting room and tiny kitchen off to the side, became the Mushegans' new home. The two older children slept on the sofa, and Janet, the youngest, slept on a bed cushion on the floor. Their kitchen table was so tiny that unless the families ate meals together in the ranch house, the Mushegan children ate their meals off the ironing board.

Since the independent church in Los Angeles still expected the evangelistic team to conduct a series of services, the Harvesters decided to go ahead with their trip. But in accord with God's amazing provisions for them, they agreed unanimously to return to Phoenix to settle down. The Lord had so obviously directed them with tangible, wide open doors.

The services in Los Angeles provided indisputable confirmation of God's presence and anointing on the Harvesters. Scores of people were blessed each night as the Paulks and Mushegans ministered to them. This outpouring of the Holy Spirit's blessings signified "signs following" evidence that God honored their ministry's direction.

However, the moment they arrived in Los Angeles, they faced a strained reception again. Harry's family asked questions concerning slanderous reports they had received through telephone calls from Atlanta. Even facing this humiliation required a deliberate act of faith and will for Earl to minister in the services in Los Angeles. He stood before the people as a wounded man, feeling tremendous emotional pain, praying for answers to give hope from the Lord to all of them. In such a fragile state of mind, Earl was amazed that even in brokenness his preaching flowed as powerfully as he had ever known.

The services provided the entire group with an understanding of their identities as Harvesters. They also shared memorable times together on the trip. Harry's brother, Mac, took all of them on his yacht to Catalina for the day. The moment that Don looked across the ocean to shore at the smog hanging over Los Angeles, his stomach churned with instant sea sickness. Though the group genuinely sympathized with Don's nausea, the memory of Don's "bout on the high seas" always brought laughter to his family, remembering how they shared the physical, psychological trauma with him.

The Harvesters returned to Phoenix feeling refreshed and ready to take the next step in God's plan. Within days after Nap and Dorothy moved into their new house, Earl and Harry bought the other two houses from them. They gratefully acknowledged the tangible resources that God had provided as they settled into becoming permanent Phoenix residents. They began to explore their beautiful city: playing golf at local courses, reading about Phoenix's sports teams, taking the children to museums, etc. They enrolled the four older children—two from each family—in local schools in early September. Though occasionally intimidated as the new kid in school, Alan Mushegan was impressed with all the Mexican children in his classes. Of course all four children received attention

from their classmates whenever they spoke with drawl-
ing Southern accents.

The ministers held daily morning and evening services at the little downtown church in order to build a
congregation. Immediately people began coming to the
services and eagerly joining the newly organized
church. Services each morning ministered prayer and
teaching to meet individual needs. The evening services
were conducted more like evangelistic campaigns with
the men rotating their turns to preach.

God assured Earl repeatedly in those services that
the spiritual anointing of the Lord flowed in his
preaching and ministry to meet people's needs. As he
opened the scriptures and delivered the messages that
God would give him to speak, he felt the undeniable
warm moving of the Holy Spirit rise and flow from him.
Response from the people attested to God's presence in
his words and ministry. The little prayer group quickly
grew into a congregation of over one hundred people.
The Lord repeatedly reminded Earl when he ministered that the calling on his life was irrevocable.

Earl opened his spirit to move however God would
lead him, promising to obey whatever instructions God
gave. Gradually, the Lord began confronting the warfare that inflicted deep emotional wounds in Earl's
spirit. Myrtle kept the children one evening for Earl
and Norma to see their first movie, *Ben Hur.* Because of
the ingrained Church of God teaching about the sin of
going to movies, Earl felt somewhat spiritually rebellious as he entered the dark theater and sat down
beside his wife. But as he watched the story unfold, he

quickly became absorbed in the plot of the movie. He sensed consuming waves of the Holy Spirit washing over him. He watched most of the movie through vision blurred from endless tears. He knew that God was washing away all traces of poison he carried inside—temptations to avenge himself which would surely lead to bitterness.

In one scene, the mighty military warrior, Judah Ben Hur, was offered water by the teacher from Nazareth on a dusty path. The soldier had been captured by the enemy. Ben Hur said that Jesus' kind eyes "took the sword out of my hand." Though Ben Hur had been betrayed and was totally justified in his desire for vengeance—not only for himself, but also for the pain of those he loved—he laid down those hurts later at the cross of Jesus Christ.

Earl fought to control his emotions. In the first movie theater he had ever walked inside, he talked with God about the sword he grasped tightly to defend himself. He would allow Jesus to take it out of his hand. Seeds of bitterness surfaced inside him; his tears cleansed his heart. Earl finally felt inner freedom, gradually glowing with a warmth of forgiveness he had almost forgotten he could feel—both for himself and for others. Numb caverns in his mind filled with peace. Letting go of anger toward people who had hurt him, he resolved that God alone would stand against all the rumors, lies and vicious attacks. God alone would deal individually with people deliberately attempting to destroy a man He had called.

With calm resolution in his spirit, Earl also searched

for the reality of peace in his circumstances. He continued groping in his mind for specific ways to fit together the splintered events of his preparation: the lessons he'd learned, his past accomplishments in ministry and the goals for this new ministry. Somehow the pieces of the puzzle still didn't coincide. He continually tried to make everything come together. Too many questions still remained unanswered. He applied to teach at the University of Arizona over the protest of his family who insisted that God never called him to preach and teach school at the same time.

In those weak moments when he still felt himself suspended between the life he had known and yet so far from fulfilling dreams of what could be—without any clues as to how to accomplish those dreams—he could only cry out to God. He asked God to somehow make him feel contentment if this ministry were indeed His perfect will. At times his tears flowed as if he were grieving for something he had lost, yet he knew undoubtedly that God was leading them. The blessings were obvious. Provisions for his family and the mighty anointing on his ministry were undeniably from the Lord. But something was still missing, causing him restless, tormenting frustration. Overwhelmed with periods of deep contemplation, sometimes he withdrew completely from the family to think and pray and rehash the same old questions.

Finally, Harry Mushegan sternly warned Earl that he had cried out for answers long enough. Earl listened to Harry's strong direct words, spoken like a father correcting a child. He told Earl that the periods of desolation he was experiencing were not from God. The calling on their new ministry was not only valid but also full of promises and hopes and even fruit already confirming God's direction. God would accomplish great things through them. If Earl ended his questioning and instead began seeking God's will in confidence, God would speak further direction to him.

At the Tuesday morning service people sang hymns and choruses, prayed and shared together encouraging testimonies and scriptures of edification. Earl had been at the altar praying and ministering to the people. As he turned around to walk toward the first row of pews, he suddenly felt himself unexplainably caught up in the Spirit. He knelt down at the bench to steady himself. He began to see a panoramic vision within his mind in distinctive, unmistakable details. Except for a peaceful inner assurance, he would have been frightened by the clarity and certainty of the scenes as he heard the familiar voice speaking to him.

First, God told him that he must return to Atlanta. In the most unlikely location for Earl Paulk to be, God would raise up a mighty church of powerful spiritual demonstration to all the world. This church would be known for its restoration of people who had been wounded, hurt and abused by life's storms and religious traditions. This church would be a "City of Refuge" for those needing forgiveness and healing love.

He saw unforgettable individual faces of people as God spoke to him. They were a diverse blend of every race and culture. He saw hundreds of youth, elderly people, families walking side by side, people in wheel-chairs and some who were sick being helped by others into the doors of the church. People were coming to this worship center from every direction from around the world.

In the vision, he stood inside a building with glass doors as well as glass across the front from the ceiling to the floor. He knew in the Spirit that he was inside the church God was calling him to build. This place was not like any church he had ever seen before. People would come here to receive ministry at all hours of the day and night. They would be restored and given new hope and purpose. He sensed the vibrant, pulsating energy of life in this place, a place filled with anointed zeal, recognition of God's goodness and people who were strong and confident in God's sure Word.

In this church God would raise up people who truly knew His compassion, people who would hear His voice and move according to the Spirit's direction to love and restore others. This would be known as a mighty church of spiritual demonstration in the last days. People from all over the world would come here to see firsthand the things that God would do by His Spirit.

This church represented a "Joseph" ministry to the universal Church. The dreamer who was sold into Egypt, stripped of his heritage and put into prison would in the end offer solutions for the famine in the land to his brothers locked away in legalistic tradi-tions. In a time of need, God would allow him to minis-ter to those who intended him harm. His ministry would offer solutions in a spirit of forgiveness and healing. God promised Earl Paulk that those things in his life which were intended for evil would eventually be used for good to bless the world.

He had no idea how long he had basked in God's presence, caught up in a heavenly realm beyond time or place. When he stood up, everyone who attended the morning service had already gone. He felt such peace inside, yet his mind was drained of conscious thought. He felt weak. He walked with shaky steps. God had spoken clear direction, beyond all he could ask or think. He understood like never before the reasons that the biblical patriarchs built altars to God at the places and times that God would speak like this. The sense of the divine presence of the Lord lingered within him.

Like Jacob who spoke with the Lord at Bethel where God changed his name, Earl Paulk would never regard his calling from God as he had before. Now he understood Moses' response when he heard God's voice in the desert in the burning bush. God called him to return to the place where he least wanted to go to accomplish an absolutely impossible task. Like the Apostle Paul who received a vision of Jesus Christ totally changing his direction, Earl vowed to be true to the heavenly vision entrusted to his spirit. He would never again for a moment pull away from the calling of the Lord on his life.

Earl walked outside the doors of the church into the yard to see a man excitedly talking to Harry Mushegan. They motioned for Brother Paulk to join them as the man spoke with obvious enthusiasm, describing his impressive proposal. The man told the two pastors that he had the financial resources to build a major church in that city. He also intended to build a church-sponsored school, a counseling center and other additions as the Lord directed in a great work for God in Phoenix, Arizona.

Without hesitation, Earl told the man that God had spoken to him through a vision. In obedience to the Lord, he must return to Atlanta. Both the builder and Harry Mushegan stared at Earl Paulk in astonishment. Earl's answer was so spontaneously shocking, Harry Mushegan knew instantly that his brother-in-law had heard from God. Harry immediately felt the Holy Spirit quicken his own heart in unalterable confirmation which made no sense to his mind of reason. He simply trusted the reliable "knowing" in his spirit.

They arrived back home where God further confirmed His direction "through the mouth of two witnesses." Two letters sent from Atlanta arrived that day, one from a man named Roy Robinson and the other from John Bridges. Both letters urged Pastor Paulk to return to Atlanta to begin a new independent church. Both letters—written by men with no knowledge of each other—indicated strong personal loyalty, support and the firm belief that Earl Paulk's ministry had been cruelly maligned because of his spiritual leadership potential.

Norma, Myrtle and Don also agreed wholeheartedly that Earl had heard a clear word from God. They began to channel their thoughts and plans to follow the Spirit, receiving direction as Earl shared with them the vision from God. A few days later Don flew from Phoenix to Atlanta to begin meeting with the two men who had written the letters and any other people who knew God had given them a desire to join this bold ministry, a church which would surely face many tests.

The families needed to sell their two houses as they prepared to travel again. The children said goodbye to their newly-acquainted classmates, explaining that they were moving back to Atlanta. With even less money and fewer tangible resources than when they arrived in Phoenix, the families left after ten weeks of seeking direction, deep inner healing and mighty spiritual confirmation. None of them would ever be the same again.

The little church in downtown Phoenix—raised up just before they arrived and flourishing in membership as a sign to them of God's anointing on the Harvesters—closed within a few weeks after they returned to Georgia. The place that God had provided for them to live—property providing not one, but two furnished houses—sold quickly.

Once again, God had given a vision to a man in the desert. True to His Word and His ways, God seldom chooses leaders who are strong and confident in their ability to succeed. He usually finds a man who is broken and contrite, a man marked as a worldly failure who feels ready to die. From seeds which fall to the ground, God grows mighty trees which stand tall and straight and strong. Birds nest in their branches. These trees bear fruit in its season, and their leaves do not wither. And like a mighty tree planted by streams

of living water, God made a covenant with His visionary that if he walked in obedience, true to the mission
he had received, whatever he did would prosper.

8

CHAPTER EIGHT

No city is more beautiful than Atlanta, Georgia, in the fall of the year. All summer the lush green foliage clothes rolling red clay hills which support a steel and concrete metropolis. By mid-October, green leaves gradually die, painting a flaming, breathtaking spectrum of color throughout the city. Finally, bare branches, intertwined and lacing one tree to another, brave the chilly winter winds.

Atlanta: Sherman's proudest torch of triumph in the Civil War—scenes immortalized in Scarlett O'Hara's frenzied ride through the burning city in the 1939 movie classic, *Gone With the Wind*. A city revived: gloriously rebuilt from the shame of slavery and the

defeat of Southern aristocracy. A city whose symbol—
the phoenix—rises miraculously from smoldering
ashes to spread its wings victoriously and soar again
into the heavens.

Atlanta: called the "little New York of the South," a
"city too busy to hate"; the complex, cosmopolitan
gathering place for small town youth with big city
dreams; industry, railroads, corporations, regional
offices, restaurants, traffic jams; the major airport,
train, trucking hub of Southern connections and
transportation.

Atlanta: the birthplace of the Civil Rights Movement, N.A.A.C.P., "Daddy," Coretta and Martin
Luther King Jr.; Ebenezer Baptist, separated by skin
color from thousands of other Baptists in the Bible
Belt; home of militant black racists and the Ku Klux
Klan; culture and agriculture blended in high-
fashioned businesswomen and men who live only one
or two generations away from the farm.

When Don Paulk's plane landed at Hartsfield Airport in Atlanta, he felt like a trailblazer on a special
assignment. He had been sent ahead to pioneer a new
church in a city brazenly hostile to his family. No one
could predict the actual volume of support. Don only
counted on the writers of those two important letters
which had awaited Earl Paulk at his house in Phoenix,
confirming that memorable day when God changed all
their plans.

The first meeting of people interested in forming the
new church filled Roy and Faith Robinson's living
room. Invited friends, neighbors and curious people

listened attentively to plans about the kind of church the Harvesters would build. The majority of the people at the meeting were detached from membership or regular attendance at any particular church.

Don Paulk emphasized to the group that the new ministry did not intend to proselyte members from any churches in the area where people were receiving solid Bible teaching and satisfying spiritual fellowship. The Robinsons, for instance, had grown up in a Presbyterian church, but they had followed Earl Paulk's ministry for many years and considered themselves to be under Brother Paulk's covering. The Harvester ministry would be dedicated to "scattered sheep," wanting and needing spiritual restoration and direction. Don shared from his spirit the hurts, experiences and finally the dynamic commission his family had received from God during their few months' excursion from Atlanta to Phoenix, and now in their plans to return to Atlanta.

Among approximately thirty people sitting in the living room, many responded with encouragement to Don after hearing him share the vision of the Harvester ministry. They were eager to move forward with specific plans for the new church. John Bridges—one of the two writers sending a letter to Earl Paulk in Phoenix—and his wife, Dottie, who had a Pentecostal Holiness background, were fully supportive. Others wanted more time to consider their commitments to this new controversial church. How could a small congregation support the large Paulk family? How would the controversy surrounding the new church affect their own lives?

Don related the mixed reactions from people attending the meeting to Earl and Harry by telephone. Just before leaving Phoenix, Earl responded to Don's report by sending a check for $1,000 to Roy Robinson. The money was used as a down payment on an inner city church building, St. John's Lutheran, which Roy had discovered would be sold soon. The building had beautiful stained glass windows, handcarved woodwork and an old John Brown pipe organ that made strange sounds resembling a fog horn on a rainy day.

St. John's Lutheran Church was located in the Inman Park area, a tarnished, transitional neighborhood. At one time the area had been an affluent subdivision with large two and three-story mansions and was regarded as one of Atlanta's finest neighborhoods. By 1960, the area had fallen from grace into notable disrepair. Many stately homes were divided into multifamily dwellings rented to transient families, usually with lots of children spilling out into the busy traffic. Farm workers looking for work in the city rented portions of the houses and crammed their large families into a few rooms. Like most transitional neighborhoods in the inner city, Inman Park filled its quota of seedy characters overcome by the lures of alcohol.

The Paulks and Mushegans spent their first night in Atlanta with Earl and Myrtle's younger sister, Ernestine, and her husband, Wallace Swilley. The Swilleys served as the Georgia Youth Directors for the Church of God. The next day the Paulks and Mushegans drove to the vicinity of Inman Park looking for a place to live

216

near the church. As they sat in the car at a traffic light, they prayed together for God's clear direction. The light turned green; the prayer ended. On the other side of the intersection sat a moderately sized brown house with a "For Rent or Sale" sign posted in the front yard. They knew instantly that God had answered their prayers. The brown house was less than three blocks from the church building, and the families moved into the house the next day.

Life in the brown house was cramped and crazy, but cozy. The adults were very conscious of the fact that the house was never intended to accommodate two families. They carefully monitored rotating playtimes so that no more than two of the six children ever played in the yard at the same time. They hoped to avoid neighbors' questions about how many people actually lived in the house.

Norma and Myrtle learned to be very creative cooks. They stretched their food budget with potatoes, beans, eggs, and occasionally they had hamburger. They prepared meals with appetite-pleasing versatility in quantities large enough to feed an army. "Basic food, no privacy and no money for extras" quickly became a way of life for the Harvesters. Their adjustments required a good sense of humor to accept the difficult transitions, the downward topple from the respectable, comfortable status of their lives only a few months before.

Earl's disappointment with life in the brown house had nothing to do with status or physical adjustments. He had told Norma that God had spoken to him that their house in Atlanta would have a room with seventeen windows. She had laughed, replying that a room like that would indeed be "a sign" from the Lord! Not surprisingly, no such room existed in the brown house. Earl decided that either he had thought up some wild fleece on his own with no spiritual significance whatsoever, or the families would live in the brown house only a short period of time.

Shortly after the families settled into communal living in the brown house, they traveled to Cleveland, Tennessee, for a Thanksgiving visit with Earl Sr., Addie Mae and the rest of the family. Don and Clariece were occupied with making final arrangements of their wedding plans, which included several family members in the ceremony. The rest of the family excitedly discussed all the possibilities and plans for the new church in Atlanta.

Earl's family were relieved to observe his calm emotional equilibrium well intact. Outwardly he seemed to have recaptured his old confidence—yet in many ways, Earl Paulk was a very different man to his family. His level of faith and certainty of direction amazed them. Still, he answered their questions with a broken spirit. Old traces of youthful personal ambitions had vanished, powerless now in charting his decisions or life goals. He'd paid the price to follow the Holy Spirit. Reliance on his abilities or pride in his accomplishments had been consumed with ashes replacing accolades. Earl gave uncertain answers to specific questions about the new ministry in Atlanta. The vision admittedly existed only in unsubstantiated faith. The church revealed in the Phoenix vision still had little tangible fulfillment. Earl seldom shared the vision with anyone, yet he cherished even the slightest encouragement or confirmation to the unforgettable scene alive in his spirit.

Earl Sr. had suffered stoically through the past months. He responded to Earl's, Myrtle's and Don's departure from the denomination he had loved and given his life to serve like a man facing an irretrievable loss. For quite some time Earl Jr. had been preparing his father for his break with the denomination. But the reality of those warnings had broken the father's heart, leaving him trusting the Lord for greater measures of faith than he'd ever needed to face personal choices or professional challenges. Earl Sr. reflected on how his older son had questioned so many church policies far too often and too openly. The education Earl Sr. had been so determined for his son to pursue had molded a brilliant mind that fearlessly probed for answers at the very root of issues. Earl Jr. was unable to settle for explanations less than absolute truth. His son could have easily risen to the top position in the denomination and served well—of that Earl Sr. was certain. But whenever his thoughts concerning these events became too painful, he reminded himself that his children's lives were their own—no matter how much he loved them and would have made different choices for them if he were given that option.

Motherly protection dominated Addie Mae's reaction to any crisis in her children's lives. Theological debates were not her concern at all. With the wrath of a mother hen, she wanted someone else to blame for any hurts her children suffered. She had dutifully preached the gospel to her children while their father had preached to the world. Their hurts were hers; their successes and failures were subjectively accounted in her own mind to her personal credit or demise. Whereas Earl Sr. suffered silently except to God, Addie Mae furiously vented strong animosity toward anyone hurling abuse or criticism at her family. Her older son had been attacked directly in the same ways she and her husband had endured subtle hostility from people in the church for most of their lives. A lifetime of unreasonable expectations and demands had finally found a cause to vent those pent-up feelings.

The alumni of Lee College held an annual tag football game on the playing field during the Thanksgiving holidays. Earl accompanied his family to the game knowing that his presence would surface varied reactions, raised eyebrows and lively conversation among many of his old acquaintances. Earl saw a familiar man walking toward him around the edge of the playing field. His head was down, but his facial expression and posture were drawn, strained, almost as if he were searching for words to convey the difficult message he carried which he needed to communicate.

The State Overseer during Earl's final year at Hemphill nervously extended his right hand to Earl Paulk. "I owe you an apology," he said. The man's hand trembled as Earl took it. "I let others influence me not to read the letter you left the church. I'm sorry. I regret that decision so much. The board was afraid of generating too much sympathy for you. I hope you'll forgive me."

The letter Earl wrote to his congregation could easily have arrested or even prevented many of the rumors circulating. With no explanation given to them, people in the church quickly opened their imaginations to wild speculations. Earl would never have believed that the rumors and lies could have become so unreasonably absurd.

And now the man who could have at least attempted to minimize the slander against the young pastor stood before him, extending his hand, making an uncomfortable, strained apology. Earl Paulk firmly grasped the man's hand with gratitude for his courage in admitting a mistake that had caused Earl and his family such undeserved hurts. Having resolved to resist any temptations toward bitterness and revenge, Earl only wanted healing and restoration with all those who had compounded the price he paid for his decision to leave the denomination.

"I accept your apology," Earl said. The State Overseer had followed Earl's recommendation for the pastor to replace him at Hemphill Church of God. Earl had named three possibilities for his successor, strongly endorsing one pastor, Paul Laverne Walker, over the others. Both Earl Paulk and Paul Walker shared a strong Pentecostal heritage from their fathers' ministries. Both men were highly educated, tolerant toward others' opinions and open to change under the Holy Spirit's direction. Both men were born leaders. Earl believed strongly that a man as richly endowed with leadership qualities as Paul Walker could ably preserve and continue to expand many of the positive, progressive strides made at Hemphill during his eight years of ministry there. Earl Paulk's perceptions proved to be totally valid. Hemphill Church of God later moved to Mt. Paran Road in Atlanta and was renamed Mount Paran Church of God, still a mighty, flourishing Pentecostal church in the city today.

Other confrontations with Church of God leaders underscored the totality of Earl Paulk's break with his parent denomination. He made an appointment to meet with the denomination's General Overseer during his visit with the family in Cleveland. Earl hoped to reestablish credibility within the ranks of the denomination during the interim period of establishing his own independent church in Atlanta. Earl held tremendous love and respect for so many of the pastors in the denomination, and those affections would never change. God had truly taken the sword out of his hand in Phoenix, Arizona. Now he could easily reach out to offer peace and reconciliation, even to brothers who had intended harm to him.

Earl told the highest church official his perspective on the Hemphill issues. Earl openly admitted his mistakes. He easily answered all the questions the church official asked, explaining thoroughly any unanswered or untrue accusations circulating in the denominational whirlwind. Earl finally told the church leader, "I have always been a man under authority. I'll go anywhere to minister under your authority, but I must preach. My call to the ministry transcends my call to this denomination or to you." Earl knew his words, spoken hard and directly confrontive, underscored the constant, motivating question in his mind, "Shall I obey God or man?"

The church leader dramatically put one wrist upon the other and said in an apologetic tone of voice, "Earl, my hands are tied!" Other Church of God pastors privately offered Earl their support and encouragement in beginning the new church. One leader confidentially admitted to Earl that he would likely be in the same situation soon. Pastors contacting him almost unanimously encouraged him to continue preaching. Although the majority of pastors Earl had always respected were sympathetic with his position, others felt angry and threatened by his return to Atlanta. His accusers would have preferred him to remain in Phoenix rather than become a visible source of contention to the denomination by returning to face his challengers. His return to Atlanta forced certain critics to face the very issues that had caused him to leave the denomination. Earl Paulk genuinely wanted peace between his brothers and himself. Ironically, his forgiving attitude only seemed to engender greater hostility, and perhaps even fear, in his accusers.

After his official release from the spiritual covering of his denomination, Earl sought out eldership to whom he could submit the Harvester ministry. He called his old friend from the Atlanta Christian Council, Pastor Ralph Byrd of Faith Memorial Assembly of God, and submitted the vision God had given to him. Earl also contacted G. R. Watson, pastor of Riverside

Church of God, to ask him to serve as a trusted spiritual advisor to whom he could submit his ministry for direction.

Spiritual authority and submission were written so indelibly in Earl's spirit that he didn't dare move in ministry without the covering of spiritual counselors and eldership. These two elders became the dual witness for critical decisions in the early days of the Harvester ministry. Both mentors encouraged the Paulks and Mushegans to move with the vision God had given to them. In daily matters, the spiritual agreement of Harry Mushegan and Don Paulk were vital to Earl's confidence in God's guidance of the ministry. As he had learned from childhood, Earl never even considered moving independently of the principles of unity and eldership within the Body of Christ.

Gospel Harvester Tabernacle held its first service at the St. John's Lutheran Church on Sunday afternoon, December 5, 1960. The Lutheran congregation was still using the church for Sunday morning services until the construction of their new sanctuary was completed. Thirty-nine people gathered at that first service. Twelve of those people were members of the ministering family.

Years later, in his book, *Divine Runner*, Earl Paulk described his fears, and even near failure, to minister at that first Harvester service.

"There were stairs that led to the pulpit area from the basement. I entered the back door into the basement unobserved. My heart was pounding like a kid running from a dog. I got about halfway up the stairs and my heart simply failed. My flesh said, 'No way.'

"Years of preaching and serving people unfolded before my eyes. I wanted so much to run away and hide. My body was trembling, my mouth was dry, my ears were ringing and my eyes began to fill with tears. I turned to walk slowly back down the stairs and go back to the house we had rented some two blocks away. I reasoned that my brother-in-law, Harry Mushegan, and my brother, Don, could carry on the service. Inside I knew full well that the people had come to greet me and hear me preach.

"I reached the bottom of the stairs and stood gazing at the floor, when my ears picked up the song being sung in the sanctuary. They sang, 'Amazing grace— how sweet the sound—That saved a wretch like me!' My tears of fear and frustration turned into tears of joy and a holy calmness possessed my entire being. I remembered the hour that I had felt the call of God to preach His Word.

"I straightened my tie, wiped my eyes and held my head high as I turned and walked back up the stairs. I opened the door that led past the huge pipe organ where my [future] sister-in-law, Clariece, was playing. She smiled as I passed by and I moved to sit in the chair behind the pulpit in full gaze of the congregation. But now I could hardly wait to minister to the people from God's Word. My flesh had been overcome." (Earl Paulk, *Divine Runner*, 1978, pp. 100-101).

Every comfort or possible security was carefully, deliberately knocked from under Earl to make him dependent on God alone. One rainy night Earl received a call from his dad to meet him at the St. John's Lutheran building. Earl Sr. brought a wealthy minister and coin collector to see the building in hopes that he would make a financial contribution to the ministry. As they walked through the building, Earl pointed out the distinctive features in the church's architecture and excitedly shared with the man the plans for the new church. At the end of the tour, the minister cordially thanked Earl for showing him the building, wished him well in his ministry, and drove off into the night with Earl Sr.

Standing in the rain watching the car drive away, Earl felt that familiar shadow of desolation fall over his emotions. He knew that his dad would be greatly disappointed also. Momentarily, he sensed a calm inner assurance rising within him. He must listen to the Holy Spirit and never again depend upon his own understanding. God would teach him higher ways to walk. God would uncover more dependable sources of supply to him if he simply would trust the Lord for provisions.

Don and Clariece were married in a large, exquisitely formal wedding in Cleveland, Tennessee, on December 16, 1960. Like royalty, Clariece walked down the aisle on her father's arm. Otis Miller was a successful builder, and Clariece's family had never known economic struggles as the Paulks had. The Paulk family agreed to shield Clariece from realizing how poor her new family was. Earl Jr. was buying a triplex near Emory University as an investment. Don and Clariece moved into one of the apartments, awarded to them to enjoy newlywed privacy, while Earl's and Harry's families continued to live in the brown house. Clariece's childhood dreams had come true. She was the wife of a pastor in an independent church which needed her musical talents full-time.

The new bride and her brother-in-law, Earl, had numerous personality clashes. Clariece was outspoken and opinionated. She grew up in a household with strong matriarchal input, which had instilled perfectionistic, high achievement expectations in all the Miller children. Of course, the Paulk household was strongly patriarchal in its decision-making. Even when Earl Sr. traveled from home, young Earl stood as the head of the family, caring for his mother and younger siblings. Clariece soon discovered that adjustments to married life included far more than getting along with easy-going Don. She also gradually became aware that she was living in a struggling financial crisis. She served the church not only as the organist, but also as church secretary with responsibility for the church's financial records.

The small congregation needed $30 thousand to purchase the St. John's Lutheran Church building. The amount might as easily have been $30 million in relation to their ability to purchase the facility. The church's weekly tithes and offerings averaged about $120. Earl's and Harry's salaries varied, depending on the church's total weekly offerings, but each man usually made about $30 a week. If the tithes were down, many weeks the pastors received no salary at all. Don's salary averaged between $15 and $20 each week—after all, Don did have the luxury of his own apartment and no children to support!

With the family's agreement in prayer and all the faith he could muster, Earl made an appointment with C. Payne McMurry, president of DeKalb Federal Savings and Loan, to apply for the $30 thousand loan. He humbly told Mr. McMurry that God had directed him to ask the bank president for the money. He had no collateral, and of course, he realized that the bank made home loans—not loans to purchase churches. Mr. McMurry reacted to the request with reasonable, professional indignation. Of course the bank couldn't accept those terms! Why should they?

Earl quietly answered the bank president's irritation with his request by saying that he had done just as God had instructed him to do. Whatever happened with the request for funds at that point was not his responsibility, but became Mr. McMurry's decision. Earl thanked Mr. McMurry for his time and left the office.

When he returned home, the family waited eagerly to find out the results of their prayers. They asked almost in unison whether he had gotten the loan. Earl replied, "No, not yet, but we will!" Ten days later the telephone rang early in the morning. Earl recognized the bristly manner of Mr. McMurry over the telephone. "Pastor Paulk, will you please come get the money for that church so that I can get some sleep!" The bank made an unprecedented loan for the total funds requested to a church with no collateral. C. Payne McMurry, calloused, practical financier, became a close, trusted friend of Earl Paulk's.

Christmas 1960 could have easily become an

unhappy memory for the Paulk and Mushegan children. The timing couldn't have been more precarious financially. Stretching their resources for food and shelter took a miracle every week—anything more than that was totally impossible. With Christmas carols and seasonal festivities surrounding them everywhere, the parents felt apprehensive for their children's sakes since the array of presents they normally received were simply beyond their means.

One evening the families returned home from church to find a lighted Christmas tree with wrapped gifts for everyone under it. Three men in the church, Jack Brewer, Hirim Wilkie and Tom Shurlin, decided that the pastors' children would enjoy the celebration of God's gift to the world with other children everywhere. Specific items in the carefully wrapped packages were soon forgotten, but the tender kindness of those three men would always be a sacred, precious Christmas memory to those children and their parents. The sensitivity and love of those men on that Christmas became the most treasured gift of all.

The Harvesters needed to find a way to alleviate the financial crunch on the ministry and their families. Earl was offered several teaching contracts at local colleges in Atlanta, but just as when he considered teaching in Phoenix, he knew that he would be moving out of God's will to sign a teaching contract now.

The three men contacted Clyde Hannah, pastor of the Church of God in Tucker, who worked as a building contractor as well as a pastor. Earl told Clyde that they wanted to work with his construction crew just like any other men he would hire. Don, Harry and Earl were hired by Clyde who paid them an hourly wage to build houses. After a few weeks, Harry couldn't tolerate the physical stress any longer. He had problems with his feet which prevented him from handling the physical demands of construction. The Harvesters decided that Harry would visit the congregation and be available for pastoral ministry while Earl and Don continued to build houses.

Earl discovered that working in construction was tremendously therapeutic for him. He enjoyed physical labor, and working with his hands allowed him plenty of time to think. The physical aspects of construction especially appealed to him by making use of his athletic prowess. Both he and Don quickly got into great physical shape. They were tanned from working outdoors even during the winter months, but they became very weather conscious—often working in snow, rain and even attempting painting contract jobs when the temperature was so cold that the paint rolled up the walls.

Never accuse the Harvesters of hoarding their money! With extra income from the construction jobs, they managed to meet the $262 monthly loan payment to DeKalb Federal Savings and Loan as well as paying $50 a week for a radio program on WGUN. The vision God had given to Earl included an outreach ministry which had to begin somewhere! Office supplies that first year remained under $10 per week.

Expenditures for the first four months in the Harvester ministry were $5,529.41. That total included all the salaries of the staff—$927. The largest purchase during that period was a grand piano which cost $650. The greatest expenditure in the ministry was the $950 for radio air time—more money than the total salaries. From the beginning, the heart (treasure) of the Harvesters was spent on outreach ministry!

The church financial records show that of the $5,250.39 incoming receipts in those first four months, only $3,011.67 came into the treasury through tithes and offerings. Special offerings for pulpit furniture brought in $210.12. The furniture actually cost the church $290.45. Another notable item in the church's financial records shows that Reverend Paulk and Reverend Mushegan contributed $1,648.60 in gifts to the church during the first four months—a little over $200 short of being twice the total salaries of the church! The total balance of receipts and expenditures from January to April 1961 left the church with a deficit of $179.02.

A large white house, the church's manse, came with the purchase of the St. John's Lutheran Church building. The house became a tremendous confirmation of God's direction to Earl. As they inspected the house before buying it, Earl and Norma walked into an upstairs bedroom which had once been an enclosed porch. Earl counted the windows in the bedroom, ". . . fifteen, sixteen, seventeen! Yes, this is the right house!" Again, God confirmed to Earl Paulk that they lived in the center of His will.

For several months after their return to Atlanta, people who had perpetrated controversy and scandal concerning Earl's ministry at Hemphill called him on the telephone at home, visited him at the church on Euclid Avenue or sent word to him in letters.They expressed their regret at having caused such devastation to him and his family. Earl agreed to see some of the people most responsible for the painful, damaging rumors—knowing that the spiritual principle of grace and compassion from God for his own life depended on his willingness to forgive others. Many times Norma, Myrtle and Harry would be present for those conversations, both to confront any attempts to inflict more wounds, and also to confirm the genuine healing that God had begun in many hearts.

Earl sometimes talked to people in Sunday School rooms at the church while Harry, Myrtle and Norma sat in the sanctuary, easily monitoring the conversations. People they had known from the past usually began by asking about his family's well-being and their new life since they left Hemphill. Earl often noted that his visitors looked tired, their faces bearing worries and judgments which had become permanent burdens. Finally, the apology would pour out with a variety of reasons for the harmful words spoken carelessly or even deliberately. Few people ever imagined that they could enter into such cruel abuse—much less that they could have actually contributed to it. And now the lies they had told reverberated endlessly, regardless of their own regrets or apologies. Who could have known that everyone would suffer such pain from careless words? Could he possibly forgive them?

Earl felt almost numb inside as he listened to the

apologies he had heard so many times before. He felt as if he were an observer repeatedly watching this scene instead of living it. He asked himself what was the appropriate feeling toward these people. Pity? Hate? Could he really forgive them and totally forgive himself for having made irresponsible judgments in meeting their spiritual and emotional needs?

"I just want to ask you one question," he spoke firmly, always surprising himself that his voice carried such calm, confident control. "Why did you say all those things about me after I left Hemphill? Why did you try to ruin my ministry and my personal life?"

Though their answers varied, the emotions were always the same. People found themselves trapped in a deceptive web which distorted their judgments, cluttered their perceptions and made Earl Paulk the target of all their fears about life. Earl assumed the blame for any unanswered questions or disappointments they had ever felt toward God. If their pastor left them without a word when they needed him, perhaps God would leave them, too. All the cherished understanding about the Lord that their pastor had opened in their hearts was suddenly called into question. They lashed out in defense of all the tender areas in their spirits that they had trusted Brother Paulk to know and understand. Suddenly, they were ready to believe the worst about him to shield themselves from spiritual hurts and disappointments. But their defensive attacks had turned on them. God judged them by their own accusations hurled toward the pastor. Now they had to answer to God for wounds they had caused both in Earl Paulk's life and in themselves.

At least once, Earl took the initiative in seeking out confrontations in order to end damaging rumors. Earl had heard from people that a certain man waited anxiously to settle the controversy between them. Earl wondered why the man didn't just call him as others had done, or simply come by the church. As Earl and Don were riding through downtown Atlanta one day, Earl saw the man directing traffic at a high school crossing near Piedmont Park. He instructed Don to stop the car and let him out. He stood facing the man reported to be a great enemy. Rumors had warned Earl that the man would be angry, accusing and perhaps even violent, but the preacher was confident in this confrontation for one reason. Earl knew that when they finally stood face to face, both men would be forced to acknowledge the truth about accusations against the preacher.

The man looked apologetically into Earl's eyes. He admitted that in many ways he had been wrong, even sharing responsibility for pressing Earl to make mistakes which he could exploit. He was sorry for the damage to Earl's ministry, and he asked him to forgive deliberate harm to his reputation. He knew that the pastor's intentions had always been only to help him and his family grow spiritually. Could Earl ever forgive him?

Forgiveness isn't difficult when a man knows that God has used painful circumstances to change his direction for higher purposes. Admittedly, that change required hard lessons. The devastation of sin against another person, even when God eventually turns sordid events around for good, always leaves many innocent people coping with the shambles of its stormy path. But Earl knew that God was with him. He preached a message he lived: God's grace and His infinite power to heal and restore any aspect of life that was maliciously destroyed. He freely extended to others the grace which he received from God for himself.

With spiritual confidence, Earl Paulk easily forgave his enemies. More than ever he could separate a person's surface intentions in harming him from the real warfare attempting to destroy his calling from God. Earl's real enemies were never flesh and blood. Dark, powerful spirits despised God's anointing on this pastor. With that understanding, Earl could forgive people easily, but he learned well the spiritual lessons of this mighty shaking. These lessons were vital to the compassionate visionary ministry God had called him to implement. Intense spiritual warfare had always been, and would continue to be, a daily way of life as long as he lived to see the reality of a vision.

Faith Memorial Assembly of God asked Harry Mushegan to be their assistant pastor, a temporary assignment which became an unforeseen, extended commitment. During that period of time both Harry and Myrtle began to realize that God was leading them to establish a separate, independent church duplicating the spirit of the Harvesters. In June 1961, the Mushegans left Gospel Harvester Tabernacle to begin their own sister church on the north side of the city. Many aspects of this physical separation were difficult after the close loving bonds all of them shared through the greatest trials and struggles of their lives. But as God opened doors to the Mushegans with numerous prophetic confirmations and provisionary miracles, the direction of their ministry became certain.

Earl and Don continued working in construction to ease the financial burdens of their growing church. Don and Clariece moved into the white house with Earl, Norma and the girls who by now had adjusted to a close, sometimes chaotic, family atmosphere. Earl and Don became so proficient at building houses that Clyde Hannah suggested to the pastors that they do their own contracting. As they continued into the second winter in the construction business, the two pastors tried building several houses on their own. Just as they began to enjoy the tremendous financial benefits from their newly-acquired skills, the Spirit of the Lord spoke to Earl to give up construction altogether.

At first Earl couldn't understand the reasons for God's instructions. They could finally afford a few extras in their tight budget. The church was growing steadily and paying its bills on time. Their additional work was not detrimental to the work of the ministry. In fact, the income was a positive benefit. As Earl began seeking sure direction from God, the Lord showed him how dangerous money from a "second career" success could become to his first calling. God helped Earl understand the reasons He never allowed him to teach or excel in any professions which could pull him away from God's perfect will for his life. The road was becoming more and more narrow in relying on natural abilities to get through a crisis. God refused to allow His visionary church to be built by the work of natural abilities or skills.

After Earl and Don left their construction jobs, God gave Earl a creative idea on how to supplement the ministry's finances. Every week Earl and Clariece printed sermon outlines to send out to hundreds of pastors across the nation. These outlines cost twenty-five cents each, a commitment of only one dollar each month. The low price and practicality of these outlines caught on with pastors across denominational lines in all locations of the nation. The outlines suggested three titles for the sermon, then gave a written introduction and scripture reference on a given topic. The message was the body of the outline with scripture references to support each point. Finally, a conclusion was written in paragraph form to complete the outline.

Four of the best sermons were selected each month by "Mr. Outline" to send to subscribing pastors. No one ever knew "Mr. Outline's" identity. By the end of the sixties, hundreds of outlines were mailed each month. Earl's preaching was consistently interesting, practical and spiritually meaty. A combination of lifelong training in the scriptures, talented oration, acute perception of human behavior and close communion with the Lord continued to produce exceptional preaching. God blessed the preacher's ministry by reproducing his sermons, through "Mr. Outline," hundreds of times in hundreds of pulpits.

The sixties were turbulent times. The Civil Rights Movement engaged the South, as well as the entire nation, in sit-ins, marches, picketing and violent civil confrontations. Harvester Tabernacle was located near Ebenezer Baptist Church, the civil rights' bulwark, in Atlanta's downtown. Since Earl continued to be notably associated with racial issues from his signature on the well-publicized Manifesto, he became a friend of the renowned King family. He served on a committee called "Concerned Clergy," which addressed inner city problems, as well as on a board headed by a wealthy Atlanta businessman, Ivan Allen, called "Board of Reconciliation." This board discussed problems in the city specifically related to racial prejudice.

Earl and Don noted one particular situation that caused their blood to boil. A chain of produce markets located in poor sections of the inner city were selling supposedly "fresh" fruit and vegetables which had been thrown out by other markets in the city's finer sections. Since so many residents were unable to travel outside their neighborhoods to other markets, they were forced to buy inferior produce at high prices. Earl and Don personally checked on the source supplying the wilted fruits and vegetables to these markets. When they discovered that their suspicions of the supply source proved to be accurate, they were determined to take action.

In a meeting to discuss what action to take, "Daddy" King (Martin Luther King, Sr.) leaned across the table toward the pastors, pointed his finger right in Earl's and Don's faces, raised his eyebrows as he glared at them and charged, "Are you boys ready to go to jail for this?" The question was certainly sobering, but the answer was already decided in their hearts. Yes, they would willingly go to jail, if necessary, to defend people who were immorally trapped by social corruption and oppression.

They picketed the markets which were eventually closed because of the publicity the protesters generated. Within a few days of closing the markets, the owners slapped Earl, Don and others who had joined them with a million dollar lawsuit. Of course, the litigation was only a threat which the owners hoped would take the heat off their operations. Though the lawsuit made the front page of the Atlanta papers, naming Earl and Don among the perpetrators, the case never went to court and the chain of markets shut down permanently.

The congregation at Gospel Harvester, like people all over the nation, continued to struggle with the conflicting issues and adjustments surrounding racial integration. Earl remained firm in defending human rights, civil rights and racial equality in every area of life. But the real test to the congregation came when black students from Atlanta University—personally invited by Earl—began to attend Sunday services. Hidden prejudices in some of the people in the church surfaced immediately. Hearing about integration in Sunday morning sermons was one thing; living with integration was another. Why did their pastor insist on making them prove—not just racial tolerance—but also unity? Some disgruntled members left the church.

One tense Sunday morning, Earl stood at the pulpit extolling "unity" from his heart as thick hostility hung over the congregation sprinkled with invited black visitors. Confrontations were imminent—both inside and outside the church doors—since the community's reaction to the church's "liberal" racial stands generated violent threats. An elderly white lady, Sister Ida Sanders, got up from her seat and walked to the altar of the church. Earl had fasted and prayed continuously for God to break prejudical bondage over his people. The moment Sister Sanders stood to her feet, Earl recognized that the woman was moving under a powerful anointing. Ida Sanders almost never spoke out publicly. Any member's overt interruption of a service was extremely rare.

The little woman began pacing back and forth in front of the altar, walking with the confident stride of a seasoned warrior ready to issue orders for battle. Earl backed away from the podium, fervently interceding for the complete spiritual breakthrough he could almost taste. Sister Sanders got quickly to the point. God wanted her to say some things that the people had better hear whether they liked her message or not. She'd lived in the South all of her life. She had lived with as much prejudice as anyone, but Brother Paulk had told them the truth. "They had no right to call 'common' that which God had cleansed," she charged, referring to the Apostle Peter's own divine confrontation with prejudice against the Gentiles in a heavenly vision recorded in Acts 10.

Sister Sanders preached a dynamic sermon, perhaps the message God had prepared her all her life to deliver on that one appointed day. Meanwhile, a nervous usher motioned for Brother Paulk to come quickly. Outside the church a group of neighborhood brawlers were gathering, ready to attack the visitors as they left the church. The group had armed themselves with axe handles, rakes and other weapons in preparation for a confrontation. They stood against a brick wall in front of the church, waiting for the black worshippers to exit.

Earl's heart raced almost audibly. He rushed out a back door of the church to face the mob alone. He felt himself coming against a wall of hatred. "Put away your weapons!" he commanded with authority. "No one is going to hurt anyone!" As Earl stood defiantly, boldly glaring into one face after another with courage imparted from deep within his spirit, one by one the agitators walked away. By now the congregation emptied out of the doors of the church, safely and quickly dispersing in every direction. Earl rejoiced that day in the victory for which he had prayed, but he knew that occupying the enemies' territory would never be a simple matter. Racial prejudice was a demonic cultural stronghold. Only God's intervention could loosen the deeply ingrained, bloodline bondage in people's hearts. Interracial unity of spirit—as Martin Luther King Jr. had prophetically envisioned it—remained only a "dream" seen from the "mountaintop" in the sixties. Earl Paulk would settle for nothing less than seeing the reality of that mountaintop dream lived out among Christian people.

The congregation continued growing. Soon the small St. John's Lutheran building barely contained the Sunday morning congregation. A much larger church,

Missionary Alliance, was for sale. The church was also located on Euclid Avenue just down the street from St. John's. Missionary Alliance leaders contacted Earl, hoping to sell their sanctuary to the Harvesters. Like before, Earl visted Mr. McMurry at DeKalb Federal about a loan to purchase the second church building. This time Mr. McMurry saved time by ushering Earl to a bank official's desk where the loan was quickly processed—again with no collateral.

The Harvesters decided to use the St. John's building as a fellowship hall since the distance between the two church buildings was less than a block. St. John's made a unique fellowship hall and converted gymnasium. The uneven floor from one end of the building to the other made church suppers interesting logistically. Some people sat on the high end of the room and others sat on the low end. All the tables slanted. Basketball games were especially challenging in the fellowship hall since one end of the court was high and the other was low. Joy Paulk, the family's star athlete, became expertly adept at hitting the basket from any range. Playing on the starting line-up with her high school team was a cinch considering the gym where she practiced!

Earl was so grateful for God's bountiful blessings to the Harvesters. Yet, often he felt conflicting perspectives like the Apostle Paul who wrote in the same letter, ". . . in all things I've learned to be content. . ." as well as "I press toward the mark of the high calling . . ." His gratitude to God for present circumstances must never tempt him to quench the urgency to press on toward challenging goals. God continuously stirred some undefinable, intense yearning within him. How easily his flesh could be content, even resigned, as a busy pastor in a thriving inner city church among people he loved to serve. He could have so easily, happily stopped here to rest.

But whenever his heart touched the Spirit of the Lord, he felt himself jolted into an important race: running, pressing, pushing, out of breath, but determined to discipline his body and soul to lunge toward an undefinable goal with all his strength. He knew he absolutely must press totally toward the prize of God's promises. He would finish the race like a track star giving every ounce of his being to reach the goal. And in the power of God's might, he would win the race by the blood of the Lamb, the word of his testimony and loving not his life unto death.

9

CHAPTER NINE

Gospel Harvester Tabernacle had become an inter-denominational church without efforts or deliberate strategy to make it so. The transitional nature of the Inman Park area established the church as a "catch-all" for people whose churches had moved from the inner city neighborhood. The doctrines of the church were clearly Pentecostal-flavored, yet the worship and preaching were notably more reserved than old line, shoutin' holiness churches. This Charismatic church pulsated with life without dramatic emotionalism—unless, of course, an emotional response became the mood the Holy Spirit prompted for a particular service. People from every denomination found something familiar as well as something new whenever they visited this church.

The philosophy of the Harvesters stated, "Put your best foot forward!" Earl, Norma, Don and Clariece did just that as they prepared for the services each week. Clariece was a dreamer who believed that the very best of every musical world could be captured in the worship at one church. She searched for ways to take the classical reverence and liturgy of "high church," the expertise of the world, the natural, God-given musical talents of Pentecostals, and the joy and uninhibited praise of black soul singers—all melted into one pot, using the best of all musical traditions to magnify the Lord.

Clariece remembered the words of a music professor who told her college class, "People don't know what they like . . . they like what they know." Clariece Paulk believed that God would raise up the Harvesters to flow freely in every expression of praise and worship to Him. Her openness to innovative ideas unlocked the doors to anointed demonstrations of worship through diverse, combined talents expressed in musicians and artists.

No matter what size congregation attended a service, Clariece prepared the music and Earl preached from the depths of his heart as if the handful of people receiving their ministry numbered thousands. They began each service assuming it would be their greatest ever. Don and Clariece worked together with the choir. Don ministered with an excellent singing voice and worked well with people, motivating them easily with his humor and charm, while Clariece selected the repertoire and arranged all the music.

The Harvester Trio—Norma singing alto, Don, tenor, and Clariece, soprano, sitting at the piano—practiced every Saturday night for their song, scheduled in the service just before the preacher marched confidently to the pulpit. The Harvester Trio labored over their song (sometimes "working through" disagreements about the arrangement), while Earl studied for his sermon in another room. When the musicians finally settled on the finished product, they called the preacher to hear their song and give his approval. Other musical selections opened people's spirits to bless the Lord and receive the preached Word of God, but the Harvester Trio sang songs to inspire the preacher!

Earl and Don gave Clariece the freedom and encouragement to try creative, innovative modes of worship. Earl emphasized the necessity of singing "music with a message," so Clariece carefully scrutinized all the lyrics. Many times she changed words of songs to suit whatever message God was speaking to their church through the preaching. They insisted that worship and preaching flow together. They avoided the "pilgrims in an alien land" themes or songs which stirred people's emotions to laughter or tears without ministering to their spirits. Good feelings or sentimentality were worthless unless they positively affected lifestyles!

Clariece had been trained as a concert pianist, but she bravely blazed new trails in worship with pioneer determination. Through trial and error, she rearranged scores, taught children's graded choirs, piano lessons, and even introduced "interpretive movement" (they wouldn't dare call it "dance") to their church. She attended musical workshops to glean ideas from the biggest churches in Atlanta.

When she first saw "interpretive movement," she was enthralled with the beauty and depth of worship in physical expression. The Harvesters tried it right away—on Easter Sunday morning with a full house. No one complained. Pre-teens Beth Paulk and Cindy Bridges wore unoffensive, floor-length dresses and simply used their hands to "interpret" the music.

Clariece was especially inspired with their move to the larger sanctuary at First Alliance from St. John's Lutheran. With the balcony in the new church she could now plan worship services complete with the dramatic effects of an antiphonal choir of angels. The "Word" songs hit popularity in the late sixties as the Charismatic sweep through denominational congregations always included singing scriptures. The Harvesters sang some "Word" songs in which scriptures and music were well synchronized (which was rare), but hymn arrangements of songs with lasting, edifying messages made up the bulk of their musical repertoire. When the contemporary sound hit the gospel music scene, all the teens in the church wanted to form a band. The Brothers and Sisters became their contemporary group, accompanied by guitars with a sound system Pastor Don operated from underneath his pulpit chair.

Year later Clariece reflected on the early days of the Harvester music program whenever pastors from around the world asked her for the Harvesters' "secrets" in worship. Clariece would answer their questions by saying, "The word 'no' was never in our vocabulary. We used whatever God put into our hands at any given time. We didn't wait until every detail was 'perfect' to use it."

Not only did they never reject new ideas, but also they rarely turned down an invitation to minister. They directed inner city choirs for underprivileged children, participated in community Easter and Thanksgiving services, sang at rest homes and prisons, took every cancellation for an early morning televison program, *Sunday Morning Sing,* because the producers knew they could be scheduled on short notice. They also sang for the Union Mission every month, joined a mass choir for *Behold The Man,* a passion play presented at the Atlanta Stadium, sang for Billy Graham Crusades scheduled in Atlanta and prepared a program for the Atlanta Boys' Clubs every Christmas.

Never saying "no" also applied unreservedly to their open door policy toward anyone coming to the church to worship. Earl was challenged one day as he stood in his front yard in a conversation with a well-known neighborhood "hippie," an intelligent pseudo-philosopher named Skinny Watson. Skinny was certain that the preacher wouldn't want him and his freaky friends to visit the church. Earl enthusiastically promised Skinny that he and his friends would be warmly welcomed by the Harvesters.

The next Sunday morning, halfway through the

sermon, Skinny and his entourage of fourteen friends paraded down the aisle where an usher seated them on the front rows as he had been instructed to do. Most of the group were barefooted, unkempt, long-haired youth, many of whom lived in the park and looked and smelled as if they did! Earl stopped in his sermon to welcome the first time late visitors. The congregation, following the lead of their pastor, lovingly surrounded the "guests" at the conclusion of the service with warm personal greetings.

Skinny Watson and his friends continued coming to church—always arriving late. Finally Earl gained their trust and love so that he could "pastor" them in basic church etiquette for the consideration of others. He asked them to arrive at church on time and to wear shoes. By then the church had become a source of food and clothing (shoes included), so Skinny and his friends readily agreed to the preacher's requests.

Earl easily assumed a substitute "father" role in the lives of the youth in his church and in the neighborhood. He was the first one they called from jail or when they were in any kind of trouble. Earl easily and quickly formed a trusting rapport with youth—even rebellious runaways and social dissidents—because he was one preacher who allowed them to voice their complaints. He understood their dissatisfactions with superficial social values. Earl loved instead of condemning them, covered their faults instead of judging them, and he always told them the truth whether they liked it or not. This preacher was "for real." These kids could spot a phony—and particularly a religious one—

miles away.

One night a group of Skinny's friends asked Earl to come pray for a girl who was sick with a high fever. He accompanied them to a large house divided into multi-family living quarters. Earl walked through rooms divided by sheets hanging over ropes, stepping over mattresses and personal belongings spread out on the floor, even stepping over sleeping bodies to get to the sick girl. She was delirious with a fever and undoubtedly should have been hospitalized—even for the physical protection of others in the house. Earl knelt down on the mattress. He gently put his hand on the girl's hot forehead as he prayed. The girl responded almost immediately to the pastor's prayer for her. The next week she accompanied her friends to the church and prayed for salvation in that service.

Another interesting member of the church was a black man, John, who was an epileptic. Earl never believed that demonic oppression caused all epilepsy, but the numerous confrontations he faced with John's condition certainly gave him reason to believe spirits were involved in this case. Often in the middle of sermons, John would have epileptic seizures. Of course the commotion distracted the congregation and alerted Earl to a spiritual confrontation. He would stop preaching, go quickly to John and command the convulsions to cease "in Jesus' name." In a few moments John smiled at the pastor who would help him back to his seat. Earl calmly returned to the pulpit and immediately picked up the message right where he left off.

To underscore their dependency on the Lord, the

Harvesters fought determined, dedicated persecutors of their ministry, who continuously badgered them with threats intended to discourage and torment them. One afternoon Earl and Clariece were working in an office at the back of the church building. Suddenly, a bullet shattered a window, lodging in the wall only inches above their heads. Once someone threw a fire bomb on the front porch of Earl's house, but the flames miraculously extinguished as it rolled across the porch. Threatening telephone calls to Earl's house were the worst form of chronic harrassment. Anonymous vulgar threats ignited Earl's fatherly protection for his girls. He issued a rule forbidding Becky, Joy and Beth to answer the telephone at home.

Despite threats, the Harvesters pressed forward with all their strength, taking every opportunity God gave them. Earl was elected the Chairman of the Bass Community Council, a civic organization including representatives from business, social and civic clubs. Don and Clariece also served as officers in the organization at various times. The council's purpose was to enhance recreation, health, education and youth facilities. The slogan of the council was "Dedicated to Creating Community" which provided the Harvesters with an excellent secular infiltration of the gospel message.

People often regarded the Harvester ministry as a "family operation," but even their most vehement critics were seldom aware of the full extent of ministry throughout the Paulk clan. Like the biblical priestly tribe of Levites, children growing up in the Paulk household had deep roots in the ministry that anchored all six Paulk children for life. Good trees continued to produce good fruit.

Myrtle and Harry Mushegan's three children, Harolene, Alan and Janet, contributed their gifts of singing, teaching, counseling and preaching to the ministry of their parents' church. The sister born after Earl, Ernestine, married evangelist Wallace Swilley. With their two sons, Duane and Mark, this talented musical family traveled all over the country in their ministry bus, even touring abroad from their home based in Atlanta. Don's twin sister, Darlene, married Jimmy Swilley, sister Ernestine's brother-in-law. Jimmy and Darlene Swilley affiliated with the Assemblies of God. Jimmy became the senior pastor of Faith Memorial in downtown Atlanta—a church already joined with strong spiritual bonds to Earl through his close association with its former pastor, Ralph Byrd. Darlene and Jimmy had one son, Jimearl, who grew up as an anointed musician and songwriter as well as serving as his dad's associate pastor until he established his own church.

Baby sister Joan joined Gospel Harvester Tabernacle as a charter member. Even as a teenager living in Tennessee with Earl Sr. and Addie Mae, Joan wanted to be involved in the new ministry at her brothers' church. Joan attended Lee College for a year where she met and fell in love with a Church of God preacher's son, Donnie Harris. Joan and Donnie were married at a large formal wedding at her church in Atlanta. Within a year, Donnie and Joan moved to Atlanta where Donnie worked for General Motors. Their first baby,

Donald Paulk Harris (called "Dana"), was born in a miraculous birth in which the doctors held little hope that the baby would survive the delivery. Dana was a beautiful baby, noted for winning baby contests based on his good looks and captivating congeniality.

Donnie and Joan were the kind of attractive young couple who drew other young families to the church. They were enthusiastic, supportive and totally involved with every aspect of the ministry. Joan became the lead soprano in the choir, taught little girls in Sunday School, and rallied the congregation to follow her brothers' directions in various projects. She wanted desperately to work at the church full-time, but Donnie had old-fashioned ideals about his wife staying at home which he refused to compromise. Instead, Joan became the chief volunteer—on a moment's notice for any job that needed doing!

In December 1964, Joan was nearly killed in a car accident that broke both her legs in several places, totally crushed one ankle and left her in a body cast from her waist to her ankles. Miracle baby Dana, only a year old, was pinned under the front seat unharmed. Joan faced several days of a horrifying nightmare, told by doctors that they needed to amputate her legs immediately. She begged doctors to wait at least two days so that her family could pray. Earl, Harry Mushegan and Ralph Byrd surrounded Joan's hospital bed and interceded for her. The doctors were astonished with Joan's physical improvement in that two-day period, but they assured her family that she would never walk again. Joan immediately answered her life sentence to a wheelchair by saying, "Yes, I will. Donnie and my brothers will teach me how."

Joan battled through months of excruciating pain with an unbending determination to walk. Norma, Clariece and the Paulk sisters took turns cooking and cleaning for Joan while Donnie, Earl and Don prayed with her and supported her efforts through months of tottering baby steps. Joan Paulk Harris was a woman whose spirit was invincible when the going was tough. Donnie would come home from work to see her standing at the kitchen sink in her body cast from her waist to her ankles. As she had promised, Joan walked again. She was free from any traces of the accident except a warning that she could never carry another baby to full term. Doctors told Joan that her lower bone structure was altered beyond supporting the additional weight of pregnancy.

Don and Clariece added a new responsibility in 1965 with the birth of LaDonna Louise Paulk. LaDonna looked like her grandmother, Louise Miller, for whom she was named, but her personality was the perfect combination of her two parents. LaDonna was practical and precocious like Don, yet outspoken, expressive and creative like Clariece. Clariece had cut out a picture in a magazine of her "ideal" little girl. She began asking God to give her a child like the one in the picture. A photograph of LaDonna, taken when she was the same age as the little girl in the magazine, absolutely defied comparison. The child in each picture seemed to be the same. LaDonna became a "daddy's girl" at an early age. Don willingly assumed many of the child care responsibilities since Clariece was involved in so many aspects of church ministry.

Don Paulk was an exemplary father, exhibiting tender character traits which were necessary on a broader scale in his counseling and administrative roles in the ministry. Don was—by necessity—often caught in the uncomfortable position of voicing the practical, realistic side of the visionary dreams that kept Earl and Clariece going. He often battled his calling from God to be "the heavy," a role providentially necessary to bring balance and credibility to the Harvesters' staff and leadership.

Don unavoidably felt his brother's shadow over him at times. He was understandably offended by comparisons of his own ministry with his brother's. Don knew in his spirit that in God's will no one was born to run in "second" place. After years of questioning and working through one situation after another to discover the meaning of his unique identity in this visionary ministry, Don's spiritual talents flourished. His ability for capturing details and depth that other people missed combined with his exceptional communication skills to produce an extraordinarily gifted writer.

Don Paulk made peace with God and himself, realizing his personal potential and value in the discovery process—value not just to Clariece and his brother who obviously needed his input, protection and care—but as a priceless, genuine, unduplicated gift to the ministry of the Harvesters. No relationship exemplified the Kingdom of God more than the love and unity between blood brothers working together in the ministry in one accord.

Earl and Norma bought a two-bedroom house in Decatur for $12,500 and moved in with the girls. Both Becky and Joy finished high school at Decatur High. Becky enrolled at Georgia State University, taking a heavy schedule of English classes. Becky was a very unusual girl: bright, optimistic, very close to her family and feeling absolutely no pressure to date. Earl often said that Becky had "his spirit." Her heart was totally given to the ministry at their church. Often Becky would write open letters to the congregation admonishing them to be more faithful in their church attendance. Of course, the letters were never printed, but they developed gifts of strong exhortation in Becky's spirit. As the oldest daughter she "mothered" people, showing a maturity toward her family and friends that brought out the best qualities within them.

Sometimes Earl expressed concern that Becky wasn't a more typical teenager—in love with a different boy every month. She would rather go with her dad to school football games than with her girl friends or a date. Whenever he would talk to Becky about her social life, she would smile with mature understanding at her dad's concern and tell him, "Daddy, we both know God has someone for me. Whenever it's the right time, he'll come along. I just don't think the Lord wants me to worry about that now."

He did "come along." Sam Lalaian was a Californian Armenian related to Harry Mushegan. Sam came from a very strong, Spirit-led family who knew how to seek God's direction for every decision of life. The

Armenians' lives were spared in leaving Russia by knowing how to move by prayer and prophecy; therefore, every aspect of their lives was unquestionably a spiritual matter. Sam had gone to spiritual counselors about whether marriage was God's will in his life. He was past thirty already, and his life was certainly fulfilled as a high school teacher, counselor and football coach. He received a strong directive prophecy which included a physical description of the woman God would give to him.

The moment he saw Becky Paulk, a meeting arranged by Aunt Myrtle and Uncle Harry whom Sam was visiting, he knew with certainty that she would be his wife. Everything about her—looks, personality, spiritual depth and maturity—exactly fit the prophetic word he had received. She was beautiful and perfect to him, but he couldn't let her know all the feelings stirring inside. He would wait, give her time to know him— more than anything, he wanted her to love him.

Becky was amazed at how easily she understood Sam from the few days they shared together before he returned home to California. They corresponded faithfully. Becky couldn't exactly pinpoint the time when she first knew she was in love, but she spent months wrestling with the complications of their long distance relationship. Could she possibly leave her family and the Harvester ministry? Did she know him well enough even to consider marriage? Earl suggested that Becky fly out to visit Sam and his family before she committed herself to any decision. The visit settled the matter for her. Yes, she would marry this man even if it meant uprooting all she had ever known and loved in order to share his life.

When Sam spoke with Becky's dad about marrying her, Earl consented with only one request. Earl asked Sam to allow Becky to stay near her family for a brief period of time after the wedding before taking her away from them. Earl's request was easily accommodated since Sam taught school and enjoyed extended vacations. Becky and Norma planned her wedding, set for her parents' anniversary, July 5th. The women debated whether Earl should conduct the ceremony or simply give away the bride. Earl finally decided for them by saying that he just wanted to be "a father" that day. Don Paulk, Harry Mushegan and other preachers in the family conducted the ceremony.

The newlyweds spent the first few months of their marriage—Sam's summer vacation—living in Don and Clariece's guest bedroom. The "adjustment" months flew by quickly as Sam and Becky prepared to leave for California, shipping their wedding gifts ahead of them. The entire family flocked to the airport when the couple left, everyone crying, feeling as if they would never see their Becky again! Becky seemed to be following almost exactly in her Aunt Myrtle's footsteps—marrying an Armenian from California she knew through correspondence, leaving her family behind to live with him on the West coast, feeling the painful separation from her family's ministry that was her very heart and soul.

Becky's comparison with Aunt Myrtle's life continued when within a year she and Sam moved back to

Atlanta. No one would have ever predicted that they would be back—Sam, least of all. He was as closely knit to his own family as Becky was to hers, even more so in some ways because of the Armenian language, cultural traditions and history of struggles. Clearly, God led the couple back to Georgia. Sam would have never made that choice arbitrarily, and though Becky was terribly homesick for months, she was totally willing to live in California for the rest of her life.

Changes in the school system specifically relating to Sam's position as a school counselor began their realization that God was changing their direction. Sam's greatest longing had always been to be a cattle farmer—a remote dream which suddenly seemed viable. Sam's family were strongly opposed to their leaving California at first. They diligently began to seek God's direction in behalf of the young couple. In a Sunday morning church service, a prophecy was given over Sam that God was moving him and he must not resist the changes taking place in his life. That prophetic word received repeated confirmations. Against any personal preferences in the matter, all agreed that Sam and Becky would be moving.

They came to Georgia to test the waters for fulfilling the things God was clearly speaking to them. Unlikely doors opened easily. Sam made an offer to buy a farm, located about thirty miles from Atlanta, that was ridiculously below its value or market price. The owner accepted his offer. For years after they moved to Georgia, Armenian relatives visiting Sam and Becky on their cattle farm spoke prophetically concerning their calling and ministry from the "holy ground" where God had led them.

Of course, Earl and Norma were thrilled to have Becky and Sam back with them. They knew that God would sovereignly join their spiritual gifts to the vision of the Harvesters. Meanwhile, their second daughter, Joy, had a teenage crush on a soldier, Steve Owens, who had once dated Becky. Steve's parents often attended their church and Joy noticed Steve's accompanying them to church occasionally. Steve was handsome, polite and respectful—in church. The wild side of Steve's nature was easily understated—even overlooked—by those who saw his tremendous spiritual potential.

By his early twenties, Steve had been kicked out of one college for breaking rules, had flunked out of another college for spending too much time partying, and had finally joined the Army to "get his head together." The Army had recruited a man who knew the full meaning of a weekend pass. Long ago he had left behind his legalistic Pentecostal heritage in favor of drinking parties and barroom banter. Steve was well on his way to the tarnished future of an alcoholic after a tour in Vietnam. But true to the clean-cut side of his dual nature, Steve regularly corresponded with wholesome Joy Paulk, the preacher's daughter.

Steve came back to church after being discharged by the Army because his father was seriously ill and his family needed him. After several trying months of searching for purpose in his life, Steve had made a new commitment to the Lord. He also very much wanted to date Joy. Earl had always taken a special interest in Steve, even occasionally inviting him to their house after church on Sunday nights. Steve was very attracted to Joy whom he had watched grow up from a gangling little girl into a beautiful young woman. But Steve recognized that he and Joy had many major differences—age, experience and friends.

After heart-rending prayer about the matter of dating Joy one Sunday night at the altar near the end of the service, Steve walked right into Joy standing in front of the church talking with her girlfriends. Joy called Steve aside with all the hesitation of a young girl captured in an elusive, hopeless infatuation. She asked Steve if he would take her to her Junior-Senior Prom. For Steve Owens, that invitation signified one time in his life when he definitely heard a direct, spontaneously clear word from God.

Joy was popular and athletic. Earl and Norma had been so proud of their starting line-up star on the basketball team. They sat in the gym at every game, cheering for their daughter and her predominantly black teammates. Joy was also noted as a natural comedian. Her commentary on her life always entertained people with some hilarious "disaster of the moment." Underneath the comical, dramatic surface lived a young woman who was a serious romantic with tremendous spiritual depth and perception. Steve Owens tapped the serious side of Joy's nature. Steve and Joy loved those inner qualities in each other which they perceived, but the inconsistencies of their personal temperaments caused numerous clashes in the relationship. Both were strong-willed. They dated Joy's entire senior year and were married the week after Joy graduated from high school.

The marriage had a stormy beginning. Joy didn't know about Steve's drinking habits when they married, and she felt uncomfortable socializing with some of his friends. Steve didn't realize how dependent and insecure Joy was. She even had to ask him what she should order in a restaurant. Steve had quit his job at Georgia Power Company to become a full-time student at Georgia State University, and Joy was working for Allstate Insurance Company. They always seemed to be pulling in opposite directions.

In the role of their pastor, Earl carefully tried to mediate their differences. Steve resented his father-in-law's advice as an intrusion into their privacy. Steve blamed Earl's sheltering protection of his daughter as being part of "Joy's problem."

Earl would simply back off and love Steve—going out on Saturday mornings to play tag football with him so that he could check his breath for beer. Steve was tremendously talented vocally—doing an unbelievably professional imitation of soul-singer Ray Charles. Earl fasted and prayed consistently for God to intervene to save the marriage. Most of all, Earl prayed for a breakthrough in making Steve Owens into the powerful spiritual man he could be. Steve had a God-given honesty and warmth that drew people to him, and his vocal talents, raised to a spiritual level, could open people's spirits to God's altars.

Most of Earl's problems in the late sixties related to

family matters and routine pastoral responsibilities. In contrast to earlier times, Earl enjoyed a calm, peaceful period of ministry. The strength of the church grew both numerically and spiritually. Weekly income in tithes and offerings averaged from $350 to $550. They faithfully paid DeKalb Federal the $756 each month for the two church buildings. Earl's salary for the first quarter in 1967 was $1170 or $97 per week. Don earned about $80 per week. The church also employed part-time nursery attendants and maintenance personnel.

The first indications that the plateau period was ending began when investors and builders bought property in the Inman Park area to re-build houses in mass renovation projects. Suddenly, it seemed as if everyone clinging to the charm in the old neighborhood either made plans to move away or planned to renovate their property with little concern for the existing community. People in the church spontaneously began exploring the Atlanta suburbs for a suitable location in which to move their church. A lady in the church who worked in real estate recommended a six-acre tract of land in south DeKalb County, a growing area populated by middle class families. Gradually the consensus of the church leadership was that the church should move.

To say that Earl had a strong spiritual leading away from Inman Park would be erroneous. He listened openly to the discussions, weighed the various recommendations, and waited for God to speak a sure word to him. He surveyed the land in south DeKalb that others recommended purchasing. Earl compared his inner conflicts on the matter with Jacob's return to Bethel. He had heard God's voice and obediently followed God's will in the inner city—of that, he was certain. The vision God had given him in Phoenix was far from realized, yet he admittedly had no strong convictions that the church's future was necessarily tied to the Inman Park area. But Earl needed to be sure in his spirit about the move. More than anything, he wanted to be in the center of God's will.

As Earl walked on the six-acre tract of land feeling pressed for a definite decision concerning the purchase, he asked God if this were the "promised land" for their church. Earl knelt down beside a little pine tree. As he broke off a branch, the Spirit of the Lord spoke distinctly to Earl's spirit that this was the place where He was leading the ministry. God promised him again that this church would minister to the world. Once he had definite assurance from God, Earl urged the congregation to make preparations to move. Years later Earl would hear again and again (from prophets who had never heard about God's promise to him) the words of the prophet Ezekiel:

Thus says the Lord God: "I myself will take a sprig from the lofty top of the cedar, and will set it out; I will break off the topmost of its young twigs a tender one, and I myself will plant it upon a high and lofty mountain; on the mountain height of Israel will I plant it, that it may bring forth boughs and bear fruit, and become a noble cedar; and under it will dwell all kinds of beasts; in the shade of its branches birds of every sort will nest. And all the trees of the field shall know that I the Lord bring low the high tree, and make high the low tree, dry up the green tree, and make the dry tree flourish. I the Lord have spoken, and I will do it." (Ezekiel 17:22-24)

The Harvesters put the inner city churches up for sale and negotiated with the bank for a loan to purchase the new land to build their sanctuary. The terms of the loan were pending the sale of the churches in Inman Park, but Earl wasn't worried about finances after he received clear instructions from God. Together Earl and Don proposed that they build an octagon-shaped building. An architect in the Mushegans' church drew up the plans from Don's rough drawing. Both the Paulks and Mushegans built new Harvester sanctuaries using the same floorplan—the Mushegans' in Atlanta's northwest, the Paulks' in the southeast.

For obvious reasons related to the transitional area, no one seemed to be interested in buying the inner city churches which were for sale. The approval of the loan began to be highly questionable from the bank's perspective. Earl remained firmly confident. On the last day that the loan contract could be approved, the churches sold. Whether God wanted to prove His sovereignty in the matter or simply build the people's faith for greater things about to happen in their little church is only conjecture. But the move to Flat Shoals Road in Decatur was similar to Israel's crossing the Red Sea for some of the Inman Park Harvesters.

The men and women of the church worked nights and weekends to complete the construction of their new sanctuary. The pulpit area in the new church sat in the exact spot where Earl had broken the twig off the pine tree when God instructed him to proceed with the move.

Many men with no construction skills whatsoever labored diligently with hammers and saws to build their new church.

The congregation moved in and began holding services long before the construction was completed—a pattern which would remain a standard in the Harvester ministry with rapid changes and constant construction and re-construction of facilities. The floor was concrete and the people sat on rented chairs. Choir members' heads almost touched the ceiling since the choir loft (literally, a loft) was built over the bathrooms located in a hall behind the pulpit area. A partition between the bathrooms became the baptistry.

Norma was quiet with her opinions, but crystal clear Clariece openly expressed her disenchantment with the new building. They had moved a long way from euphoric stained glass windows and the creative versatility of a balcony! After years in a busy, downtown area with constant traffic, they felt isolated in the country, surrounded by quiet woods beside an out-of-the-way two-lane road. Within a mile down the road, the Assemblies of God were also building a new church—a much larger, more elaborate sanctuary than the Harvesters had built. Surely that location would affect the Harvesters' ability to draw resident Charismatics from the surrounding neighborhoods. A large, established Baptist church was located directly across the street. The Harvesters both looked and felt like the new kid on the block!

Social snobbery in south DeKalb County in 1972 was blatant. The upwardly mobile middle class bought the spacious homes in the area—typically three or four bedrooms, two or three baths, den, living room and dining room, and of course, a two car garage! Most of the white residents were on the run from black neighbors who were in determined pursuit and only a few subdivisions away. South DeKalb was populated with committed "white flight" residents who had already moved once or twice before to avoid black infiltration into their neighborhoods and were ready to move again at the first sign of "block busters" targeting any houses down the street.

Housing construction in the area was booming. Subdivisions sprang up overnight. Because they were in the Chapel Hill subdivision, the Harvesters elected to change the name of their church to Chapel Hill Harvester Church. Of course, the members always encountered the question, "What is a Harvester?" Many people in the area soon began referring to the church simply as "Chapel Hill." The congregation of several hundred people grew steadily with long-term visitors becoming actively involved in the ministry. People often attended church for months before they were ever given an opportunity for membership.

One member, Charles Bonner, was even elected a deacon before he actually joined the church. Charles, his wife, Corrinne, and their teenaged son, Wes, were typical of many people coming to Chapel Hill Harvester Church. They came disillusioned and hurt, seeking a refuge to heal their spiritual wounds. Many people found themselves painfully alienated from churches where they had worked as leaders for many years.

Among issues igniting controversy and division in mainline denominations, the baptism of the Holy Spirit was the most explosive. Wes Bonner received the baptism of the Holy Spirit, and through the positive changes they observed in his life, the entire family soon experienced this new dimension in their relationship with the Lord. When people refused to renounce or compromise their spiritual experiences to be accepted in their home churches, often the most peaceable alternative was to leave the church for greener pastures. The Harvesters received these people as scattered sheep, just as God had called them to do.

Charles Bonner was a successful builder with experience constructing shopping centers and housing subdivisions. He lived near the church in a large house complete with a huge recreation room in the basement. Earl asked him to teach the Career Class in Sunday School at his house since the church had little space for classes. The class met at Charles and Corrinne's home until Charles completed building the fellowship hall extension to the sanctuary in November 1974.

The Harvesters were growing internally also. Joan Harris once again defied doctors' predictions by giving birth to a beautiful daughter, Deanna Joan, in 1968. Joan's pregnancy created the circumstances to cultivate Deanna's dominant spiritual trait—a child of extraordinary faith.

Clariece often compared herself with the woman in the Bible who petitioned the unrighteous judge until he granted her request. Clariece's petition to God was for a son. Donnie Earl Paulk was born in 1973, an answer to

Clariece's fervent prayers. Don often said that he raised LaDonna, and Clariece raised Donnie Earl whose idealistic, adventuresome temperament definitely emerged from the Miller genes.

Earl and Norma became grandparents. God never promised Earl a son, but He did promise to give him seven grandsons, a promise he shared openly. Several of those grandsons were born in the early days of the ministry on Flat Shoals Road. Danny, born to Becky and Sam in 1972, grew to be a very intellectual, spiritually discerning young man, mature, serious and committed to spiritual values, as well as an outstanding basketball star. Danny's brother, Jeffrey, was born in 1975. Jeff emerged with an outgoing personality—peer-oriented, yet also intellectual like Danny. Jeff won his school spelling bee and often set the academic standards for his classmates.

Joy and Steve's first child, Andy, was born in 1973. Andy was the first baby dedicated in the newly-built sanctuary. Andy seemed to take after his parents with obvious musical, dramatic talent and inborn showmanship. He displayed a notable ability to open his spirit in worship.

Meanwhile, Norma Paulk adapted enthusiastically to her role as doting grandmother. The children called her "Mimi," and her close loving relationship with her daughters' children undoubtedly became one of the richest blessings God could have given to their lives. The boys regarded their grandfather as a prophetic spiritual voice with comprehension of his message beyond their years or experiences. With an astute determination to fulfill their heritage, they took careful notes during their grandfather's sermons, embellishing God's Word as their parents encouraged them in preparation for their own ministries in the Harvesters' future.

After Donnie Earl was born, Clariece temporarily curtailed her frantic pace. Don hired Dottie Bridges to help with the church's growing clerical responsibilities. Within a short period of time Dottie became Earl's secretary. Dottie and her husband, John, their two daughters, Cindy (who lives forever with the distinction of being the first Harvester baby) and younger daughter, Teresa, had persevered throughout every phase of the Harvesters and knew the ministry inside out.

Dottie added a delightful, refreshing sense of humor to the staff. She always picked up on the lighter side of any situation or crisis which proved to be a tremendous asset in keeping Earl in balance. Earl loved to tease her publicly, embarrassing her as being scatter-brained and unreliable and blaming her for his own oversights. But Dottie truly brought notable, professional efficiency to the office.

Earl also taught Dottie, John and Norma how to play tennis. When Norma and John dropped out of the lessons, Dottie became the preacher's most reliable tennis opponent. John Bridges also served a vital role in the ministry: first, by the important letter he wrote to Earl in Phoenix, later as the church's Sunday School Superintendent. In the early years of explosive growth, John served as the financial comptroller—though he also maintained a full-time career working as a corporate credit manager with Swift Company.

In May 1974, the Bonners' son, Wes, began taping Earl's sermons. The tape ministry began with a cassette tape player sitting on an altar rail. Wes got up from his seat halfway through the services to turn over the tape. Copies of taped messages were sold from a shoebox. New members of the church were relieved that they didn't have to continue relying on their memories and notes alone to preserve the excellent messages they heard consistently.

Other new members also joined the ministry as staff personnel. Lynn Mays led a ladies' prayer group which had begun meeting at the church on Tuesday mornings. Lynn had moved from Baltimore, Maryland, with her husband and four children. Lynn's heart had been stirred after hearing a youth leader in her church in Baltimore who had returned from a conference in Atlanta. The youth leader prophesied that Atlanta would one day be "the spiritual capital of the world." The prophecy specifically relayed a vision in which anointed fires beginning in Atlanta would spread to cities around the globe. Lynn's thrilling reaction to the prophecy remained a lingering mystery to her. Why should a housewife living in Baltimore be so moved in responding to spiritual fires igniting in a city where she had never even been? Within a short period of time, Lynn's husband was tranferred to Atlanta and she understood her reponse.

Living in Atlanta, Lynn spent her days as a suburban wife and mother. She patiently sought God's direction, knowing with certainty that God had called her into the ministry. For many years she ministered from her home to neighbors and friends. They, in turn, brought other friends to receive her counsel. Her housewives' coffee breaks with her neighbors inevitably turned into Bible teaching and ministry sessions. Often Lynn prayed for neighbors, then for their relatives and friends whom they would bring to her to receive the baptism in the Holy Spirit. God greatly blessed Lynn's willingness, openness and obedience in serving Him. Lynn easily loved people with a pastor's heart at whatever opportunity God gave her to minister.

In what seemed to be a contradiction to Lynn's naturally soft-spoken manner, her ministry gifts included spiritual discernment and deliverance of people from oppressive spirits. These spiritual gifts from God were almost startling to Lynn at first. She would sit in the little Baptist church she was attending at that time and visibly see various spirits oppressing members of the choir.

She visited Chapel Hill Harvester Church seeking spiritual teaching in an atmosphere where ministry flowed freely. She was impressed by the pastor who delivered quality biblical teaching and sought the Holy Spirit's direction for God's people. The messages challenged Lynn to expand her love for others as well as stretch her faith in spiritual growth. She and her family joined the church and almost immediately members of the church responded to Lynn's sensitivity to their needs. They began going to her to receive deliverance and counseling.

Earl was somewhat skeptical of deliverance ministries. In some circles "casting out demons" seemed like emotionalism or sensationalized melodramas with people choking and vomiting at an altar. He definitely believed in the biblical authority for deliverance from demonic, oppressive spirits, but as with many aspects of the Charismatic flood of "hyped pseudo-spirituality," Earl demanded valid proof of God's power at work. He saw much abuse and misunderstanding on the subject of deliverance.

In a dream, God told Earl to ask Lynn to lead the Ladies' Prayer Meeting on Tuesday mornings. He felt inner resistance in asking Lynn with so many unanswered questions about her ministry in his spirit, but he willingly obeyed the Lord. If Lynn's ministry were valid, good spiritual fruit would quickly prove itself. He saw her in the hall after a service and obediently asked her to consider leading the Tuesday meetings. Lynn replied that she would pray about the matter and give him an answer in a few days.

Several days later, Lynn paid Brother Paulk a visit in his office. Lynn told the pastor that many of the women in the church were afraid of him. She challenged his tight reins on "emotional displays" by saying that such restrictions also inhibited true ministry of the Holy Spirit and the free flow of valid ministry gifts. The answer to justified caution at "emotionalism" was spiritual discernment, allowing real ministry to flourish and "fleshly displays" to be judged and admonished.

At first, Earl couldn't understand her challenging

observations. Then Lynn began to press the pastor about the call of God on his own life—revealing a comprehension of the Phoenix vision of the church without ever having heard it. The confirmation was bold. Leaving his office, Lynn told the pastor, "I don't just want to join this church. I want to become a joint in this body."

Earl prayed about the conversation. He knew that the Holy Spirit must operate in mighty power to build the church God had shown him in the Phoenix vision. He believed that the body of Christ must be "fitly joined together" to fulfill God's purposes in ministry. He also knew that deliverance from evil spirits is valid evidence that Kingdom authority has come to earth. As he opened his spirit, he recognized the consistent fruit of Lynn's ministry in numerous lives. God began to give him some of the most powerful sermon series in his entire ministry on "Sound Doctrine" and "Body Life." This teaching opened the faith and responsibility of his congregation to new spiritual depth and began working maturity in their spirits—responsibility for individual growth as well as helping others to grow.

Lynn had just been elected the first woman deaconess (later the Harvesters appointed deacons as the church grew) when her marriage ended. She had totally submitted herself to the authority of the church in situations concerning her marriage—hanging on through years of financial struggles and turbulent circumstances. Earl had insisted that Lynn try everything possible to hold her marriage together as a leader in the church and a spiritual example to others. She and her husband had sat regularly in counseling sessions with the pastor for over a year. Lynn had followed the pastor's counsel explicitly, going beyond the second and third mile many times hoping to break the bondages over her family. She agreed to proceed with a divorce as the only solution after totally submitting every aspect of her marriage to six elders in the church for their decision. Whatever they said, she was willing to do. After careful deliberation'and prayer, all six men recommended a divorce on clear scriptural authority.

Earl knew that even recognizing this woman's ministry would be a tremendous risk for the Harvesters. The authority of women in ministry was controversial enough, much less a divorced woman. With all the accusations of the past threatening him like an alarm blaring in his thoughts, Earl took the risk. How could he possibly deny the spiritual fruit of this woman's ministry and the total submission of her spirit to God's voice? On the Wednesday that Lynn's divorce was finalized, Earl preached that night on the subject "Divorce." Lynn told Brother Paulk earlier that day that she wanted to sit on the back row for the service, but Earl insisted that she sit on the front row and challenge any oppression or guilt which could war against her calling from God. From that day, Lynn never felt any power in Satan's accusations against her in regard to her divorce.

The risk was worth taking. Lynn Mays became a vital link in the City of Refuge that God called Chapel Hill Harvester Church to be. She was both a recipient and a channel of healing compassion and restoration to others, first receiving God's restoration for herself and her children, then ministering hope and deliverance to desperate people with nowhere else to turn for help. People set free from bondages by God's power working through her ministry had no criticism for Lynn as a woman, her marital status, or the church where they had finally found solutions.

The deliverance ministry at the church became widely utilized by other pastors in the city. Atlanta's mental health hospitals and clinics often sent those whom they considered to be "impossible cases" to Chapel Hill for prayer. Discernment from this woman, and others like her whom God raised up in the ministry, became more and more vital to God's plan. Almost overnight the little church's membership exploded.

As people flocked to the church, Earl prayed that God would give him greater sensitivity. He always said that the one thing he wanted people to remember most about him was his love for them. How greatly Satan had attacked that ability to love people. Of course, the greatest area of attack came in areas of trusting others. Earl learned to depend on the Holy Spirit's protection in order to ignore mental threats as he opened his heart to people. How could the ministry at Chapel Hill ever become that City of Refuge without personal vulnerability, building solid relationships and taking risks by trusting "the Christ" in one another? And as the love of Christ flowed freely in Earl Paulk's ministry toward the people whom God entrusted to his care, that perfect love of the Holy Spirit cast out all fear.

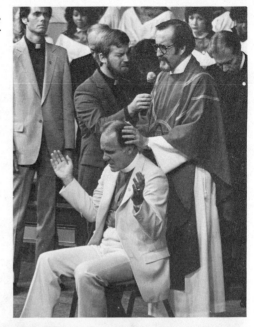

Consecration of Pastor Earl Paulk to the office of bishop by Bishop Robert McAlister (Rio de Janeiro, Brazil)

t's your free part."

Judge yourself at the table of the Lord.

International Communion of Churches, College of Bishops (l to r) Tito Almeida, Robert McAlister, John Meares, Benson Idahosa, Earl Paulk, Herro Blair, Harry Mushegan

Gold and Silver Day — (1980)

Possessing the Land (198...

The Groundbreaking (1982)

The Wilderness Experience —
One bitterly cold winter and two sweltering summers in the tent (1983-84)

"Behold! It is done!"
Bishop Benson Idahosa

Loving the sheep

The Founders
K-Center Dedication Day
September 30, 1984

Covenant Brothers
Bishop Paulk, Bishop Meares
and Pastor Reid

ALPHA with Youth Pastor
Duane Swilley

Over 100 Central American pastors attended
Atlanta '85. Their flags graced the balcony.

Pastors Sam Lalaian and Lynn Mays ministering life at
"Life and Growth In The Spirit" service

Worship the Lord with the Chapel Hill Harvester Church Concert Choir and Orchestra, K-
Dimension Singers and Pastor Steve Owens.

The Presbytery
of
Chapel Hill Harvester Church
March 1986

...rvester Television on location: (from left)
...na Harris, Reggie Lancaster, Clariece
...ulk, Patti Battle, Ron Gaither, Beth Paulk
...nner, Earl Paulk, Greg Hall (front)

The First Satellite Uplink
(1983)

Chapel Hill Harvester Church Staff
February 1986

"I have a word for you from the Lord."
(with Rev. Jim Bakker at PTL, 1981)

Earl Paulk and Robert Schuller

Ready for battle from "Seed Power"

Rev. T.L. Osborn at Chapel Hill Harvester Church

Clariece Paulk at the Bosendorfer Concert Grand Piano

Sharalee Lucas and Tony Washington with the K-Dimension Singers

Buck, Reba and Dottie — God's gifts to us

*Dony McGuire
"Upon This Rock"
1985 Dove Award*

The Don Paulks
Clariece, LaDonna, Donnie Earl and Don

Beloved sister
Joan (Paulk) Harris
who went on to be with the Lord on May 26, 1985

"By your fruit you shall know them"
(standing from left) Andy Owens, Timmy Sam Lalaian, Steve Owens, Joy (Paulk) Owens, John David Owens, Wes Bonner, Beth (Paulk) Bonner, Rebecca (Paulk) Lalaian, Sam Lalaian, Jeff Lalaian, Danny Lalaian. (sitting from left) Britt Bonner, Norma Paulk, Penielle Bonner, Earl Paulk, Jesse Owens.

10

CHAPTER TEN

People who joined Chapel Hill Harvester Church in the mid-70's learned to "move with the cloud." In only a five-year period the church grew so dramatically that people who joined a close "family" fellowship either adjusted to rapid growth or moved on to smaller churches with less expansive visions. The "old timers," members of the church before 1975, fondly recalled Wednesday night Bible studies that ended with Earl calling the entire congregation around the altar for individual ministry and prayer. Everyone knew everyone else: their needs, strengths and weaknesses. Whenever members missed a service, dozens of people asked them the reasons that they were away. Soon the large crowd made finding specific people impossible without a designated meeting time and place.

Earl loved the personal interaction of a small congregation. The one aspect of growth that tormented him was the possibility that people were left unattended in their needs for ministry. For years he had checked on people who missed Sunday services with telephone calls on Monday or Tuesday. He personally had made all the hospital visits. He took his charge from God seriously to "watch over souls" with eternal accountability.

Suddenly he didn't even know the names of people who sat in his congregation after they had joined the church. He depended on others to inform him about emergency situations in people's lives. He could no longer attend personally to everyone's daily needs for ministry. Could he find other pastors with his conscientious spirit who would love and minister to people just as he would himself? He rarely prayed without reminding God of that pressing, dominating concern.

Family life was busier than ever. Both Earl and Don moved into a neighborhood near the church along with John and Dottie Bridges and many other Harvesters from Inman Park. Beth was a high school senior in the fall of 1977—intelligent, beautiful and madly in love. She and Wes Bonner planned their wedding for December 16th, Don and Clariece's anniversary.

As often happens with "the baby" of the family, home life for Beth was notably less sheltered and sedate than for her two older sisters. Whereas Earl and Norma sat dutifully at home watching the clock as they waited for Becky and Joy to get home from dates, Beth found herself wishing that her parents would slow down to a more predictable pace. She often called home on Friday and Saturday nights to tell her parents that she would be a few minutes late or to ask permission to extend her curfew, only to discover they weren't home yet themselves.

Wes continued volunteering with the tape ministry at the church as well as having responsibility for adjusting audio during the Sunday and Wednesday services. Fortunately, the recording equipment had improved, automatically producing cassette tapes of the messages. Wes worked weekdays with his dad in construction, especially on completing a house with a huge bay window in front where he would live with his beautiful bride.

A traumatic series of events surrounded Beth and Wes's wedding. Norma and Beth planned details of the momentous occasion with all the pomp and pageantry expected of the preacher's daughter in a growing church. Of course, Norma threw herself into every aspect of the preparations with excited anticipation. Two weeks before the wedding, Norma fainted in the bathroom, hemorrhaging from bleeding ulcers. Earl carried his wife into their bedroom and called an ambulance while he prayed over her and commanded life into her body.

For several days Norma was in intensive care receiving continuous blood transfusions. The family kept a constant vigil at the hospital until Norma was out of danger. Meanwhile, Beth debated about proceeding with her wedding, which seemed like a trivial matter next to her concern for her mother. Once Norma's physical crisis passed, Earl assured Beth and Wes that they should continue with their plans. Joan, Clariece, Becky and Joy took charge of the details of the ceremony, floral arrangements, food and decorations for the reception. Beth kept her mother informed of the last-minute wedding preparations as she sat at her bedside.

Norma left the hospital on Tuesday before the Friday night wedding. She looked pale and felt weak, unable to finish the tablecloths she intended to make for the reception. In spite of her ordeal, Norma was grateful to the Lord that she would see her precious baby daughter walk down the aisle on her daddy's arm. The day of the wedding Earl received a call from Greenville that Norma's brother had died. He decided to wait until after the ceremony to tell Norma about her brother's death, realizing that she could do nothing about the situation. She was certainly under enough emotional stress with Beth's wedding and physical stress with her own recovery.

God's glory only shines through broken vessels. He will not allow His majesty to be tarnished by selfish motives, human egos or prideful plans. God had found in Earl Paulk a man who would listen to His voice and speak whatever He told him to say. The little church built on a muddy hill in south DeKalb County was almost like a spiritual experiment—controversial, bold, eager to make a difference in the world by pleasing God. In the late 1970's, God required brokenness prior to a tremendous flood of spiritual blessing, explosive growth and bountiful harvest.

God dealt powerfully in preparing members of Earl's family for their calling into the work of the Harvesters. Steve Owens' talent in singing and leading worship began to flow with the anointing that Earl had always envisioned God would give to Steve when his heart was right. Though Steve always perceived himself as being reserved, his exuberance in leading worship demonstrated dynamic freedom of the Spirit.

Steve was looking for a new job in 1978 when Earl finished writing a book on jogging as a physical/spiritual exercise called *Divine Runner*. Earl asked Steve to help him market the book while he continued going to job interviews. During the days that Steve worked at the church, Dottie Bridges often asked him to counsel and pray with people who showed up unexpectedly needing to see a pastor. Soon people specifically asked for Steve to counsel with them.

God used several situations to confirm Steve's call into full-time ministry. He visited Mr. Sykes, a dying, elderly man at the Veteran's Administration Hospital. Mr. Sykes was not a Christian. Steve talked with the man, ministered love and tenderness to him and prayed with him to receive Jesus Christ as his Savior. When Mr. Sykes died a few days later, Steve's account of the man's salvation was the greatest comfort to his family. The family asked Steve to preach the funeral. The experience amazed Steve, but he also experienced a tremendous sense of God's anointing and immeasurable confidence.

Several weeks later the staff sat around a table in a

planning session for Holy Week services. Earl made assignments for the nights when Don, Sam and Lynn would preach. Then he said, ". . . and Friday night I want you to preach, Steve." Clariece burst out laughing. Earl glared at Clariece, underscoring his seriousness. He turned to Steve who also smiled in agreement with Clariece. Steve never forgot his father-in-law's words, "I cannot call Steve into the ministry, but I will do everything possible to open doors for whatever God is doing in his life. I certainly won't stand in God's way!"

Earl was just as adamant in allowing his daughters to develop their spiritual gifts in the ministry of the Harvesters. Becky, his spirit, taught the Bible with anointed exhortation. She enrolled in an independent study seminary course to gain a historical, scholarly perspective of scripture. But Becky's understanding of God's Word and ability to teach came from God alone. Joy, his laughter, wrote plays, acted in comedies and serious dramas, and sang the messages her daddy preached. She also organized sports activities for children, utilizing her natural athletic abilities. Beth, his song, led the young women in the church to become their best for God by practical application of the messages they were taught. Beth was the poet, writer and singer. She not only set the example for others in her sweet, loving service to God, but she also developed into a gifted teacher.

Earl often said that the greatest proof of genuine ministry was to have one's children join their lives in service to the Lord. Though many times "the family" became a point of contention among Harvester critics, the dedication of Earl and Norma's children lived as undeniable confirmation that good trees produce good fruit. The fact that Earl's brother, sister, nephew and their families also worked in the ministry added further confirmation. The Paulks understood service. Earl's three daughters as well as their husbands gave their lives to Kingdom work. Becky joined her husband serving on the Presbytery of the church. Both Joy and Beth sang every service with the K-Dimension Singers, who opened the hearts of people in worship to receive the spoken Word of God. Earl never apologized for developing his children's abilities to fulfill the calling of God in their lives. Further emphasizing that conviction, he never backed away from proclaiming their family's intention of raising the grandchildren to work in the ministry also.

And God continued to add to that corps of "ministers in training" for the next generation. In 1978, Becky gave birth to Timmy Sam, the large "baby" of the Lalaian household, who quickly grew to equal the size of his older brother, Jeff. In 1979, Beth and Wes had their first baby, Britt, whom people often said looked like his grandfather Paulk. Later that same year, Steve and Joy had Jesse, a serious child who required constant intercession for physical battles attacking his life.

Clariece faced the greatest test of her life in the late 70's. When a surgeon told Clariece that her mother, Louise Miller, had cancer, she panicked. This was the mother who stood as an invincible tower of strength to her children. Louise had insisted on high goals and the pursuit of excellence. Clariece's mother could be credited with Clariece's musical accomplishments by the way she required her daughter to practice, practice, practice—and punished her if she didn't. Now Louise Miller lay dying and the excellence of all her cherished goals and possessions could not help her.

Clariece desperately wanted to be brave and confident in this test, but inside she crumbled. When she heard the surgeon say that the tumor in her mother's stomach was inoperable, her legs trembled, her tongue thickened and she couldn't remember her own telephone number to call Don who waited at home in Atlanta with the children. For the first time she realized how completely sheltered her life had been, how unprepared she was to face losing someone so precious to her.

For several months Clariece drove to Cleveland, Tennessee, as soon as the weekend services were over to sit at her mother's bedside. Louise had bitter memories of disagreements with legalism in Pentecostal churches. Church laws had made her feel judged and unworthy of God's love. As Clariece shared simple truth, faith and the love of Jesus with her mother, Louise began to realize how she had filled inner voids in her life with pride in her children and material assets. Now all she wanted from her daughter was to hear about Jesus. Clariece gratefully poured out her own love for Him in the last conversations she and her mother shared.

Clariece did her crying, struggling and questioning

of her own faith back in Atlanta to Earl, Don and Lynn Mays. Earl sternly challenged Clariece to trust the Lord. She knew the language, behavior and expectations of faith as a minister's wife. She could give answers to anyone else in her situation. But suddenly, unless verbalized faith became dependable reality, she would die of grief.

Clariece experienced a great spiritual victory. Her mother's death gave her confidence in the Lord which would never fail her. She often shared with people that the experience changed her from being "a Martha" with so many things to do for Jesus into "a Mary" who could simply sit for hours in adoration at His feet, totally fulfilled just to be near Him. Earl had been with Louise Miller in the hours just before she died. At the funeral, Don sang *It Is Well With My Soul*, and Clariece played the piano. At Chapel Hill the next Sunday, Earl preached a special tribute to Louise Miller, a sermon entitled "An Elegant Lady."

The overshadowing of the Holy Spirit, the Comforter, was a reality to Clariece in a way she never would have understood otherwise. She said that she almost felt her mother sitting beside her at the piano as she played sometimes, sharing the fullness of joy, peace and knowledge of God's presence and love. In brokenness, Clariece Paulk's spirit burst into higher realms of worship than she had ever known. Her victory opened the door for thousands of people to join her. In brokenness, worship at Chapel Hill Harvester Church soared freer and higher with fresh anointing.

Other family members also needed preparation for

ministry in the church. Joan's husband, Donnie Harris, was a man with the perseverance to make the television broadcasting dream a reality. But first, Donnie's spirit had to be in tune with the pastor and the vision of the church.

On June 7, 1978, Earl announced to the congregation that they were going on television. They contacted a group known as T.C.I. to produce television programs that would share Chapel Hill's vision with the world. The next Monday morning, Charles Bonner brought an electrician with him to build two platforms for television cameras. The following Sunday morning the Harvesters taped their first television program which aired that night at midnight on Channel 36 in Atlanta.

Every week the Harvesters taped the Sunday morning and evening services and hand delivered them to be broadcast on Sunday night at midnight. The Harvesters were totally convinced that all of Atlanta sat up on Sunday nights just to see Chapel Hill! The congregation had to adjust to "thinking" television for the services. When necessary, Donnie Harris insisted that the entire congregation sit on one side of the sanctuary to insure that the television audience saw a good crowd at church. Members who owned a real estate company, Faith Realty, financed the purchase of Chapel Hill's first television equipment in September 1978. Besides the weekly services, the new equipment was used to tape a Christmas special of the entire Paulk-Swilley-Mushegan-Harris clan which was broadcast in December on two Atlanta stations, Channels 36 and 46.

In early January of 1979, Earl asked Donnie to join the full-time staff to head the television outreach. Greg Hall, a young man from Tifton, Georgia, who worked with Donnie through T.C.I., also joined the staff, working full-time in audio and television production.

Earl commissioned the television department to pursue markets to broadcast the Sunday services. The Harvesters purchased time on Channel 22 in Savannah, Georgia, and were even offered free time on DeKalb Cablevision. In late 1979, they broadcast the *Harvester Hour* in Portsmouth, Virginia, and Leesburg, Florida, by CBN's flagship station. Inevitably, the television exposure brought hundreds of local people to the church to "experience" Chapel Hill firsthand.

Another family member and his wife, Duane and Sunny Swilley, joined the church in 1976. After graduating from Georgia Tech, Duane left his parents' evangelistic ministry to establish himself as a businessman in Atlanta. Earl was very aware of Duane's leadership potential, but he felt restrained in asking his nephew to serve in any spiritual position in the church. Earl's sister, Ernestine, and her husband, Wallace, were heartbroken with Duane's career decision. They had hoped their two sons would continue to travel with them in the ministry after completing school.

Duane finally took the initiative by asking his uncle to allow him to work with the youth of the church. About the same time some church leaders came to Earl with urgent concerns about their children's involvement with drug traffic at a local high school. Earl called a meeting of leaders to pray for specific direction in addressing the teen drug problem. That prayer meeting, with leaders on their faces crying out to God for their children, resulted in Duane's beginning a youth Bible study at one of the member's house. Within a few weeks the number of people attending the Bible study dwindled to only three people: Duane, Sunny, and Ann Harold, a teenager who had offered her house as their meeting place.

Duane finally began to understand God's requirements. Feeling like a failure with little confidence in himself and wondering if God would still use him, Duane made a serious commitment to the ministry that drastically changed the direction of his own life. He set spiritual priorities. Sports, money, ambition—those things would never make him into the man God had called him to be. As he opened his spirit to God's will, the Bible study gradually began to grow. Soon crowds of teenagers were spilling throughout the rooms of the house, out the front door into the yard. Kids were coming from everywhere and bringing their friends with them. Of course, people in the neighborhood registered their complaints about the meetings—noise, heavy traffic and groups of black and white kids praying in tongues in the front yard!

Earl told Duane he felt that the Bible study would explode if they brought it back to the church. Duane consented but held strong reservations that kids really needing ministry would come to church to receive it. Few teens were convinced that the church offered any answers to their problems. Young people's stereotyped views of church services connoted a quiet atmosphere, a boring lecture and traditions which were totally irrelevant to the world where they struggled daily with sex, drugs, social and family pressures. But Earl knew the vision God had given him included thousands of young people—in church!

Earl believed that kids had a certain "sound" that communicated to them. While leading evangelicals issued stern warnings about the satanic influences of rock-and-roll music, Earl took another risk. He knew that the church had to capture young people's attention. Music with "their beat" became a "candy" ministry, attractive bait that opened thousands of young people to the gospel of Jesus Christ. Facing harsh, highly vocal reactions from religious leaders, many parents and an assortment of dedicated critics, Earl gave the signal to form a contemporary band. The band combined guitars, drums, trumpets, and hand-clapping, foot-stomping, hip-shaking rhythms in words conveying the messages Earl preached. Earl named the ministry "Alpha": the name of a band, a service and an innovative ministry concept that quickly represented the beginning of "new life" to thousands of young people.

Teenagers packed the fellowship hall set up with chairs. The band—Clariece at the piano, Duane on guitar—joined recruited musicians in the church who played drums, guitars, etc. LaDonna Paulk and Cindy Bridges sang old songs with a "new sound," communicating an "old message" that revolutionized young people's lives. Within a year, teens lined the walls of the sanctuary in "standing room only" capacity. Altar calls at the end of the services brought hundreds of people to the front of the church to pray. High school football players, cheerleaders, homecoming queens and student body officers, parents, teachers, even youth leaders at other churches came to Alpha out of curiosity about the methods and remarkable results.

The Alpha controversy raged in the community. Some church people refused to allow their children to associate with other kids getting off drugs and "going straight." Persecutors resented hearing the conversion testimonies reported weekly after the Monday night meetings. Some people—both church goers and those who weren't—insisted that Alpha was a cult. No one in south DeKalb County who knew of Alpha remained indifferent to the Alpha phenomenon.

Another source of irritation toward Alpha was that many of the teenagers attending each week were student leaders in other churches in the community. Many times those churches resented divided loyalty— especially since Alpha taught the validity of the baptism in the Holy Spirit. A pastor at a church within a few miles of Chapel Hill wrote a tract denouncing the baptism in the Holy Spirit and gave copies to his youth group to distribute at school. Several churches fired youth pastors who had encouraged their kids to attend the meetings. These youth pastors were convinced that Alpha was not proselyting, and their own groups reaped the positive fruits of Alpha's emphasis on commitment and lifestyle. At local high schools, Chapel Hill Harvester Church became known as the "Alpha Church." The subject generated hot classroom debates among students and faculty as everyone seemed eager to voice strong opinions on the subject.

People often wondered about the secret to Alpha's success. Was it the music? The charismatic leadership? The peer group acceptance? A writer with the *Atlanta Journal and Constitution* wrote a scathing article entitled "The Alpha Imperative" that focused on the opinions of disgruntled critics of the ministry. Instead of hurting Alpha's popularity and effectiveness, the article solidified Alpha's support among teens who were experiencing love, acceptance and the most positive understanding of life they had ever known. The controversy also brought more kids to the church to investigate Alpha for themselves.

Earl plowed through the community and media attention focused on the youth ministry with characteristic boldness. He knew well that spiritual breakthroughs inevitably generated warfare—the book of Acts all over again! Alpha was a genuine move of God, one important facet of a comprehensive heavenly vision. The danger now focused on the "youth movement" becoming a separate cause from the primary thrust of the church. This problem always killed the purposes of God in channeling youth energy and spiritual zeal. Alpha's impact and influence were undeniably supernatural, but careful discernment in the raging storm surrounding it was essential to producing lasting fruit. Meanwhile, hundreds of families and adults with a burden for youth ministry joined the church.

The drug problem diminished at the high school

which prompted parents to pray for solutions months before. The school was the only one in the area to undergo the racial shift from predominantly white to black students without violence. Bible studies began meeting every morning in local schools where students prayed for peace among their peers and wisdom for those in authority over them. Teenagers began to understand evangelism as a lifestyle witness—an individual commitment to responsible Christianity.

An economic recession in the mid-70's slowed the building boom in south DeKalb for the rest of the decade. Wealthy investors who continued to build throughout the recession labeled the south DeKalb area as unstable for construction development. They predicted an inevitable population shift from white to black residents. Over several months, two south DeKalb high schools required police protection for their students after racial riots broke out on school parking lots. Suddenly residential families felt threatened by violence.

Families moved in panic, justifying racial prejudices with excuses such as "fearing for their children's safety" or concern for "quality education." People posted "For Sale" signs in their front yards throughout the well-manicured neighborhoods. One black family moving into a neighborhood surfaced prejudices in white families living up and down the street. Beautiful homes in the area sold well below the market value of identical houses in other areas of Atlanta.

Having already come through area transitions and with firm assurance from the Lord, the Harvesters disregarded ridiculous scare tactics and rumors that caused others to sell out. Several established families in the area, those owning thriving businesses or involved in some of the other larger churches in the community, also dug in their heels and refused to budge.

Private schools sprang up overnight in south DeKalb—some even sponsored by area churches— with the purpose of maintaining racial segregation. Within a five-year period, the black student population in one school grew from twenty to eighty-five percent. Many teachers and administrators also reacted to scare tactics by requesting transfers to other schools in the northern districts of the county. Transitions of personnel inevitably caused instability in neighborhood schools. Students reflected their parents' prejudices. People were either moving away or explaining to others the reasons they had decided to stay in south DeKalb.

Of course, Chapel Hill Harvester Church welcomed new neighbors with open arms and openly challenged those who didn't. Earl thanked God for years of preparation in leading his ministry to this location. The racial blending at Chapel Hill demonstrated hope to the surrounding community. In their panic and uncertainty, people carefully noted the church's positive declaration of racial unity and harmony. While political forecasters made gloomy predictions about the quality of life in south DeKalb, Chapel Hill Harvester Church burst with life, vision and plans to build new facilities to accommodate increasing crowds of people and expanding ministries.

In 1980, a young couple at Chapel Hill made an appointment with Earl to share their burden for the desperation of unwed pregnant women. After praying about the matter, Earl encouraged them to stay open to God's confirmation of their calling. The couple shared their home with one pregnant woman until her baby was born. Then they purchased a larger home near the church which they called *House of New Life*. The couple, along with their four small children, provided a family atmosphere surrounding young women until their babies were born. Labor support "mothers," women in the church, volunteered to walk with these mothers-to-be through childbirth classes, labor, delivery and the recuperation period after the baby arrived. Many other churches and ministries visited the *House of New Life* as a model for other homes for unwed mothers throughout the country.

The *House of New Life* ministry created the necessity of providing an adoption agency, *In His Care*. The agency was licensed by the State of Georgia in 1981. Initially, all babies for adoption came from residents at the *House of New Life*, but soon women living in their own homes contacted the ministry about selecting Christian families to raise their children. *In His Care* placed children in strong, verifiable Christian homes which demonstrated the love of the Lord as a first priority in family life.

Other ministries were born out of people's needs for restoration. Earl noted a group of men whom he discerned were still in bondage to homosexuality attending the services regularly. Many times Earl addressed the subject of homosexuality in his sermons, but instead of fiery condemnation of their lifestyle, he focused on Christ's restoration and liberating power to forgive and heal. A few of the men responded to the message by renouncing homosexuality completely. They submitted their lives to the spiritual authority of Chapel Hill's ministry.

A ministry to people directly affected by homosexuality as well as their families, *Challenge*, began meeting every Friday night. One of the men restored through Chapel Hill's ministry and his wife, whom he married at the church in 1981, led the group. *Challenge* provided individual counseling for inner healing, support group counseling and educational presentations. People desperately seeking help in coping with homosexuality began driving from distant cities to attend the meetings.

A member who was a recovered alcoholic and his wife began a ministry to others struggling to overcome alcohol and drug addictions. The *Overcomers* ministry began meeting every week to share the victories and struggles of chemically addicted individuals and their families. Many people came to *Overcomers* through the church's counseling ministry. *Overcomers* opened its ministry to halfway houses, hospitals and other community organizations. *Overcomers* also expanded its support group programs to include family members of the addicted, adult children of alcoholics, people under emotional stress, those desiring to quit smoking and overeaters—each group providing its own ministers whom God had restored and renewed in a church called to be a City of Refuge.

Other ministries under Human Services began simultaneously—a ministry to retarded and mentally ill patients in regional hospitals; nursing home visitation which provided a Sunday service every week; a ministry called *Living Waters* which provided food, transportation, clothes and practical help such as shopping, banking, etc. to disabled people confined at home; a *Prison Outreach* ministry offering counseling, tutoring, information and job placement help on release from prison.

The church also provided free counseling services which met a variety of needs. Spiritual counseling from the pastors on staff as well as academically trained counselors were available to people who needed spiritual and emotional help in addressing their problems— all without cost. Counseling services included financial, vocational, pre-marital, marital, personal growth, parent-child, inner-healing, sexual and deliverance counseling. Teams of volunteer telephone counselors ministered during Chapel Hill's television broadcasts as viewers called in their prayer requests or asked for information. The church also provided a full-time *Intercessory Prayer* ministry.

Other innovative ministries began at Chapel Hill including an *Artists Guild, Garden Guild, Political Action Group, International Relations, Friendship Force, Puppet Team, Literacy Action Group*, and even a businessmen's group, *The 300 Company*, which encouraged starting small profitable businesses to utilize entrepreneurial expertise in financing projects at the church.

Two specialized fellowship ministries also offered counseling and restoration by personally giving that special, caring touch of Jesus' love. *Super Saints* began as a fellowship for senior members of the Chapel Hill family. They sponsored monthly fellowship suppers, frequent bus trips to the mountains and the beach, fun activities such as talent shows, aerobics classes and 50th anniversary parties for their members. *Super Saints* also became a dependable volunteer corps. They often gave their time to mailouts and telephone counseling as well as providing "Spiritual Grandparents" to children in the church from broken homes, one-parent families, or children needing extra attention and love.

Hebron Singles ministry reached out to older singles—many who were divorced—with social activities, projects which included restoring an old house for their meetings, conferences, and close, loving relationships. *Hebron* also ministered to the children of single parents in fun activities, dramas and "family" days filled with physical/spiritual interaction of parents and children.

Hundreds of small fellowship groups began meeting throughout the church in members' homes each week. *Covenant Communities* filled the need for close, personal ministry and opportunities to form nurturing relationships that were often lost in large churches. Leading the way in the *Covenant Community* concept were *Alpha Covenant Communities*. *Alpha* divided young people into groups for individual ministry and discipleship training. The personal, one-to-one ministries had over 600 participants under the care of 140 elder disciples who led Bible studies and fellowship activities.

Alpha Covenant Communities gave an excellent opportunity to develop spiritual leadership among the youth in the church. Many young people began to realize that they were called into the ministry, so the Presbytery of the church selected a group of youth leaders as candidates for the *Timothy Program*. The *Timothy Program* aimed at training young men and women for full-time pastoral ministry. Besides actual ministry experiences working with pastors in hospital visitations, children's ministries, etc., various groups also traveled on evangelistic trips to Jamaica or to churches affiliated with Chapel Hill Harvester.

In 1980, the fledgling Publications Department of the church began publishing a monthly newspaper named *Harvest Time*. The newspaper recorded the rapid chain of events happening in the ministry as well as publishing selected sermons by Pastor Paulk. Pastors Don and Clariece Paulk wrote almost the entire publication in its early days which was mailed free to an ever-increasing mailing list of visitors and people responding through television outreach.

God abundantly answered Earl's concern for adequate pastoral care by sending a choice group of pastors who joined their hearts to the ministry of the Harvesters. Many of these pastors also brought highly technical, occupational skills as well as pastoral gifts for ministry. One pastor previously worked as a construction engineer; another was a successful real estate agent; another was a practicing dentist; another had been a high school teacher and coach. Several pastors had served previously as senior pastors in their own churches—one a long-time friend of the Paulks from an established Church of God family; another, a senior pastor with a particular burden for international outreach.

Members of the church were divided into groups under the watchful care of these pastors who gave the people the personal time and attention required of a good shepherd. Nine of the eighteen pastors comprising the Chapel Hill Harvester Church Presbytery served as shepherding pastors. Other members of the Presbytery either headed a specialized ministry or led a weekly teaching service—such as Lynn Mays and Sam Lalaian. Lynn and Sam ministered anointed spiritual gifts on Tuesday mornings at "Life and Growth in the Spirit," a dynamic prophetic ministry which expanded the calling of the ladies' prayer meeting.

As Earl Paulk shared his vision from God, the words became spiritual seeds scattered by the wind into the cultivated soil of numerous lives. The quickening of one man's promise from God into the hearts of many people is the mystery of the Holy Spirit stirring those who are "called" and "chosen" by God to do specific work for Him in the earth. The vision of Chapel Hill Harvester Church challenged men and women with pioneer spirits to lay down their lives to make an eternal difference by following God's Word and the leading of the Holy Spirit.

But in spite of repeated confirmations, a sure foundation, a spiritual vision unfolding before his eyes and
God's daily provisions to him, Earl Paulk was hardly
prepared for the full impact of God's calling on this
church. How could anyone understand fully the mission of this miracle sitting on a muddy hill on Flat
Shoals Road in south DeKalb County?

As Earl faithfully held to the hard lessons and painful preparation for the path where God had led him,
revelation from God's Word suddenly began to shake
Earl's long-held doctrines. His ministry would never be
built on popular consensus. Like a paradox in scripture, a man who loved to serve the Lord as "a peacemaker" felt himself on fire with the Word of truth
which cut, divided and shook God's people with bold
challenges. Earl opened his spirit to receive fresh
insights from God's altars. He spoke powerful
revelation—clear, direct, uncompromised. In order for
God's people to dwell in a dimension of righteousness,
peace and joy, they must first open their spirits to the
fire of Kingdom revelation.

The messenger was fearless behind the pulpit, yet he
often broke into tears in his office only minutes after he
had obediently admonished his people with "hard sayings." God demanded obedience from this messenger, a
demand to deny his emotions, preferences and natural
diplomatic tenderness. Earl Paulk proclaimed prophetic truth to his congregation as well as to his generation by television outreach. He boldly delivered the
truth God gave to him. Then he often heard the mes-

sages repeated back, leaving him feeling like a man listening objectively, wondering himself at the full meaning of God's revelation message to the Church. He was a reluctant prophet. He never sought the calling or the gift. The personal price of his calling was too great for him to have sought the gift. But Earl Paulk had learned obedience through the things he had suffered. And many people heard with joy the anointed, timely truth that the Spirit was speaking to the Church. A prophet of the Lord was preparing them— and himself—line upon line, precept upon precept—for world confrontations.

11

CHAPTER ELEVEN

The world was dark and quiet outside the bedroom window, a shadowy time just before daybreak. Earl opened his eyes still seeing the vision. The incredible dream struck him to the core of his being, still electrifying his mind and spirit, piercing his soul with resplendent light. His pillow was saturated. Even his ears were a reservoir collecting the tears he had wept uncontrollably. How could he ever explain what he had seen? What could be its meaning?

Behind his pulpit later that Sunday morning, he told the congregation about the vision. He said that he had stood before the throne of God experiencing "energy" and "creativity" as tangible substances. A rainbow surrounded God's throne, a spectacular spectrum in motion, swirling in distinct colors of emerald greens and royal blues in shades which blended together in vibrant, pulsating intensity. He had stood in a realm which permitted him to understand the universe, creation and God's absolute authority—not understanding in human concepts, but understanding in experience, understanding beyond communication through language and perceptions.

His voice broke often as he spoke. He stopped talking, wiped away tears, breathed deeply, swallowing emotion as he tried to continue relaying the vision. The message's impact filtered through the spirits of hundreds of people hearing it. Some thought the pastor was losing his mind. He needed a long rest, perhaps a retreat somewhere with time to pull his emotions together and face reality again. Others watched and listened to the preacher tell his incredible story as if they were viewing a program on television, wondering what sort of plot would unfold, who would emerge from this scene as the villain or the hero. Some people felt hostility rise within them. Why didn't he read scripture? Who did he think he was, substituting these emotional dramatics for a real sermon?

A few heard the message with quickening excitement—realizing with the preacher the correlation of his vision with John's on the Isle of Patmos. They didn't know the vision's meaning either, but it whetted their appetites with a foretaste of indescribable promises. The preacher's words were part of the puzzle, the vision, the undefined destiny of God's calling them individually and corporately in their generation. God had said to the preacher, "I will show you what is taking place so that you will understand." Then God had shaken him from a scene of magnificent, glowing virtue to a dark dimension of crying and groaning that caused him to feel almost unbearable grief. Under the heaviest emotional pain his soul had ever known, he awoke. Then God said to him, "Now I will give you understanding of the Revelation."

In the months that followed he searched, prayed, asked and repeated insights God spoke to him, unfolding the last book of the Bible, the Revelation of Jesus Christ, like a man miraculously receiving his sight after a lifetime of blindness. The Bible was a new book. Its meaning opened in richer, deeper truth than he had ever known before—not in any way changing foundational principles of repentance, salvation, baptism, etc., that established relationship with Christ—but adding immeasurable immediacy to every familiar scriptural principle. He talked with a God in "the now," no longer focusing on "futuristic" or "escapist" hope as the message of the Church. The possibilities of living today in a Kingdom mentality staggered his imagination and ignited his spirit with the urgency of its implications!

Pieces of the puzzle fit together quickly. The teaching he had done on "Body Life" launched ministries of restoration, deliverance from the bondages of Satan in people's lives. From "Body Life," God had directed Earl to teach "Spiritual Authority." For months he had preached "The Kingdom of God," sermons on the

Kingdom mind, Kingdom giving, a Kingdom spirit, Kingdom lifestyles.

The truth was really so simple, so obvious. God's "Kingdom" had a King. Somehow Church doctrines seemed to miss the significance of Christ the King, reigning on earth in dominion, authority and power, conquering world systems through His people. The Church was too busy singing about "cabins in gloryland," "flying away," and "getting to heaven." Many Christians hoped and prayed to hang onto their salvation until judgment day or until Jesus came to rescue them out of their troubles—whichever happened first. Now Earl asked people to consider how His Kingdom would come "on earth as it is in heaven." How would heaven and earth come into unity in the "culmination of all things"? What part did God's people play in this universal war of human history? Suddenly, mysteries began to unfold.

Every principle of scripture—the commission to live like Christ in the present world—took his mind to the Garden of creation to discover God's original purposes and intentions for creating man and woman. God's original plan had been to establish a kingdom to overtake the universal chaos which resulted from Lucifer's rebellion. That plan hadn't changed. God now cultivated a garden in the world called His Church. Since creation, world forces had struggled unceasingly against the fulfillment of God's plan, attempting to conceal the identity of God's people. Often even "the elect" were deceived. Jesus had come with one life-changing message, "The Kingdom of God is at hand!"

Jesus' ministry communicated and demonstrated a new order, a new breed of mankind with every truth necessary to establish a Kingdom theocracy on earth. Then Jesus commissioned His disciples to follow His example through the power of the Holy Spirit given to them at Pentecost.

Centuries of traditions, dogmas and doctrines had diluted Christ's commission so that the Church became a powerless and divided institution with no strategy for warfare, no recognizable generals and undisciplined, untrained soldiers. But the authority to fulfill God's plan waited, held in mystery, fully available for that one generation who would live out God's adequate witness by demonstrating His authority over world systems to powers and principalities. In every worldly kingdom—the arts, finance, sports, politics, education—God's people would demonstrate His alternative plan, offering the world a choice between light and darkness, truth and deception. That generation's witness would set the standard by which God could judge the world.

The "pearl of great price" was the Kingdom on earth, a costly treasure worth giving one's life away to purchase. Earl ate, drank, slept, talked and preached the Kingdom—the nowness of God, the reality of "God in the flesh" in His Church; Christ in us, the hope of glory. He pressed people to live out responsible Christianity as "manifest, bold sons and daughters" of the Kingdom. But proclaiming the Kingdom of God ignited the wrath of the opposing kingdom. Satan attacked the leadership of the Harvesters, generating widespread criticism throughout the church, stirring discord, disunity, misunderstanding and rebellion.

Many people left the church, questioning its calling, angry with its administrative decisions or disagreeing with the teaching they heard on national Israel, the "rapture" and man's responsibility in last day events. They wanted "God is love" sermons that emphasized "grace" instead of responsibility in daily living. Kingdom theology demanded total allegiance to Christ—allegiance calling for hard choices and self-sacrifice. Prophetic exhortation from elders warned Earl repeatedly not to look at the faces of people as he preached, but he often felt the same kind of hostility bounce back from his words as in the early days when he preached against racial prejudice. Some of the leadership—even family members—cautioned him against speaking things God told him to say.

People grumbled and complained. Any challenge to church traditions sparked friction, and the challenges were numerous. Teaching on spiritual authority struck harsh chords in many people. Some decided Earl wanted to be a dictator. He always received hostile letters after powerful Sunday sermons. But he refused to compromise the truth God would give him in the early morning hours when he prayed, or in the shower, which became one of his favorite places to converse with God.

Forces became more powerful, both for and against the ministry. Great ministers from around the world came to the church to confirm the mighty move of God among the Harvesters. John Meares from Washington,

D.C.; Benson Idahosa from Nigeria; one of America's greatest missionaries, T. L. Osborn, and his wife, Daisy; Dr. Judson Cornwall and his sister, Iverna Tompkins, both of whom moved to Atlanta and joined the church; Bishop Bob McAlister of Rio de Janeiro, a close friend of John Meares—all encouraged, exhorted and blessed the ministry. Approximately seventy-five to one hundred new members joined the church each month. The ministry now required thirteen full-time pastors and forty full-time staff personnel to meet the people's needs.

Ministries grew, expanded, developed leaders and prospered in spite of pockets of turmoil and strife. The warfare remained constant, requiring committed people to grow rapidly in spiritual maturity. Earl often taught that the mark of spiritual maturity was discernment. People who endured the subtle testing and sometimes violent shaking of attacks against the Harvester ministry became true leaders in God's army.

Many fell away—not necessarily from the Lord, but from the uncompromised calling on this church. The church's core took responsibility for Kingdom demonstration seriously. Deception crept into places of great influence. People who were "religious and sincere" sometimes left the ministry with their own little flocks following along behind them. Earl wept over them in intercession, but he refused to back up one step. A committed core endured. They grew stronger as God opened deeper revelation to them.

While inner turmoil raged and powerful anointing flowed in the weekly services, a nightmare gripped

311

Atlanta beginning in 1979. Black children, primarily young boys, were disappearing. Many were found dead days later, floating down a river or thrown in the underbrush of a wooded area. Black parents in the church shared their personal terror with Earl. Their children felt threatened; fear dominated their thoughts. The entire city lived under a strict curfew for children in public places.

Earl counseled distraught parents and children, but he became publicly involved in the "Missing and Murdered Children" cases at the request of the NAACP's president, Dr. Frazier Ben Todd. On February 14, 1981, Earl made a television appeal at the end of the *Harvester Hour* television program to the killer(s) of the Atlanta children. That day an advertisement had run in the *Atlanta Journal and Constitution* stating, "If you are responsible for the crimes against our children, this television appeal is to you. Watch Saturday, February 14, Channel 46, 11:00 p.m."

In a five-minute appeal, Earl offered himself to mediate communication between "the killer" and the police or the community. He told "the killer" that he knew a tormented mind suffered because of an inability to control violent actions. He assured "the killer" that the church could offer restoration and forgiveness—even a public platform to speak grievances—so that he could be helped. He pleaded with the perpetrator of the crimes to end the assaults tormenting the city.

The next day calls began coming from the supposed "killers." Many of the calls were obvious hoaxes. On February 16, Earl received a series of calls that never lasted more than a few seconds. The caller instructed him to go to a local television station for the 6:00 p.m. news broadcast. He went immediately, but no communication came to the station. Within a few hours, the same person called again, instructing Earl to go to another television station for the 11:00 p.m. broadcast. Again, there was no contact. At 11:30 a.m. the next day, the caller telephoned Earl saying that he was disappointed that he was not on camera during the news broadcast. Earl assured him that he had followed his instructions.

On a Sunday afternoon, Earl preached at a city-wide rally held at Chapel Hill at the request of the NAACP. His scriptural text was Ephesians 6, emphasizing the battle between God and powers and principalities, light and darkness. The next day during a staff meeting, a caller telephoned the church identifying himself as "the one Earl Paulk was trying to reach." Earl rushed to the telephone to speak with a very nervous man who hung up after only a few seconds, saying he would call back. Within an hour he called back, but refused to set a meeting time or place. He called a third time, still evasive about meeting with Earl.

Meanwhile, network news personnel contacted the church to ask whether any calls had been received in response to the appeal. They alerted the FBI who joined the news media in several weeks of constant surveillance of the church. The FBI took the reins in handling the calls, and news reporters stationed themselves at the church for any leads from the callers. On February 28, Earl made another appeal to the killer on

313

the *Harvester Hour* broadcast. The same caller talked with Earl for the last time only three days before the twentieth victim, thirteen-year-old Curtis Walker, disappeared. The child's body was found on March 6, caught on a log in the South River adjacent to the church property—one-fourth of a mile from the doors of the church.

Associated Press, United Press International and numerous national publications carried the story. Earl was interviewed by television reporters from all major networks, including *NBC Magazine* with David Brinkley. The ministry was bombarded with news reporters who were trying to fit together clues leading them to the murderer. Calls and letters poured into the church from Christians around the world who were praying over Atlanta. Chapel Hill scheduled an around-the-clock prayer vigil including other churches who interceded for a swift intervention for the crimes. The warfare was clearly kingdom against kingdom. Within a few months, a suspect was arrested in the cases and later convicted for committing two of the crimes with "incomplete but related" evidence in the other cases.

Many people battled the church for their efforts in appealing to the killer. Though Earl received overwhelmingly favorable response in letters and calls of gratitude to him for taking whatever action he could, he also received accusations from people who believed he was trying to become an overnight celebrity by capitalizing on the plight of murdered children. The critics' perspective was tragic, but the implications of their complaints uncovered serious attitudes that stretched

314

beyond a single issue. Many people—both Christians and non-Christians—resented a pastor who took social action in challenging life and death situations. Society would never trust a church which assumed more than a passive, peaceful, "Santa Claus" role toward social problems.

Kingdom against kingdom warfare inevitably caused conflicts and misunderstandings. Earl often reminded people that Jesus' proclamation that He was "a king" led Him to the cross. Society welcomed a church's social benevolences of providing food, clothing and shelter to people. They even tolerated reports of healings and miracles with skepticism and scorn. But once God's people began to touch world systems with Kingdom authority, they must prepare to give their lives in confrontation.

Bill Hamon, an anointed prophet of God, visited the church in the summer of 1981. Earl called the staff and church leaders together in a special service to open their spirits to God's prophetic direction. For several hours the Spirit of the Lord spoke over individual leaders in confirmations and exhortation. The prophecy was thrilling and timely, yet in many ways unsettling to Earl since it pressed him to take bold directions. To Earl the Lord said:

"The Lord would say to you, 'My son, I called you in your early days. I called you to grow. I said, "I'll make an oak tree out of him and not a blowing sapling that bends with the wind." I began to work with you, My son, and I dealt with you and I shook you to the right and to the left. I limited you so that you could not go and run with the crowd. You could not understand in those early days why you were not one of the bunch; why you didn't fit and flow as the others did; why there was a call; why there was a zeal; why there was a seriousness about you that others didn't understand. You didn't run with them in lightness and frivolity. But there was a hunger for God to be glorified and for God to give the anointing that flowed in your life. You said, "God, there's more . . . there's more . . . there's more . . ." A hunger in your soul and a longing in your heart was birthed in those days.

'And you said, "God, how can this ever be? How can this be fulfilled?" And in your church affiliation at that time, you did not see how it could be fulfilled.'

"Then the Lord said, 'I've released you. I've opened the heavens before you and given you unlimited opportunity.' And now the Lord is saying, 'Son, I've brought you to a place. There's no ceiling over your head and no bounds around your area. I've given you unlimited opportunities to reach out, bless My people, build My work and establish My Kingdom in the hearts and lives of men and women.'

"And the Lord says, 'Son, I'm going to bring you forth like never before. I've worked on other churches and other people. I've worked in other places, but they haven't been faithful or followed through. But I'm going to use you. I've taken you through the fire. I've brought you through the flood. I've taken you through the winter, into the summer and through the spring.'

"The Lord says, 'Son, I've killed the self-ego. I've killed the kingdom-building attitude in you, and you've come to the place to build My Kingdom—to build My work and do My ministry.'

"And the Lord says, 'I'm going to open up new doors beyond your wildest imagination, and you have a big mind and a big understanding. But you've seen nothing yet to what I'm going to show you can be done! I'm about to bring a new revelation to the Body of Christ, and I've prepared your spirit. I've made a Joshua-Caleb spirit out of you, and you're going to lead My people into the promised Canaan Land! You're going to lead men to the fruitful land, bring forth My glory, establish My people, build My work and possess the promised possessions.

'You'll be like Caleb of old. You'll say, "Yea, though I'm this age, yet I'm still as strong as any young person in my church. I'll go in and possess the land. I will build the work of the Lord." '

"And the Lord says, 'Son, I'm going to release a greater working of miracles in your life, like the signs of the Apostle Paul, signs and wonders. I've called you and told you over and over again—in your spirit—I've put an apostolic mantle to build and establish My work in the land and address My ministers.'

"You've said, 'I don't want to promote myself or exalt my office. They will recognize me when it's time.'

"And the Lord says, 'Son, it's time! Hallelujah! You're going to come to the place that you're not self-conscious about giving glory and honor to the position I've called you. You won't exalt yourself. You won't promote your position, but you won't be ashamed or self-conscious about it either. You will know that you are what you are by the grace of God. You'll say like the Apostle Paul, "I am what I am! By the grace of God, I'm an apostle called to build and establish the Church." '

"The Lord says, 'Son, the apostles and prophets established the church in the beginning, and the apostles and prophets will put the finishing touches on it. I've reserved and saved you for this day and hour that you might bring My Church to maturity—that you might bring them to function.

'There's going to be fingers go out from this place. It's going to expand and extend. If you'll remain humble and guard My people and keep your ministries pure and humble . . . if you'll correct, straighten out, line up, cover and protect, preserve and love them, I'll cause them to stand beside you. I'll weed them out, and bring others in who have no desire but to build My kingdom . . . no ego or self-promotion, but desire to glorify My name.

'You've said, "Lord, give me men like that . . ." and I've given them to you. They will stand beside you and My work will be built! Hallelujah!' "

Then Bill Hamon turned to the staff and added:

"I saw something in the Spirit that I should pass on to you. God has called this man to build a work in this area that others have tried and failed. But I saw in the Spirit, any co-laborers with him who rise with personal ambition, getting resentful, feeling they don't have enough recognition—bigger and greater than people are allowing them to be—God is going to move them out and move someone else in. If you are going to demonstrate the Kingdom of God, you must develop a servant attitude . . . not seeking for position or power. Forget position and power. If you've got it, live up to it. But if you don't, don't worry about it. Just flow!" (To Earl Paulk) "I've sensed some key brethren here that God has given to you. There will be one or two who will stick their heads up, and God will have to shoot it off for them!"

Bill Hamon prophesied over Norma Paulk about reactivating ministry gifts in her life as well as the battles she waged in praying for her husband. The prophecy also said:

". . . You're going to travel with him. He's going to start

traveling more in days to come. He's going to go out and establish those who are struggling in little works, and the apostolic ministry shall go. He'll stand and preach and teach and prophesy, but you'll prophesy, too . . . I saw you stand with your husband. There are going to be little branch churches develop out of this church. He's going to go out and you're going to go with him to lay hands on pastors and elders, ordain them and set them in the work as God prophesies over them . . ."

Archbishop Benson Idahosa from Nigeria visited the church in the fall of 1981. God had given him one phrase to speak to the Harvesters, "It is done!" He told the Chapel Hill congregation that within three years their sanctuary would be used for Sunday School and children's church. But "It is done" was God's contingent promise to covenant people. If the Harvesters were learning anything from consistent Kingdom teaching, they knew that God's promises required obedience and faith. Earl believed that Abraham, the father of the household of faith, was possibly one of many whom God called into covenant promise. The difference between Abraham and other men was that he both heard and obeyed God.

God gave Earl a simple plan to share with the people to bring them into covenant obedience: On Fridays, the church would fast until the evening meal and pray for the ministry. They would wear a round rainbow pin to symbolize their covenant with God as an outward witness to the world—the pin had a "K" at its center representing the Kingdom of God. Covenant people would give an additional ten percent of their incomes as well as the tithe. Earl suggested a special day of

319

giving every tenth Sunday to allow people to give one week's salary to God on that special day of giving, but many people preferred simply giving twenty percent on a weekly basis.

Earl asked God to give him a way to express his own covenant in addition to leading the people in obedience. He was prepared to shave his head, grow a beard, even go naked as Jeremiah had done if God required that from him! Instead, God showed him an area of prejudice in the Church which was seldom addressed that would further stretch the Harvesters as a bridge ministry. As Earl sat at a traffic light, he saw a priest standing on the corner. God spoke to Earl, "Wear a clerical collar to confront conservative prejudices toward the ecclesiastical branch of the Church." How clearly Earl recalled attending camp meetings in his youth where the preacher was sure to get people stirred up if he criticized ministers who "wore their collars backwards." Other pastors on the Harvester Presbytery joined Earl in wearing clerical collars as well as full vestments to serve the Eucharist. Inevitably, the collars caused fundamentalists' blood to boil!

The Sunday congregation was overflowing, bursting at the seams. Charles Bonner led a work crew to knock out the back walls of the sanctuary to double its seating capacity. Still people packed into the building, filling the chairs along the back wall the first Sunday they opened the new section. The Harvesters also built a gymnasium with a kitchen and classroom space surrounding the gym floor which they named the "Paulk Activities Building." Within a few weeks the additional classrooms were also too crowded to accommodate all the children comfortably. The ministry purchased seventy-four acres of land adjacent to their own in 1980 where they proposed to build a new sanctuary and other facilities for ministry.

The construction crew also worked on reconstructing existing space into offices for pastors and staff. The prayer chapel was divided into three offices. Every storage closet now contained a desk, a telephone and bookshelves. The staff and the building grew, even adding trailers for offices and storage. Crowds packed the pews to overflowing—chairs in the aisles and out the open doors into the halls leading into the sanctuary for two services on Sunday mornings. Sunday nights' overflow crowds watched the evening service on a television monitor set up in the choir room.

Earl's family also continued to grow. God had promised to give him seven grandsons. Six grandsons were already born, and two daughters, Beth and Joy, were pregnant. Both daughters were hoping to have a girl. One Saturday night Earl had a strange dream in which he kept calling the name "Penny" which connected in his spirit with a biblical name, "Peniel," where Jacob wrestled with God. The name meant, "I have seen God face to face, yet my life has been spared."

During the morning sermon, Earl's spirit quickened when he saw Beth sitting in the congregation. "Beth, God has given me a name for your baby. Study Genesis 32 where Jacob wrestled with God." Later that afternoon, Earl called Beth and told her that her baby should be named "Peniel" or "Penny." He laughed,

"I've never heard of a boy named 'Penny,' have you?" God told Earl that this child would be one of that generation who would see God face to face. Penielle Brooke Bonner (called Penny Brooke), the little cheerleader among all the Paulks' grandsons, was born in March 1982. A beautiful son, John David Owens, was born to Joy and Steve in October—a child whom God had promised would have an extraordinary gift of joy.

God kept saying, "Build My Church!" to Earl's spirit. He led the congregation to a large field on the property for "ground breaking" one Sunday morning in which he combined the two morning services into one service for that special day. They had begun the service at the sanctuary by writing out their covenants with God on flat sticks which they burned as an offering to God at the proposed building site. The people followed Earl and Norma, Don and Clariece, the Presbytery and staff in a joyful procession, singing, waving tree branches. In a breathtaking blessing from God, the people looked up into a clear, blue sky to see a perfectly formed rainbow around the sun! Everyone saw it—a miracle—as God responded to their covenant with Him by a sign in the heavens.

But crossing the Red Sea and manna from heaven didn't necessarily make God's people obedient. Earl fought ridiculous battles and accusations—making him weary with trivial matters which constantly diverted his attention from the real issues at stake. When God's direction seemed most clear, people would get distracted by some minor skirmish which would blow up to major proportions, always causing "little ones" to stumble and fall. Financial giving was sporadic—commitment to God one week and new cars, clothes or vacations the next. Leadership battles raged continuously. Some people asked, "Does God only speak to Moses?" Every ministry decision resulted in a leadership tug-of-war to decide who was in control— winners and losers. Earl hated heavy-handed decisions which people pressed him to make. Was this the promised vision? Where was the demonstration? Why fight the very soldiers God had commanded him to lead?

He would leave these people and start again. Somewhere, someone would understand the vision from God, deny themselves and do God's will. Bishop Bob McAlister visited the church in the fall of 1982 and recognized Earl's weariness from the first moment he saw him. Earl told the Bishop from Brazil that he would submit a drastic decision to him concerning the future of the church. He was willing—even wanting— to lay it all down and walk away. He was also willing to stay and fight to the end if God only required endurance from him. Either way, he must know immediately. God had trusted him with revelation that some people, somewhere, must implement.

In the second Sunday morning service, Bishop McAlister called Earl Paulk to the platform. He said to the congregation, "God wants a bishop in this place." Bishop McAlister laid his hands on Earl Paulk's head to commission him to the office of bishop—a biblical term meaning an overseer of the universal Church, one who assumes responsibility for the welfare of other leaders and their parishes. The Chapel Hill Harvester Presbytery surrounded their Bishop who sat in the chair crying like a baby. His weariness lifted as even greater responsibility covered him like a mighty mantle. Underneath all the discouraging conflicts in the church, God saw open hearts, fertile ground in a hidden core of people dispersed among hundreds of others who sat together in the congregation watching a new Bishop cry.

In November 1982, Chapel Hill Harvester Church hosted its first national pastors' conference, Atlanta '82, attended by over three hundred pastors from forty-eight states and three foreign countries. Bishop Paulk, Iverna Tompkins and Dr. Judson Cornwall shared insights into their ministries with visiting pastors in straightforward question and answer sessions. Afternoon sessions of the conference "showcased" the ministries of Chapel Hill in informal, multi-media demonstrations presented by the leaders of each ministry.

Visiting pastors were especially interested in observing Chapel Hill's successful youth ministry which played "Christian rock" music, the innovative worship with versatile modes of expressive adoration to God, and various specialized restoration ministries. Many of the pastors attending the conference returned to their churches with new thrusts in their messages. A conference at Chapel Hill Harvester Church guaranteed ample servings of spiritual meat that required months to chew and digest. Pastors called, wrote and visited the church daily, asking Earl Paulk to serve as their Bishop in counseling, direction and spiritual covering.

Powerful revelation in Earl's messages seemed to trigger physical attacks in his body. He battled chronic kidney stones for several years, many times preaching in excruciating pain. He held on to the pulpit, drenched in cold sweat while he defied satanic oppression through diligent faith and endurance. He boldly delivered the messages God had given to him many times during long, agonizing nights of prayer for physical strength.

Earl and Norma flew to Rio de Janeiro in January 1983, to visit Bishop Bob McAlister's church. Earl and John Meares were speakers there at an international pastors' conference. Earl was amazed at observing the poverty and spiritual oppression of Rio—a place of rapidly climbing economic inflation. The city exemplified a study in extremes—opulent wealth in some sections contrasting with destitute living conditions of cave dwellers in the mountains surrounding the city.

On a Wednesday night shortly after Earl and Norma returned to Atlanta from Rio, he became very sick. He felt all the symptoms of a virus—fever, nausea, abdominal pain. He battled through the flu symptoms into the weekend, but by Friday afternoon he began to suspect the attack was more serious. As the pain increased, Earl prayed for the strength to preach on Sunday. Only by God's overcoming grace and power, he preached both Sunday morning services as well as Sunday night—refusing to give in to the illness by asking an associate pastor to substitute for him. At the evening service he brought a message concerning the relationship between Jacob and Esau—Jacob's spirit of finally humbling himself before his brother to bring peace between them. Earl pressed the people to make eternal decisions regarding ambition or humility, a choice of conflicting kingdoms affecting every relationship and life choice.

Later at home, Earl continued to fight almost unbearable pain. He called a urologist, Dr. David Rowland, to describe the symptoms and ask for help. Dr. Rowland ordered him to go to the hospital immediately. He was admitted to Decatur Hospital about 2:00 a.m. and was given medication to dull the pain enough so that he could fall asleep.

Early the next morning, Steve Owens accompanied the nurse taking Earl to X-ray. Dr. Rowland informed Earl that a kidney stone the diameter of a nickel had lodged three or four inches into a tube leading to his bladder. The size and location of the stone made surgery their only option. The doctor ordered intravenous feeding for Earl to receive continuous fluids and antibiotics. Earl assured the doctor that he submitted fully to his authority in medical decisions, but then he asked the doctor, "What are the possibilities that this stone could move one way or the other?" Dr. Rowland smiled at his patient, knowing that Earl Paulk also submitted to a higher authority.

"It would take divine intervention," the doctor answered. "I'll be praying that by Thursday we'll have a good report." The surgery was scheduled for early Thursday morning.

Earl asked again, "Are you saying that avoiding

surgery would require a miracle?"

The doctor smiled as he replied, "Yes, Bishop Paulk, it would be a miracle if that stone moved."

The church prayed continually for the Bishop's health. Pastors came by the hospital to minister to him personally and a continuous prayer vigil was held at the church. Earl continued to follow the doctor's orders. The pastors and elders of the church met on Tuesday night to pray in unity for God's will in waging this warfare. One of the elders asked if anyone had a sure word from God concerning the situation. Lynn Mays spoke up, "I believe I have the mind of Christ in this matter. God wants to do a miracle—to raise up the Bishop at this particular time as a Kingdom witness." The elders prayed in agreement for that miracle to occur.

Earl went back to X-ray on Wednesday morning to determine the precise location of the stone for surgery. A nurse briefed Earl on the surgical procedure and the necessary preparations for the operation the next day. On Wednesday afternoon, an anesthesiologist gave him specific details on the physical aspects of surgery: the extensive incision around his side, the removal of the stone which he said would be like "bobbing for apples," the duration of pain and soreness he could expect, the weeks of recovery time without any physical movement at all.

Because Earl had experienced no pain for several days, he knew that the stone had not moved. He listened to the details of the surgery and for the first time realized the full consequences of this attack—at a time when his calling was urgently necessary in fulfilling God's promises to the Harvesters. The door to his room opened and his sister, Darlene Swilley, marched into the room like a woman going to war. She gave her brother a scripture, Psalms 20:6. According to Darlene, God had taken note of his anointed and would deliver him. Darlene insisted, "I don't care what you have heard or anyone has said. Even if you go to the door of the operating room, you will not undergo surgery!" Earl quietly praised the Lord for Darlene's proclamation.

Around six o'clock, Dr. Rowland walked into the room smiling at his patient. "You're not having any pain are you, Pastor?"

Earl answered quietly, "No, sir."

"Well, you can get up out of bed, put on your clothes and go to church tonight." Dr. Rowland looked directly at the Bishop. "I don't claim to be a prophet, but God says that I should tell you that He has something for you to say to those people tonight. God is releasing you to go and do that!" The kidney stone had miraculously traveled up the tube back into the kidney—harmless for the moment or perhaps forever.

Earl walked into the Wednesday night service while Don was leading the people in prayer for his condition. The Bishop slipped quietly to the pulpit as people were praying. When they opened their eyes, he stood before them smiling—not unlike Peter's release from prison. He shared with them the lessons he had learned in this test: relaxing in the Spirit as Kingdom righteousness, peace and joy replaced the natural inclination to fear;

receiving ministry from the Body of Christ in intercession and encouragement; allowing faith to work in his
physical body by knowing the will of God. Earl prayed
for God to give him and his church the grace to handle
this miracle with proper gratitude.

That Thursday Earl met with the church staff to
thank them for their love and support throughout the
physical test. On Friday, he felt impressed to wash the
feet of the Presbytery. He knew that they were the key
to solving internal warfare battling the ministry. Their
unity created an impenetrable wall against satanic
attacks. When the pastors were seated, Earl began to
share his most vulnerable feelings about the calling of
God on their church to be a prophetic voice to the Body
of Christ. He reminded them that John the Baptist had
preached the Kingdom, Jesus had come as a demonstration of that Kingdom, and now the Bride of Christ
must come to maturity and power—in both communication and demonstration—to bring Christ to earth as
King of kings and Lord of lords. As Earl began to wash
the pastors' feet, Don got a towel and began to wash
their feet also. A special unity of spirit bonded all the
Harvester leaders like never before—perhaps a greater
miracle than a physical one.

Another physical battle also raged that year. Joan
Harris had been diagnosed as having lymphoma during the summer of 1981. Earl had received a promise
from God that Joan would not die in that test—a promise he shared with Joan's husband and children. They
had sought direction from God together about treatment for the disease. For over a year Joan had under-

gone chemotherapy, steroid injections in her joints and regular hospitalization. Her physical attacks correlated exactly with specific attacks on the ministry—a correlation which Earl knew had spiritual significance to the warfare over the church and the lessons God was teaching the Harvesters about body life, obedience and spiritual covering.

Joan had begun working on the staff at the same time Donnie left General Motors to work in television. Joan's primary responsibility was to coordinate the schedules and appointments for all the shepherding pastors. Earl kept Joan close to him, sharing the ministry's daily victories and trials. He continued to protect her in the role he had assumed in her life since she was a baby—father, brother and closest confidant.

Joan's suffering especially related to the burden and goals of her most fervent prayers—the outreach of Chapel Hill Harvester Church. Whenever Earl began to question the ministry's vast financial commitment to television and publications, Joan was the first one to respond with unshakable affirmation of its priceless value. The messages God was speaking to the church, the vision God had given her brother, must be shared with the world if they were to follow God's mandates in responsible covenant with Him. Joan fully understood the price—financially, physically, spiritually. She grasped in demonstration the reality of overcoming faith—by the blood of the Lamb, the word of her testimony and loving not her life unto death.

In March of 1983, Earl, Norma, Don and Clariece, Harry and Myrtle Mushegan, Darlene Swilley and

John and Mary Lee Meares from Washington, D. C., flew to Benin City, Nigeria, for meetings with Archbishop Benson Idahosa. Bishop Bob McAlister and his wife, Gloria, also met the other pastors in Africa. The trip was an experience in cultural shock. They arrived in Monrovia to change planes after a harrowing landing which Don Paulk later described as "coming down stairsteps, dropping a few feet at a time."

Next they arrived in Lagos. They descended from the plane into a wall of hot, humid air which left them breathless. The taxicab ride to the domestic airport, where they would board Nigerian Airways for Benin City was, according to Don Paulk, "demolition derby time!" Don described the domestic airport as "a room that resembled the chute at the rodeo where they release wild animals." Soldiers with machine guns lined the walls, assuring that the tourists would follow orders not to take pictures. They were served hot Cokes while they sat on couches under one ceiling fan. Clariece and Darlene felt very ill and stretched out on the sofas.

Suddenly, Earl felt the grip of now familiar pain—a kidney stone attack! The heat, filthy bathrooms, armed guards surveying a boisterous crowd and sickening stench in the air were enough to cause nausea and semi-shock, but the prospects of African hospitalization sent the group into serious prayer in Earl's behalf. Dr. Rowland had warned Earl against making the trip because of the primitive medical facilities. By the time they finally boarded the plane for Benin City, the pain had subsided significantly, confirming again that the physical battle was symptomatic of insidious spiritual warfare.

The African services were worth any risk or inconvenience. Earl felt such a responsibility toward the hundreds of people who were packed close together on backless, wooden benches, listening intently to the speakers share Kingdom insights. Many wore wool suits in the stifling hot weather—clothes some had received from America. Everyone wore their best church clothes to honor the Lord and their guests.

One afternoon during the conference, the pastors baptized at a river in the region. They rode in a truck as far as they could, then walked the rest of the way to the river along jungle paths. They passed people living in primitive huts, centuries behind life in the cities. Naked children followed the pastors, curious at the invasion of these strangers, some observing Clariece as if they had never seen a white woman before. Hundreds of Africans participated in the holy sacrament at the river.

After the Nigerian conference ended, the group flew to Rome and London before crossing the Atlantic. John Meares, a veteran traveler, served as tour guide for the group of novice jet-setters. In Rome they were welcomed by Bishop Meares' friend, Pastor Silvano Lilli, a Pentecostal pastor with a growing church in the most predominantly Catholic city in the world.

Earl shared his travel experiences upon his return to Atlanta by underscoring the responsibility of the Harvesters in becoming "a storehouse" to supply the needs of the Body of Christ around the world. The "storehouse" concept called for people who understood responsibility for abundance of talents, resources and blessings from God. Again, the Bishop pressed his people to give sacrificially out of their abundance to support the work of the Kingdom in places needing provisions.

Since the Harvesters were shopping for new television equipment, Earl asked the television department to put signs on the equipment they were using which said, "Going to Brazil." Rather than selling the cameras to another ministry, Earl felt impressed by the Lord to give the equipment to a ministry needing to broadcast the gospel of the Kingdom to reach their nation. Many times when the Harvesters faced great financial straits, Earl took up special offerings for other ministries in need. This practical application of Kingdom giving, interpreted by some to be irrational generosity, sometimes brought a flood of complaint letters to Earl's office on Monday morning. But inevitably and unexpectedly, God always honored obedience in giving. However, one of Earl's greatest weaknesses was his tendency to give things away. People constantly tried to help him overcome this "character flaw" by pointing out the realities of the high costs of ministry.

Two Sunday morning services failed to accommodate the increasing crowds. Scheduling three services on Sunday mornings would not only be physically taxing on Earl and the other ministers, but also escalate current problems with parking space, traffic jams and child care. They already scheduled Sunday lunch in the activities building for the staff since they arrived at church at 8:30 a.m. and remained through morning services which didn't end until 1:30 in the afternoon. Sunday afternoons provided barely enough time to drive home, change clothes and arrive back at church by 6:00 p.m.

Financial inconsistency in weekly givings and the costs of outreach and service ministries made launching a building program almost impossible. The financial commitment to outreach ministries continuously tested the calling of the church. Earl sought the Lord for solutions. He called together pastors and church leaders with building expertise for consultation. While skilled architects drew elaborate plans for a sanctuary costing millions of dollars, an associate pastor, Dan Rhodes, began to contact tent makers to provide a temporary covering for the people until the new structure could be built. In May 1983, the congregation moved into the big blue tent, erected on the parking lot beside the old sanctuary, just in time for the Sunday evening service. The seating capacity of the tent was 2,300—with people sitting on folding, metal chairs. The tent was filled to capacity the first night.

Gospel music legends Dottie and Buck Rambo came to Chapel Hill with their daughter, Reba, and son-in-law, Dony McGuire, who won both the Grammy and Dove Awards for their album *The Lord's Prayer* in 1981. The family ministered as the Harvesters' guests the first night in the tent. Dottie had visited the ministry alone in 1981, then brought the rest of the family with her to Chapel Hill regularly, even coming for a

"Rambo Reunion" on a New Year's Eve Watch Night service.

Because the Harvesters sang numerous Rambo-McGuire songs, Clariece knew the Lord had answered her prayers by joining the spirits of those who understood the impact of witnessing through the kingdom of the arts. The Rambos and McGuires were immediately embraced as Chapel Hill "family" members. Dony and Reba, who lived in Los Angeles but spent most of their time traveling from church to church across the country in gospel music evangelism, asked Bishop Paulk (whom they called "Uncle Earl" after spending time with Duane) to be their spiritual covering. The young couple needed loving restoration. The McGuires claimed Chapel Hill as their home church. They regularly scheduled flight layovers in Atlanta to refresh their spirits whenever they ministered on the east coast. Meanwhile, Chapel Hill sent Dony and Reba videotapes of the services each week—the messages which became the source of some of the most powerful, anointed, contemporary Christian music written to edify the modern Church.

Shortly after moving into the tent, Chapel Hill hosted a conference with the College of bishops as its guests. Bishop Meares, Bishop McAlister and Archbishop Idahosa were joined by Bishop Herro Blair from Jamaica, Bishop Tito Almeida, who came with Bishop McAlister from Brazil, and Bishop-elect Harry Mushegan. The "Thy Kingdom Come" conference provided the people at Chapel Hill with a firsthand understanding of the International Communion of Churches to which Bishop Paulk had been consecrated. This new spiritual network of ministry with a world-wide vision of the Kingdom of God emerged from traditional church structures to bring spiritual unity to diverse branches of the ecclesiastical Body of Christ around the world. The College of Bishops also provided Earl access to eldership for counsel and covering to which he gratefully submitted his own ministry.

The "Thy Kingdom Come" conference opened the tangible reality of Chapel Hill Harvester's world outreach. In a dramatic demonstration of ministry following the Holy Spirit's leading, Bishop Bob McAlister released the television equipment promised to Brazil to Bishop Herro Blair's church in Jamaica. Since Jamaica had only one television station, Bishop Blair's broadcast had the potential of reaching the entire island with the Kingdom message. A television crew from Chapel Hill later flew to Kingston, Jamaica, to set up the equipment and train people to use it.

An important event was scheduled to coincide with the meeting of the College of Bishops. Chapel Hill Harvester Church honored Bishop Paulk in a celebration of consecration at the Marriott Grand Ballroom attended by over five hundred people. Each visiting bishop extended his congratulations. Earl Paulk addressed the banquet guests by reflecting on the foundations of his ministry which resisted rigid religious traditions and denominational barriers.

Earl Paulk told the guests, "I make no apology for the things God has done in my life and ministry. The last thing I ever dreamed of becoming was a bishop.

But now we are beginning to see what God meant all the time. This work is a light beaming as a testimony to the gospel of the Kingdom. This is a new day of life, vision and hope. We are a new breed of people. We are God's hand of love reaching out to the Body of Christ and to the world."

Special blessings occurred in the life of another family member as well. After agonizing months of treatment, Joan's cancer had gone into remission. The hair she had lost through treatments grew back thick, salt and pepper gray, making Joan's appearance more stunning than ever. But the beauty of her spirit was captivating. Just talking with her about casual, ordinary events of the day was an uplifting sermon. She had walked through the fire and not only survived the physical ordeal, but also grew with such spiritual depth that she became a witness to others of God's faithfulness. She was a paradox—fragile and strong, soft-spoken and bold, peaceable and uncompromising.

Earl moved Joan closer to his office, allowing her to work on the financial records of the church at her own pace—which was often hectic. Earl ordered Joan to go home to rest whenever he detected her laboring under stress or weariness. Joan's dedication to the ministry made supervision of her work schedule a difficult task. The Bishop was grateful for the victorious results in Joan's favorable medical reports, but he was cautious in his optimism. By the Spirit, he knew the battle over Joan's life persisted. Several times he shared a "knowing in his spirit" concerning the warfare over Joan in guarded confidence to ones he trusted to understand

and pray in faith for her.

God also gave the Bishop a medical miracle in his own body. For the first time in the Harvester ministry, Earl scheduled two weeks of vacation for himself, one week of which he intended to spend with the entire family at Daytona Beach. The kidney attacks continued to be a perpetual problem, unpredictable and physically debilitating. Dr. Rowland informed Earl of a new surgical procedure—performed at only two hospitals in the country—using lasers to make the incision and "blast" the stones into small particles.

Earl was admitted to a hospital in Atlanta for the first week of his summer vacation. The surgery was simple—a miracle compared to the only medical alternative available just a few months earlier. Lynn Mays had prophesied that "a ray of light" would end the problem with kidney stones long before the laser technique was known or available. With a small closed incision in his side, he left the hospital two days after the surgery and flew to Daytona with Norma to join the daughters, their husbands and all the grandchildren playing on the beach.

But this vacation was not significant for simply allowing family time, relaxation and recuperation from surgery. Earl had dreamed a strange dream which was working in his spirit with the impact of momentous, unshakable impressions. In the dream he found himself at the old St. John's Lutheran Church on Euclid Avenue in Inman Park. The church building was in shambles: boarded windows, no pews or musical instruments. People were milling about in total disorder. Earl asked God what he should say to these people. He opened his Bible looking for sermon notes when the Lord spoke to him saying, "Close your Bible. Son of man! Prophesy!"

For over an hour he preached prophetically in the dream, quoting Psalm 41 verbatim. The message was on the wounded Body of Christ, wounded from within by ". . . my own familiar friend, who did sit at the table with me." The sermon he preached insisted that the attacks on the Body of Christ were not from the world, but from Christian brothers warring against each other.

Earl returned to his pulpit to preach a five-sermon series that marked a turning point in the ministry. He began with a sermon called "The Wounded Body of Christ," and the series went on to explore the prophetic ministry, the priesthood of Jesus as a Restorer, and the meaning of the Lord's table as a place of either unity or purging. He ended the series with a sermon called "The Glorified Church," describing that mature Bride who welcomes the King. The series was transcribed immediately for publication and then distributed to pastors attending the second pastors' conference, Atlanta '83, in October. *The Wounded Body of Christ* became a book of great influence in other restoration ministries across the nation.

The dream marked a turning point in Earl's own spirit. Never again would he feel uncomfortable with his calling as a prophetic voice to the Church. He told the congregation, "In the dream that God gave me, I learned something very important. Chapel Hill Har-

vester Church in Atlanta, Georgia, is correctly called a
City of Refuge. As a City of Refuge, we have ministered
to the injured who have been left dying by the wayside.
Many, if not most, of the people in the church came to
us from the world. Their wounds were usually self-
inflicted because of sin. Although many of them
remained in the world, many more found refuge within
our walls.

"Our ministry now has a much broader perspective.
God's Church must always be a refuge for the sinner
and downtrodden person. But God has called Chapel
Hill Harvester Church to be more than a City of
Refuge. God has called us to become a Balm of Gilead, a
City of Truth, to help heal and set free the Body of
Christ. While we will continue to minister as a City of
Refuge to people such as those who are pregnant out of
wedlock, who find themselves trapped in homosexual-
ity, who are bound by drugs and alcohol, that ministry
will not be our first calling. Our first calling now is to
heal the Body of Christ. This goal should be a signifi-
cant part of the ministry of any church if the Body of
Christ universal is to achieve wholeness and unity."

Those who heard the words of the prophet lifted their
own eyes above the tent, an unlikely structure to
represent a City of Truth, to see the total Body of
Christ. Yes, the Body was indeed wounded. All anyone
had to do was to reflect on his own past exposures to
religious traditions and conflicts. Most people needed
to go only as far as their own family relationships to
find misunderstandings, bitterness and divisions in
the Body of Christ. Would the Harvesters accept the

challenge? Could they really make a difference? Would they be willing to support "a Provoker" who prophesied to unruly stubborn people, walking about in disorder in churches with windows boarded up and padlocks on their doors?

12

CHAPTER TWELVE

If unusual circumstances and strange behavior characterized prophets from Abraham to John the Revelator, then Chapel Hill Harvester qualified as a prophetic voice church. Services in a tent for fourteen months allowed people to understand the cry of the prophet in the wilderness. Someone once described the ministry as "a Rembrandt in a dime store frame." That frame swayed with the wind, leaked in the rain and sweltered like a sauna in the summertime. Unwelcome noises intruded on each service. The people worshipped spontaneously through Atlanta downpours, ignored traffic sounds on Flat Shoals Road (including sirens), and became acquainted with the frequency of jets flying over south DeKalb. Earl often told the people that God wanted their ears trained to hear! God certainly provided the circumstances to develop that discipline.

Television tape rolled while Earl preached in heat that caused his saturated shirt to cling to his body, or in freezing temperatures wearing a heavy overcoat. People watching the *Harvester Hour* broadcasts every week on national television wrote letters expressing their concern. Both Earl and the congregation appreciated their sensitivity. Never had a group of people become more conscious of the weekend weather forecasts. In the summer, they brought "funeral parlor" fans with them to generate a breeze while ushers occasionally carried out people who were overcome by more than the Spirit. In the winter ushers passed out blankets generously provided by a member who worked for the airlines. The tent included an ineffective, make-shift heating system, but most people provided their own insulation against the chill in coats, boots, long underwear, gloves, scarves and active worship that became livelier with every degree the thermometer dropped.

The most obvious perfecting that God performed on the Harvesters in the tent wilderness was in the area of arts and worship. Perhaps the environment not only required a call to commitment which pleased the Lord, but it also released buried creativity from traditions and inhibitions. Dance in worship represented celebration more than physical interpretation, becoming freer in choreography as well as freestyle response to God. The choir and the orchestra learned the meaning of flowing in worship. They played with greater freedom and spontaneity, allowing Clariece to guide them with her eye instead of by bit and bridle.

Steve Owens totally cut loose in leading worship, as uninhibited as a child playing before God in unrestrained delight. Dana Blackwood, a gifted tenor, was a special gift from the Lord whose songs often blessed the Bishop before he walked to the pulpit. Singers could sing; Dana ministered. Tent services also included visits from guest artists, each one bringing variety, flavor and seasoning to the Harvesters' worship. Of course, Buck and Dottie Rambo and Dony and Reba McGuire came "home" regularly. The Harvesters were also blessed with visits from Phil Driscoll, Andrae Crouch and his sister, Sandra, Jimmy McDonald, Carlton Pearson, Nicholas, and Sharalee Lucas. Dony and Reba brought Jerry and Sharalee Lucas for a visit at Chapel Hill shortly after the Lucases moved to Atlanta from Hawaii. The Lucases joined Chapel Hill, sharing their vision for an exciting children's ministry called WOW (Witness Of the Word), utilizing Jerry's memory techniques to instill God's Word in the minds of little ones.

Mysteries continued to unfold in revelation to the prophet who delivered strong challenges to the people. The tent wilderness purged lifestyles, tested motives and surfaced subtle rebellion in numerous areas of people's lives. Bishop Paulk preached extensively on deception in the last days and the maturing of the Bride in warfare. Alpha particularly picked up on the "soldier" concept, singing a variety of songs with lyrics steeped in military language. The New Breed, as they called themselves, trained spiritual revolutionaries to take the offensive, declaring a new day to their generation in the ancient spiritual war.

At the second pastors conference in October, Earl gave the pastors a powerful exhortation as he participated in a panel discussion. He leaned over the table, and with his finger pointed at the pastors and his eyes blazing, he declared, "Preacher! Preach the Word!" He emphasized that they were not to "look at men's faces" as they spoke the truth the Spirit put into their hearts. Pastors wept openly as the prophet's words touched their spirits and confronted anxiety in secret circumstances they tolerated in their ministries. Earl provoked the pastors to live out their callings from God in authority and power. He didn't offer them easy solutions, but the seasoned warrior promised victorious results.

Hundreds of pastors contacted Earl, requesting spiritual covering and counsel. Often pastors drove all night from distant states to sit for an hour with Bishop Paulk to receive direction and confirmation concerning the message God was speaking. Those conversations prepared the pastors for the warfare that message would surely bring.

Many young pastors walked into Earl's office who were ready to give up. They were weary with the battle; ashamed of their mistakes in ministry that made them feel unfit to lead others; resenting criticism for actions they had taken in obedience to God which their people had totally misunderstood; tired of financial and social

sacrifices their families made because of their dedication to the gospel; hurt because family and friends
thought they were wasting their potential and education with no tangible returns; tired of respected Christian leaders contradicting and criticizing the very
direction God gave them to lead their people. After
sorting through their problems, then they would speculate. Perhaps they were never called into the ministry
in the first place. Perhaps they were only called for a
season. Now God was making a way for them to walk
an easier path.

Earl listened patiently and empathetically to every
argument. He could relate to these pastors on the basis
of many personal experiences that gave meaning to the
strange, winding path of his own life. How well he
understood. How easily he remembered the pain from
exact wounds he endured, wounds healed by time with
a heavenly balm which made him grateful for the
scars. Those scars helped him to remember specific
examples of God's goodness through trials. They
increased his faith on days when he needed more confidence in God's sovereignty than he had needed the
day before.

Sometimes after a young pastor had talked out all his
disillusionment, he expected the Bishop to react by
defending the calling to the ministry and contradicting
his complaints. The Bishop seldom did. In fact, Earl
Paulk often congratulated the young pastor for his
courage. Such warfare usually indicated a valid ministry making great strides for the Lord. Any New Testament disciple could have delivered the same speech as

347

the young pastor, except that remembering their experiences with Jesus kept them running in the race with joy. He would ask the pastor whether he believed Jesus' promise of tribulation to those following Him. Did the pastor now comprehend Jesus' call for self-denial? Was he still willing "to carry a cross" daily? Did he believe Kingdom righteousness, peace and joy depended on one's circumstances?

At that response, instead of answering the Bishop's questions, the young pastor earnestly asked, "Is there no deliverance?"

Suddenly, Earl Paulk broke into a smile. His blue eyes twinkled and he leaned foward with a sure response to that question. "Yes, it's called 'the Kingdom.' " That answer was neither futuristic, escapist nor necessarily comforting to the one hearing it from Earl Paulk, Kingdom theologian. Those "seeking first the Kingdom" had made a life choice with no alternative options, no turning back. Deliverance for all believers depended on the obedience of those comprehending the costs and the rewards.

Walking narrow paths separated believers as well as leaders, "the called" from "the chosen." For all the multitudes mouthing high-sounding phrases and singing beautiful, powerful lyrics, few laborers truly sold out seeking Kingdom treasure. No one had the privilege of answering for anyone else or judging the path another walked. The only sure test of the harvest was enduring fruit which brought glory to God. Truth seekers often felt alone, but of course they weren't. God's root system around the world was almost in place, ready to shake the ground. Kingdom spirits were finding each other, causing believers on the fringe, hanging onto the safety of worn out traditions, to ask the right questions out of frustration and curiosity.

Christmas morning, 1983, was the coldest Sunday on record in Atlanta with daytime thermometers at zero degrees Fahrenheit. Many Atlanta churches closed their doors—first, because of the holiday, and secondly, because of the unusual weather for the deep South. Hundreds of Harvesters gathered in the tent wrapped in their warmest clothing. Hands and noses froze and feet grew numb within an hour. What a special day! The tenth Sunday giving was over $90,000 and the people gave to the King with joy. The worship reached such heights that Clariece insisted everyone return for an evening service—a contingent weather consideration until then with predicted sub-zero temperatures. Some Harvesters who had congratulated themselves on their tough endurance that morning could have killed Clariece, a Kingdom woman who always pushed people to the limit!

The week after Christmas the drama department, Kingdom Players, presented a three-act musical called *The Bride*. The play was written by a young man in his twenties, Gary Thurman, whose ministry gifts included "anointed ears" to comprehend the messages delivered by the Bishop and the ability to illustrate Kingdom principles in unforgettable dramatic portrayals.

The play was about the Bride of Christ growing up. In the first act, she is portrayed as an immature little girl who separates her white and black dolls to prevent them from fighting with each other. She tells herself that her prince (Jesus) is coming to take her to heaven to watch cartoons all day with no one telling her what to do. The Holy Spirit approaches her, promising that He will get her ready to meet the Bridegroom.

In act two, Satan is feeling threatened by the way the little girl has grown into a discerning young woman. Meanwhile the angels speculate that she isn't the prize for Jesus that they had pictured. She still makes many mistakes. But Jesus, who sits on the stage lovingly watching her the entire time, seems delighted by any positive signs of her maturity. He obviously adores her. The Bride reads the Bible, asking the Holy Spirit questions about Israel, denominations and her role in fulfilling end time events. She trusts the Holy Spirit's answers because of the close relationship they have developed by spending time together. She learns quickly from Him.

In the final act, Satan launches an all-out effort to destroy the Bride. He attempts to taunt and confuse her. By now she has grasped the Word so firmly that she answers Satan's deception as Jesus answered His own temptations in the wilderness. Still, at times she cries out to Jesus Himself, asking Him if He still loves her. The Holy Spirit allows her to walk in the wilderness by faith so that she will grow to maturity. After an attack, including physical rough-handling, the Bride commands Satan and his cohorts to leave. Having finally learned to use authority and dominion properly, the Holy Spirit helps her to dress for the wedding.

Together, the Spirit and the Bride declare that all things are made ready, and they bid the Bridegroom, "Come, Lord Jesus." The finale of the play is a dance between Jesus and the Bride—almost overwhelming to watch for those sitting in the audience longing to see the reality of His Kingdom on earth as in heaven.

Dony and Reba McGuire had written some of the music selected for the play. Because they were out of town when the play was presented, it was repeated for them to see when they returned to Atlanta. They spent several weeks in seclusion in Los Angeles writing a musical score specifically for the message in *The Bride,* which they later recorded. The final song, *Messiah, King and Priest,* could easily compare to Handel's *Messiah* in its heavenly sounds—music written with human talent and disciplined skill, and yet heard by human ears who immediately recognized that the source of this music is not of this world!

In his first sermon of the year, Earl declared 1984 to be "The Year of the Word in Motion." A few weeks later, President Reagan addressed delegates at the National Religious Broadcasters Association by calling 1984 "The Year of the Bible in Action." Earl cautioned his people that Chapel Hill Harvester Church would go to the cross that year—a strange prophecy that gradually unfolded painfully, almost unbearably for many Harvesters. Victory at the cross depended on holding onto God's promises, the joy set before them. Trials leading to the cross always became an individual test of enduring of misunderstandings and unfair judgments without fighting back in retaliation or defense. People were grateful to God for His prophetic preparation.

Earl traveled to the 1984 Idea Exchange in Miami where he addressed his fellow colleagues in the ministry on the subject of "Restoration." Earl, Norma, Don and Clariece attended the President's Prayer Breakfast in Washington, D. C., in early February. While in Washington, Earl and Don met with Georgia Senator Sam Nunn and Congressman Elliott Levitas to discuss human service ministries at Chapel Hill.

In late February, Earl flew to Buffalo, New York, for discussions with Pastor Tommy Reid, Bishop John Meares, Pastor John Gimenez and Dr. Ken Lipke on beginning a satellite television network to provide Kingdom theology and demonstration for local churches around the country. Dr. Lipke, a steel magnate who owned both Gibraltar Steel and Gibraltar Satellite Network, had opened his heart to the Lord through Tommy Reid's ministry. By utilizing Kingdom principles, the businessman had turned profits in his company during the "doom period" for other companies in the steel industry.

Outreach took on new emphasis in late February. In a Sunday morning message, the Bishop explained that God had given the church a message and a mission, and now He would provide the means. That service launched *Partners For the Kingdom,* a network of committed people around the world who would support the outreach ministry with ten minutes of prayer each day, at least ten dollars each month and a daily Kingdom witness. PFK members received a K-pin, the books written by the Bishop, a monthly update newsletter and the *Harvest Time* newspaper which had grown to a circulation of over 25,000. The thirty-minute, magazine format television program, *Kingdom Dimensions*, as well as the *Harvester Hour*, became the major connection in drawing new Partners beyond the walls of Chapel Hill. Many people joined PFK by telephone during the broadcasts. A member, Ken Posey, who was an executive Customer Services Representative with the U.S. Post Office, left his position to join the staff in organizing *Partners For the Kingdom*.

All the new Partners received Earl's new book, *Ultimate Kingdom*, released in March 1984. The manuscript was almost two years old before it finally reached publication. The book contained messages on a chapter by chapter study of the Revelation of Jesus Christ that Earl preached as a series after he received the vision of God's throne. People across the nation read *Ultimate Kingdom* like a break in the clouds in understanding the message of Kingdom demonstration God was speaking to His people today.

So much fresh revelation and many insights into God's Word had come to the Church since that series was delivered. An editorial staff labored over new manuscripts, recording and explaining Kingdom theology. Offices devoted to word processing and typesetting added tremendous potential to publication proficiency—a long way from the days when manuscripts were typed and retyped in the editing process.

To enhance publications, Harvester Booksellers opened a bookstore in a section of the "tent" auditorium. Wes Bonner coordinated book buying and selling as well as heading a new publishing company, K-Dimension Publishers. Acting as an independent publishing company, K-Dimension contracted book distributors to sell the Bishop's books and other books with a Kingdom thrust to stores all over the world. Wes and Beth attended the Christian Booksellers Association Convention in Anaheim, California, in the summer of 1984. They received an instant education on the difficulties of cracking the book market. After days of frustration in talking to distributors, Wes promised the Lord and himself that K-Dimension would have a booth at the next national convention.

Beginning in the spring of the year, the Harvesters were building a huge structure they called the "K-Center." In his spirit, Earl had seen the building, which he described as a warehouse. He commented that the sanctuary was as fancy as a barn. Workdays were scheduled all day on Saturdays and every weeknight when services weren't held. Businessmen, housewives, secretaries, even children, became construction workers to some degree—even if their only building tool was a broom or hands to carry scraps and trash.

Fellowship during the project became an added blessing to the ministry. Women prepared large platters of sandwiches and cookies for the Saturday work crews. People met new friends every time they hammered, sawed or painted. The people worked side by side with their pastors—building relationships and personal understanding, far more important to God than the tangible structure.

The barn began to look more like an airplane hangar,

complete with sophisticated television and audio equipment, a sunken pit for the orchestra, a baptismal pool, a parquet floor on stage for the dancers and curtains in front of the orchestra and choir, useful in staging dramas. All the construction caused what Earl referred to as a "plague of dust" which took months to settle. They dedicated the building in September 1984, a period of exactly three years as Benson Idahosa had prophesied. Also as the African prophet had predicted, the old sanctuary became children's church on Sundays, and a facility for youth and education during the week.

For years Earl had opposed opening a church-sponsored school. He firmly endorsed infiltration of Christian young people in the public school system. However in 1983, God spoke to him to begin Chapel Hill Harvester Schools as a Kingdom prototype of quality education.

The school opened in 1984 in two divisions, the School of Early Learning was under the direction of Pete Aycock, a Kingdom-minded educator committed to excellence. The School of Biblical Studies, under the direction of Pastor Bob Blackwood, offered a three-year program to train men and women for the ministry or to enjoy personal enrichment through scriptural studies. The Baptist church across the street from the Harvesters was purchased to accommodate the elementary school (with grades and enrollment increasing each year). The adult school included plans for an accredited junior college as well as the School of Biblical Studies.

Moving forward always demanded a price. Joan

received an alarming report from her doctors—a biopsy on a tumor in her cheek in the late summer of 1984 proved to be malignant. Joan again faced chemotherapy—this time in fragile health with little natural resistance to germs or infection. The doctors' alternatives were all foreboding. The treatment would be very dangerous. The hospitalization would be longer than before with no medical prognosis concerning the duration or eventual results of their efforts. But, the doctors added, they always had hope. With her family surrounding her with love and prayers as they had time after time, Joan courageously fought another round with unshakable faith, trusting fully in God's will for her life.

The Atlanta '84 Pastors Conference in October brought over three hundred pastors to the new facility, requiring shuttle services to the Paulk Activities Building for meals. Tommy Reid, John Meares, Ann Gimenez and Dr. Judson Cornwall shared the general sessions with Bishop Paulk. Atlanta '84 required headphones for over twenty-five guests from Latin America who spoke only Spanish. Three pastors on Chapel Hill's Presbytery had taken trips to the Caribbean, Central and South America in the summer to meet with church leaders and share Kingdom principles as an alternative to liberation theology.

God had blessed these missionary excursions with open doors and major contacts with officials in Pentecostal denominations throughout Latin America. Many of these key pastors came to the conference at tremendous financial sacrifices. Their zeal to learn added immeasurably to the worship and significance of the conference's content. Chapel Hill's International Outreach Department had translated *The Wounded Body of Christ* into Spanish, but the manuscripts lay on a shelf waiting for sufficient funds to publish the book.

Bishop Paulk met in a closed door session with the Latin American pastors. Speaking through a translator from the Presbytery, Pastor Pedro Torres, he challenged the pastors to take a stand against "escapist" doctrines or resorting to violence in the political upheavals oppressing their nations. With tears in his eyes and his voice breaking, Earl spoke to one young pastor about the fear he discerned in the pastor's heart. He told the pastor to get before God and settle the matter—then God would move in power like he had never imagined He would.

Just in time for the conference, K-Dimension Publishers released another book by Earl Paulk, *Satan Unmasked*. This book, which focused on deception in the Church, quickly became a best-seller with the largest distributor of Christian books in the nation. The book went into its second printing within six months. *Satan Unmasked* exposed deception in worldly kingdoms such as the kingdoms of sports, politics, finance, education and the arts. Earl wrote hard-hitting revelation on the god of mammon, preparing the seed (our children) properly, the necessity of men and women working together in ministry, the vital activation of the five-fold ministry in the last days. He startled many critics of his teaching with a chapter discussing the final generation who would "challenge death" as the last enemy.

Many critics wanted to write Earl off as a "Millennialist," a "Manifest Sons of God" or "Latter Rain" theologian. Many were disturbed with his challenge to literal interpretations in Revelation concerning "the rapture," a literal seven-year tribulation period and a millennial reign of Christ on earth. They surmised that Earl Paulk must also advocate "spiritual interpretations" of other basic edicts of faith. They were furious with his teaching on "God in the flesh" in His Church on earth—often quoting Earl's writings out of context in books and articles, attempting to discredit the Harvester ministry. One author even criticized Earl's quoting I John 4:17, "Love has been perfected among us in this; that we may have boldness in the day of judgment; because as He is, so are we in this world" (NKJ).

Instead of living out the Word of God, many Christians almost regarded the Bible itself as a god—much as the Pharisees' reverence for the Law in accusing Jesus' demonstration of love as the "living Word" on earth. As in the example of Jesus' ministry, Earl told his congregation that one of the most effective ways that Satan "kills the prophets" in the modern Church is by propagating innuendoes, false accusations and attacks on the prophet's character. Many people outrightly rejected prophetic truth in fear of "Jim Jones" types and demoralizing cults. Satan gained a tragic victory by instilling the fear of counterfeits into a generation who also received genuine revelation from God.

When given the opportunity to respond to his critics (which was rare, even though he asked them repeatedly on national television to join him in closed door dialogue), Earl answered their charges by refusing to be classified with any theories or traditions that would insulate him against truth, causing him to carry undeserved baggage of various doctrinal identifications. He charged, "I cannot see how anyone who has heard me preach would misrepresent my stands on literal miracles, demons, the virgin birth, the resurrection and the second coming of Jesus. I really believe that this confusion is an effort to withstand the real issues of today: the Church growing to maturity, coming into oneness, and becoming the witness by which God will finally judge world systems."

The Harvesters were honored with a visit from evangelist James Robison in the winter of 1984. Earl had met James Robison at his hotel when he had visited Atlanta during the previous summer. The renowned evangelist, called by the Lord to a ministry of restoration in the Body of Christ, had read *The Wounded Body of Christ* and received confirmation of many things God was speaking to him in his own ministry. James Robison had weathered attacks by many Christian brothers who totally misunderstood the calling and new direction God had given to him. He was a man following the voice of the Lord and willingly paying the price.

The worship was lively, upbeat, typical Chapel Hill style—"Glory to the Lord"! The dancers opened the service. As soon as James Robison came to the podium, he commended the choir, the K-Dimension Singers, the orchestra and dancers by asking them to participate in his crusade in Dallas in January 1985. He explained that the racial blending and the anointing on the worship at the church was among the greatest he had ever experienced—and he had spoken at the largest churches in America. "You are the church I have been describing around the nation," he said.

The choir and orchestra sold cakes after services and initiated other fund-raising projects to provide the money to go to Dallas. Many people paid for their trips themselves or asked family members to pool their Christmas gift money to help pay for the trip. Some members of the church donated special funds for people to go. Most people took vacation time from work. Of course, the church underwrote the expenses for many people who could never have afforded to participate otherwise.

Almost two hundred people from Chapel Hill went to the Dallas Crusade. Most of them flew on chartered planes, but others rode in a van caravan which also carried television equipment and orchestra instruments. The two nights and three days were exhausting and wonderful. Many pastors, most of them Baptists, opened their receptivity at least to explore more expressive worship. They asked the Harvesters lots of questions in restaurants and hotel lobbies about clerical collars, the rainbow pins, dancing in church, speaking in tongues and "Earl Paulk's church in Atlanta."

The Harvesters sang and danced *Messiah, King and Priest* under a powerful anointing. The bride in the awesome presentation stood on stage with tears streaming down her cheeks. Dony and Reba McGuire and Sharalee Lucas joined their church family to worship the Lord. They ministered with a song Reba wrote called *A People Who Were Not.* The song was written from a series of sermons Earl preached on God's peculiar people—a people who were not a people, a nation without national origin or definable identity. The final phrases of the song said, "We're not black or white, We're not bond or free, We're no earthly race, We're a brand-new breed . . . We are a people who were not, We are the people of God!" Dony also sang a song he had written from the message of *The Wounded Body of Christ* called *The Wounded Soldier.*

On the return trip to Atlanta, the van carrying television equipment burned to the ground. Four passengers barely escaped and managed miraculously to pull out some of the equipment. All the cameras—including the videotape which recorded the conference highlights and interviews—were totally destroyed. Chapel Hill had learned well how to thank God in tribulation, so instead of reacting, they responded in praise to the Lord. They understood the warfare. They knew from anointed teaching that their witness to powers and principalities of darkness never consisted of notoriety or praise from man, but trusting God in the middle of the storms. Indeed, the story of Job exemplified the witness of the Church to powers and principalities.

Flying thousands of feet in the air, returning from one of his now frequent trips to conferences, God gave

Earl a seven-year plan for Chapel Hill Harvester Church. He announced to the congregation that 1985 would be the "Year of Credibility" in the Harvester ministry. He had taught his people the value of the cross applied to their lives individually and corporately. If they had truly submitted their lives to death on the cross, God would prove them in a way that would honor His Kingdom. Establishing credibility forced people to answer Jesus' question to disciples who wanted to share His robe and crown, "Can you drink the cup?" Chapel Hill Harvester Church would continue to answer that question.

In the 1985 Idea Exchange, fellow pastors asked Earl to speak to the gathering on "Kingdom Theology." Because of other topics pastors addressed which contradicted certain principles of Kingdom teaching, Earl easily could have geared his message to gain acceptance among his comrades, simply skirting or omitting the more controversial aspects of Kingdom teaching. Instead, he barreled ahead, wide open. Speakers following Earl on the program corrected his stand concerning national Israel, obviously provoked by the content of Earl Paulk's address.

The Idea Exchange Committee asked Clariece to participate in a workshop on the arts and particularly to focus on dance in worship. As they had in Dallas, many people approached Clariece after her presentation wanting to visit Chapel Hill. Clariece knew God was confirming a desire she had prayed about for years, a conference dedicated to arts and worship. With only a few months to prepare and little publicity to

generate a large attendance, Clariece pressed preparations in the various components of the Arts Department, involving hundreds of people.

The early spring conference dedicated to "Prophetic
Worship" brought together several hundred conferees,
ministers of music, pastors, dancers and worship leaders. Bishop Paulk and Dr. Judson Cornwall addressed
the conference on worship principles. Afternoon workshops focused on particular areas in the arts: choral
music, drama, dance, orchestration—offering conferees specific "how to" demonstrations and the opportunity to ask questions. Dony and Reba McGuire and
Sharalee Lucas joined Chapel Hill's Fine Arts
Department in the services as well as workshop sessions. Dony and Reba made Atlanta their official home
early in 1985. Of course, Buck and Dottie Rambo began
preparations to move to Atlanta immediately. They
joined their children in November as official members
of Chapel Hill. Earl often expressed his thanks to the
Lord publicly for these "gifts" to the ministry!

One evening of the conference featured an original
ballet, *Seed Power*, written by Angelle Smith, a dance
teacher in the church. The ballet incorporated music
written primarily by Dony and Reba McGuire. It
depicted the heavenly struggle between demons and
angels to influence the minds of children of the Kingdom. According to the message of *Seed Power,* the
struggle for control of the human mind determined the
generation which ended the heavenly conflict.

In the middle of the ballet after Jesus and the Bride
dance together, Jesus goes into hell to take the keys of

sin and death away from Satan. He gives the keys to the Bride. The Bride trains the Seed and finally watches two children go into hell to defeat Satan as Jesus had done. In the finale, the stage is filled with children in gold metallic costumes, singing a song Reba wrote, *Ready For Battle!* Dancers dressed as sinister demons crawl up the steps to the stage while the children sing about putting on their armour. When they sing the phrase, "Satan, you hear me, I'm prepared for war . . ." the children advance with authority on the demons who fall down the steps in defeat.

On the final night of the conference, Dony McGuire sat at the piano singing a song which he had written with Gloria Gaither called *Upon This Rock*. The song expresses Kingdom theology from Jesus' own words, "Upon this rock, I'll build My Kingdom, Upon this rock, forever and ever, it shall stand. Upon this rock of revelation, I'll build a strong and mighty nation, And it will stand the storms of time—upon this rock!" The song had been recorded by singer Sandi Patti and had won the 1985 Dove Award as "Song of the Year." In a touching presentation, Dony gave his Dove Award to the man who opened Kingdom revelation to him, Earl Paulk.

K-Dimension Publishers released another book by Earl Paulk in March 1985. Earl had taught a series on Christian sexuality that caused an avalanche of mail response from the television audience in the PFK offices. The series on cassette tape had sold in record numbers. Members of the church and the television audience bought the tapes for friends and family members with problems in this sensitive area of their lives. Earl felt that worldly concepts of sexuality caused strongholds of bondage in many Christians' lives. Unfortunately, teaching on sexuality in most churches, if at all, offered little valid ministry to help believers enjoy wholesome concepts of love as God intended.

The content of *Sex Is God's Idea* utilized Earl's forty years of ministry with an estimated twenty thousand counseling sessions related to sexual problems. This subject challenged the kingdoms of darkness as much as any theological treatise on church doctrines. *Sex Is God's Idea* balanced much of the "prophetic" content of other recent books Earl had written by sharing insights derived from pastoral ministry. People following the ministry by television or publications often perceived a one-sided view of Earl Paulk, the hard hitting prophet. This book addressed serious problems with professional understanding in counseling as well as sharing Earl's warmth, humor, candor and personal experiences as a husband, father and grandfather.

Joan battled lymphoma bravely throughout the winter into the spring. Several times her blood pressure dropped so suddenly that doctors were surprised when she snapped back. Medical scientists threw out their books regarding Joan's physical condition. She seldom responded when or how they predicted. People going to the hospital to cheer up Joan often left her room feeling refreshed from her ministry to them. She told one friend, "Game time is over!" She didn't waste words in idle conversations with those coming to her bedside.

Earl responded to Joan's battle as a man stripped before God, willing to move at His command to hold onto or let go of anything. The first battle over Joan had been so clear in its outcome. God had promised Earl that Joan would rise victoriously from that test. He never doubted victory even though one perilous night he literally fought spirits of death attacking his sister as she lay in the hospital bed barely able to breathe. He had told everyone else to leave the room as he prayed aloud for hours in the Spirit. Joan later said that until he prayed, she knew she was dying. Earl Paulk's confidence rested in following God's commands. Once he received the sure direction of God's mind on a matter, he wouldn't back away or give in regardless of circumstances or the most official medical reports.

Now over a year later, Earl cried out to God again for clear direction, an immovable word concerning his sister. He would learn any lesson or take any test God gave him, but he must be sure of the Lord's voice. Until he knew a direct Word from God in his spirit, Earl ordered everyone to pray the prayer of faith over Joan, to claim every scripture on healing in her behalf. The Presbytery anointed her with oil and believed God for her total healing. When others sometimes doubted God's power, Joan herself testified to complete trust in God's will in the matter. No one in the ministry grasped overcoming faith, even "loving not her life unto death," as Joan did. Whether she lived fifty years or died tomorrow in this world, Joan was determined to be an overcomer, a demonstration of a Kingdom witness.

The "word" Earl waited for finally came. On a Monday night, he had been privately talking to the Lord, asking questions, discussing his most intimate thoughts. God spoke to Earl Paulk about "Operation Unity." Somehow God was going to unite His people supernaturally, and Earl must prepare his spirit to follow God's commands to bring spiritual unity of the Church to reality. "Operation Unity" would call for great sacrifice, involving many leaders in many places of service to the Lord around the world.

Earl talked about "Operation Unity" to members of his outreach department the next day, but he couldn't explain its meaning, strategy, or even what action he should take first—if any—until God gave him specific steps. One insight into "Operation Unity" was clear. When God spoke to him, he experienced a release concerning Joan's struggle. God's call to "Operation Unity" and letting go of Joan's battle in his spirit were synonymous within him.

Searching out its meaning, Earl began preaching a series called the "Jerusalem Happening" on April 21, 1985. He told the people that they were to pray concerning Pentecost Sunday, May 26, which he said would be a landmark day in the ministry at Chapel Hill. The messages offered a new look at the meaning of Pentecost in preparing God's people to become His witness, His standard, so that final judgment of world systems could take place. God was bringing "a people who were not a people" into one mind, one spirit, one accord, so that God could move again as He did in the upper room—this time in the culmination of all things by His reign on earth.

One Sunday night Earl called Joan to the stage to pray for the healing of people in the congregation. Pastor Don and Joan's husband, Donnie, helped her onto the platform where she sat in a chair. Before she prayed, Earl asked Joan to declare publicly her greatest desire from God. Without hesitation, Joan told the people that she wanted the Kingdom of God on earth far more than physical healing or anything else in the world. Then she cried out to God in behalf of the people, interceding for healing, restoration and spiritual life to flow among them.

Many people criticized Earl for asking Joan that solemn question and calling her on the stage to pray. However, God honored Joan's prayer with a sign in her own body. The next week they received a good medical report—no cancer cells in her spinal fluid. But she was very weak. She came to work, if at all, only a few hours at a time. Joan missed church only if she were confined to bed or in the hospital. Whenever she felt sick during the services and needed to leave, she would go to the Bishop's office to watch the service by television. Sometimes Earl urged the congregation to clap in welcoming Joan who was watching the service on the television monitor in his office. If she were confined to the hospital, she always watched videotapes of the services she missed.

Joan was in the hospital on Easter Sunday morning, feeling angry with her doctors who refused to release her to go to church. The family and close friends gathered in Earl's office before the service to make a videotape so Joan could see all the children's Easter outfits. They acted silly in lighthearted laughter when the camera was on them and cried openly off camera, consoling each other because they knew the reason this video was necessary.

Earl spent Sunday afternoon at Faith Memorial Assembly of God, Jimmy and Darlene Swilley's church. He participated in their church's anniversary service. Earl especially enjoyed seeing his old friend, Pastor Ralph Byrd, who shared incidents of the early days in his relationship with a bold young pastor, Earl Paulk Jr. Earl thanked Ralph Byrd publicly for his counsel and eldership in the ministry when few spiritual leaders believed in his calling. Earl felt he owed a great debt to this elder for giving him guidance and the courage to go on in difficult days.

Earl rushed home to change clothes for the evening service at Chapel Hill. Daughter Joy Owens had written a moving, dramatic musical about Mary Magdalene's love for Jesus called *The Rose*. The moment he opened the door at home, Norma told him to call Joan immediately. She had some exciting news to share with him.

He immediately sensed the ecstasy in Joan's voice— beyond excitement or joy. She told her brother that Jesus had visited her in the hospital room that day. They had talked and walked together. Jesus had told her about "His loneliness for His Bride, His longing for her to understand truth." Then He told her many insights concerning people who worked in the ministry at Chapel Hill Harvester Church. He spoke to her about "agape" love that would bring His Bride to maturity, a love that He longed to share with His Church. Joan asked Earl to take "agape" love from her to the people at Chapel Hill that night.

The confirmation of Joan's visitation from Jesus was lived out in Joy's play. Two songs in the play defied coincidence in confirming the events of that day. A song called *The Rose*, written by Dottie Rambo, told of the crushing of Jesus—the perfect rose—to give a permeating fragrance to all mankind. Like Jesus, Joan's message was given from a crushed rose with a fragrance affecting many lives. Another song in the play, *I've Just Seen Jesus,* written by Gloria Gaither, portrays the ecstasy of the disciples at Jesus' resurrection. When Earl shared Joan's visitation from the Lord and her message to the people, everyone felt the excitement and tears of joy those disciples knew long ago after having seen the risen Lord in their darkest hours of grief.

All the people at Chapel Hill Harvester Church, even those who didn't know Joan personally, walked through the day-by-day lessons that God taught her family. The "Jerusalem Happening" sermons were delivered from great brokenness in Earl's spirit. Joan's illness made him vulnerable, weak and tired in his flesh but strong in the Lord. He visited Joan in the hospital almost every day and brought reports and messages from her back to the people she loved so. Joan relayed her awareness of heavenly powers surrounding her to her brother—the host encamping against her, the cloud of witnesses cheering her on.

Earl opened his spirit to learn more about the interaction of heavenly beings with events on earth. He
realized fully the dangers of occult probing which is
clearly an abomination to God, but he also became
more sensitive in asking God for understanding of
familiar scriptures openly addressing the matter of
interaction between heaven and earth. One verse particularly took on new emphasis to Earl, "That in the
dispensation of the fullness of times He might gather
together in one all things in Christ, both which are in
heaven and which are on earth—even in Him . . ."
(Ephesians 1:10). Joan's illness left him living out the
meaning of "hope in the Lord." He shared privately
with those close to him that on Pentecost Sunday, God
would either raise up Joan in total health or take her
home to Himself.

Pentecost Sunday was a special day of celebration at
Chapel Hill. The people wore red clothing representing
"tongues of fire," and Earl preached the tenth sermon
in the "Jerusalem Happening" series that morning. He
reported Joan's condition to the people by saying that
anything that happened to her would be a victory to
God's glory. If the Lord raised her up, of course they
would rejoice. But if Joan went on to become one of
those intercessors crying, "How long, how long . . ."
under God's altar, then they would rejoice also. The
unity among the people was evident in the extraordinary worship and openness to the Word of the Lord.
The evening service turned into a "love feast" of music,
dancing, celebration and personal one-to-one ministry
within the church body. People lined up to embrace

Earl, Don, the Presbytery and fellow members of the Chapel Hill family.

Ten minutes after the service ended, as Earl was on his way to the hospital, Joan died. She had worshipped the Lord the entire day. Pastor Sam and Becky Lalaian, Donnie and his sister, Jackie, had spent the day in her room around her bed, joining her in praise and worship to the King. Sam would ask her, "Joan, are you tired? Do you want to rest for awhile?" Joan responded to the question with a grunting sound that obviously meant, "No, keep it up!" She died peacefully, as if she had finished—even to the last moment—all that she was supposed to do. Her final hours were spent in praise to the Lord, her deliverer, the rewarder of those who refuse release from trials in order to "receive a better resurrection" (Hebrews 11:35).

A sign on the doors of the Youth and Education Building read, "The Life and Growth in the Spirit service has moved to the K-Center to celebrate the home-going of Joan Paulk Harris." On that Tuesday after noon, people gathered together to tell Joan good-bye—her husband and children, her sisters and their families, the people who worked with her, old friends she had known since days on Euclid Avenue as a young bride, new friends, many of whom knew her best through the Bishop's love for her which he had so openly shared with the people.

Her brothers sat on the stage as speakers. Clariece was at the piano accompanying the choir and orchestra. Earl had asked Dr. Paul Walker, a long-time family friend and senior pastor of Mount Paran Church of

God, formerly Hemphill Church of God, to speak in the service also. He had called Paul Walker weeks earlier and asked him to visit with Joan.

Don's eulogy reminisced from a sensitive personal perspective. He remembered the blonde-haired little girl who sat on the curb with a dime in her hand, waiting for the ice cream truck. Paul Walker, a gifted orator, offered the glorious hope in Jesus—a hope through God's Word that was real in times like this. Earl walked to the pulpit to deliver a burning message. He said that he and Joan had an agreement between them concerning the church: no prejudice, no compromise, and no turning back in the things God had called the ministry to do. Joan's funeral sermon was "Operation Unity" through and through—less about Joan personally than about the message of Joan's life. The sermon emphasized Joan's love, her dedication and her determination to follow the Lord at all costs to take the Kingdom message to the world.

Joan was laid to rest in the family burial plot in Baxley, Georgia, the next day. The extended Paulk and Tomberlin family and friends, as well as the Chapel Hill Presbytery and members of the staff, gathered that hot May afternoon in a small family graveyard beside a sandy road. A fence enclosed several graves with Paulk/Tomberlin headstones. The family sat in chairs under a canvas canopy while friends and staff members stood around the edge of the covering. The K-Dimension singers sang *Free At Last,* a song written by Dony McGuire. Earl took the opportunity to challenge members of his family who weren't following the

Lord. He wanted them to understand how deep roots in a farming family from Baxley had grown into a strong tree, becoming a ministry to the world. They were part of that heritage which kept Joan moving forward courageously in a tremendous personal test, a heritage that meant even giving their lives if necessary to follow God's will. To many members of the family, their lives in Baxley seemed a long way from Earl Jr.'s church in Atlanta.

Earl Sr. stood beside his son and thanked God for Joan's life. Earl Sr. and Addie Mae had moved from Baxley to Atlanta in 1984 in order for their children to look after them. Since his retirement from the ministry, the man who had once preached as a tower of strength to thousands of people now worried over his cats or periodically became despondent when people didn't call him or seem to need him to minister. Addie Mae sparkled as full of fire as ever, though years of illness had taken their toll. She could tell a story from the past with total recall but often forgot current details in her life. If Addie Mae's story got a favorable response from her listeners, she might repeat the story several times for them.

Alpha held youth rallies every summer from 1979. They staged outdoor evangelistic crusades, invited guest speakers, even held two summer rallies in tents and presented major dramas. ALPHA '85 brought over one thousand teenagers and youth leaders from across the nation to Atlanta for three days of Kingdom teaching, seminars and workshops on ministry and lifestyles. Special guest speakers for ALPHA '85 included

Pastor Donnie Meares from Washington, D. C., and Lauren Cunningham from "Youth With A Mission," based in Hawaii. Earl and Duane conducted a special open forum which allowed youth leaders to ask questions.

Earl addressed the conference as keynote speaker. He emphasized the call for young people to "think higher!" He told them, "Renewal alone is not enough. We must move even beyond a Charismatic experience to demonstrate a Kingdom mentality. Kingdom thinking takes us to God's original purposes for man. Only Kingdom thinking will prepare that generation to be ready for Christ's return."

In July, Earl flew to Dallas, Texas, with his outreach staff to attend the Christian Booksellers Association convention. As Wes had promised, he reserved space on the convention floor for K-Dimension Publishers to sell books as their own distributor as well as a publisher to other distributors. What a difference a year makes! Distributing company representatives lined up to talk to Wes about international distribution of books published by K-Dimension Publishers. *Satan Unmasked* was offered in a "Best-sellers Package" by the nation's leading distributor of Christian books, and Bishop Paulk autographed *Sex Is God's Idea* as K-Dimension's newest release.

On the final day of the convention, officials notified Wes that he should sit at a special table at the awards luncheon. With over three hundred booths in its size category, K-Dimension Publishers won the first place trophy. Indeed, God had named this "The Year of Credibility" for the Harvesters.

In early August tragedy struck again, underscoring God's call to "Operation Unity" in Earl's spirit. Rudy Price, a man who understood unity in the Body of Christ as few ever have, was the first officer on Delta Flight 191 which crashed at the Dallas airport in a violent storm. Rudy, a member of a Catholic church, worshipped each Sunday morning at mass as well as attending Chapel Hill with his wife, Dawn, and children, Mike and Christy.

With an open ecumenical spirit, Rudy headed the prison ministry at Chapel Hill, attended staff luncheons and business meetings and often talked or wrote letters to Earl expressing his desire for unity among Christian brothers and sisters. Like Joan, Rudy understood the Church. The mystery of their deaths could only be comprehended with spiritual understanding. "Unless a seed die, it abides alone" (John 12:24). "For where a covenant is, there must of necessity be the death of one who made it. For a covenant is valid only when men are dead, for it is never in force while the one who made it lives" (Hebrews 9:16,17).

The annual pastors conference in November proved to be a monumental stake in the Harvester ministry. Over six hundred pastors and Church leaders, with more than one hundred representing denominations and churches in Latin America and the Carribean, gathered in Atlanta. After an afternoon closed-door session with conferees from Latin America before the conference officially began, Earl met for forty-five minutes with Vice President George Bush, a meeting arranged by Georgia Congressman Pat Swindall. That night, the opening service of the Atlanta '85 conference, the Bishop relayed the Vice President's personal greetings—especially to Latin American guests. Then Earl delivered a memorable keynote address on the seed, the Covenant, God's desire for a people, and the responsibility of those people to prepare to rule the earth as ones left behind, "as in the days of Noah," when God judged lawlessness in the land.

The conference speakers were a tremendous blessing to all the conferees but no less of a blessing to the guests than to Earl Paulk himself. Earl had stood many times like a soldier on the front lines all alone, taking jabs and abuse from people he loved because they perceived him to be an enemy. Probably no calling could be more challenging to one's confidence than to be a man called by God to be a "Provoker" to the Church. Truth spoken in love provoked conflicting circumstances, misunderstandings and accusations of irreverence to traditions which many people still held sacred. Earl Paulk realized at last that his fellowship in the ministry was not only growing rapidly but truly shaking everything that could be shaken with Kingdom truth, beginning at the house of God! Conferees were able to share the revelation of the "Jerusalem Happening" sermons in Earl's book, *Held In The Heavens Until . . .*, newly released from K-Dimension Publishers. A play written by Gary Thurman from those sermons, *The Final Witness*, was presented one evening of the conference.

Conference speakers Bishop Herro Blair, Bishop Robert McAlister, Bishop John Meares, Pastor Tommy

377

Reid, Pastor Kelly Varner, Pastor Bill Hamon and Pastor John Garlington gave one message in a variety of servings: the Kingdom is at hand! Christ in His Church (in the world) is the hope of glory! Believers must grow quickly to maturity and unity of faith in Jesus Christ to prepare to rule with the King! One classic line from John Garlington's sermon proclaimed, "Jesus didn't come to take sides—He came to take over!"

Prophecy over the ministry in Atlanta confirmed the seven-year plan God had given to Earl. Bill Hamon prophesied a world conference at Chapel Hill Harvester Church in the 1990's, a gathering of 25,000 people. Months before the prophecy, a unique worship facility had been designed by a visionary architect on staff, Norbert Senftleben. Bill Hamon called Earl Paulk "an apostle to the general Church" who would travel on every continent in the next few years "setting the Church in order." He contended that the decade of the eighties established and redefined the ministry of the prophets in the Church, but the nineties would once again establish the apostolic calling, the foundation which began and also will end the Church era.

Pastor Kelly Varner told Earl that God had given him a prophetic word for Earl two weeks earlier, then he began to read Isaiah 54, ". . . Enlarge the place of your tent, stretch out the curtains of your dwelling, spare not. . ." He repeated the words "spare not" seven times, emphasizing God's command to press forward with the message he had trusted to Earl Paulk's spirit.

God was preparing the Harvesters to "press forward" regardless of the price they must pay. Earl told his people that 1986 would be "The Year of Visibility" in the ministry. Confirmation of that visibility fell immediately in the opening weeks of the year. Earl received invitations from somewhat diverse poles of the traditional church. He was chosen as one of nine theologians from the United States to participate in the 1986 Vatican Conference—a Roman Catholic/Pentecostal dialogue—to convene in Pasadena, California, at Fuller Theological Seminary in May 1986.

While in California, Bishop Paulk would also be one of the house guests of Robert Schuller. Dr. Schuller annually invited a small group of clergymen from some of the nation's largest, growing churches to share strategy in their ministries with him in vulnerable, closed sessions. Earl Paulk had attended the meetings with Robert Schuller and Methodists, Baptists, Presbyterians and other Pentecostal pastors in 1985.

Another significant alliance confirming "Operation Unity" was an invitation for Earl to serve as one of 27 founding members of Charismatic Bible Ministries, a fraternal fellowship promoting unity which Oral Roberts initiated. Oral Roberts shared with the founding members in Dallas in January 1986, that God had called him in dedicating the later years of his ministry toward working for unity within the Body of Christ. Among other ministers represented on the board of founding members were Kenneth Copeland, Jerry Savelle, Robert Tilton, Marilyn Hickey, John Osteen, John Meares, John Gimenez and others. Oral Roberts believed that the group he had chosen for the board had the pulse, eyes and ears of the Church world.

Another book, *To Whom Is God Betrothed,* was released by K-Dimension Publishers in February 1986. In this book, Earl boldly addressed the teaching of many Christians toward national Israel as God's Covenant people. In a powerful scriptural foundation, he admonished the Bride of Christ to assume her rightful place in fulfilling the plan of God in the earth.

The Provoker stands between two kingdoms of God's people. One kingdom is still strong, having once moved under God's mighty anointing and blessings. Now that kingdom relies primarily on old methods, stories of God's voice heard in the past, rituals and routines which give them security in "no risk" religion. That kingdom protects itself with traditions. It goes through motions which once flowed with an anointing as God burst people out of old wineskins at some time in their pasts, bringing them again into worship of Him in spirit and truth. Many "nice" things happen in that Kingdom, but the electrifying glory of the Lord has departed.

Now the people in that first kingdom, who are often discontent and bored, look to the past or to the future or to the heavenlies hoping to hear from God again. That kingdom is ruled by Saul who is easily threatened. He defends past glory, yet reacts quickly to reject any reports of "other places" where God's goodness and blessings flow in abundance in these days. Saul always attacks, forcing people back into rigid, reliable formation according to his own rules, for his own glory, because of his own fears. This kingdom sows to the flesh and reaps from the flesh.

The Provoker proclaims a fresh anointing which brings depth, meaning and purpose to the past. He calls for a covenant of heart, a citizenship based on love, an inner desire to please the King. This calling requires an even greater commitment than keeping rules and regulations. Love, righteousness, peace and joy rule. This new Kingdom flows in jubilant praise, the lineage of Judah, in responsive worship to God and dancing for joy. Every citizen of this Kingdom has a special place of ministry and gifts to offer each other so that all will be whole, well and strong.

All of the five-fold ministries flow in one voice, one mind, one purpose and one heart to help the citizens grow. Tradition and ritual only serve to remind people of the reality of Emmanuel today, "God With Us." The only rules in this Kingdom forbid anything which hinders or offends the gentle Spirit of God, moving among His beloved people. God Himself dwells among people who are preparing their own hearts as the throne for the Kingdom of David, an everlasting throne for the King of kings and Lord of lords.

People entering this Kingdom must live daily as kings and priests, learning to see, hear, taste, smell and feel daily communion with the Holy Spirit, their teacher. His lessons are neither easy nor painless. Hard lessons press, shake and strip the people. These lessons accomplish whatever is necessary to make God's people into royalty. But less of them lifts more of Him up to the world as the true witness. In obedience to God, the people become like a city set on a hill, the light of the world, the glory of Mount Zion. Seekers of light look at their faces and see the glorious face of the King!

And the Provoker stands like the prophet Samuel between the kingdom of Saul and the everlasting Kingdom of David, knowing that not only has he heard God's voice and followed His directions, but also he has an eternal responsibility. He must sound a trumpet in Zion to alert the people to "make all things ready." God will guide him in dreams and visions were confirmed His word. The Provoker will take risks that would cause others to tremble. He'll walk strange paths, leading people to encircle a city for seven days, or to break a lantern and blast a horn rushing into battle, or to sit for months in a tent on a parking lot. But God will cause impenetrable walls to fall and men to drop their weapons in fear of His "people who were not a people." And to the Provoker—a chosen, loud, clear trumpet to the Church—the King will proclaim with joy, "Well done, My good and faithful servant!"

Tricia Weeks

Tricia Weeks and her husband, Alan, joined Chapel Hill Harvester Church in 1980. Tricia taught English for ten years at a high school in Decatur, Georgia, which experienced the "Alpha explosion." In 1983 she joined the staff of Chapel Hill Harvester Church as Editorial Assistant to Bishop Earl Paulk. She has assisted Bishop Paulk in writing his last six books. *The Provoker* is her first book.

Other books by K-Dimension Publishers

Held In The Heavens Until . . .
To Whom Is God Betrothed
Sex Is God's Idea
Satan Unmasked
The Wounded Body of Christ
The Divine Runner

For further information please contact—

P.O. Box 7300 • Atlanta, GA 30357